Dedication

This book is dedicated to the Magnificent Seven:
Mary Jane, Carol, John Joe, Kathy, Marybeth, Bryan, Maura

Contents

Acknowledgements

The writing and publishing of this book would not have been possible without the help of numerous people who advised, corrected, encouraged and assisted me along the way.

I would like to express my sincere appreciation to my family for their continued support and encouragement as well as their sound advice.

I would like to thank Ann Anderson and Maya Prpić who provided outstanding editorial services as well as Sharon McCully and Judith Dawson who assisted in the arduous process of preparing this book for publication. Pat Walsh and Bill Young provided technical expertise while Carl Lemyre did an outstanding job on the front and back covers and the book layout.

The Donohue family opened the doors of their homes and hearts and shared their most intimate memories and memorabilia.

Jack's former players at St. Barnabas School, Tolentine and Power Memorial High Schools, Holy Cross College and the Canadian National Teams shared their personal memories and were a tremendous help. Particular thanks go to Art Kenney, Brian and Jimmy Boyle, Steve Ryan, Jackie Bonner, Kareem Abdul-Jabbar, Richie Murphy, Jim Maloney, Billy Robinson, Jay Triano, Romel Raffin, Chris Critelli, Kathy Shields, Bill Wennington, Joyce Slipp and Leo Rautins.

Many of Jack's friends and associates spent time recounting stories and anecdotes and I would like to personally thank John Restivo, Steve Konchalski, Jack Curran, Ted Burns, the late Danny Buckley and Jackie Leaman, Walter, Frank and Tom McLaughlin, Charley Kitts, George House, Togo Palazzi and Ken Shields.

Several organizations including Basketball Canada, the Coaching Association of Canada, the Canadian Olympic Association, and the Power Memorial Academy Alumni Association as well as the Holy Cross Athletic Department and Alumni Association assisted with valuable information and assistance. Additional thanks go to CHSAA historian Joseph Dombrowski.

A special thanks goes to Barry Husk whose support and advice helped make this dream a possibility.

Introduction

I was in my first week of coaching at the university level in 1973, when the *Montreal Gazette* interviewed me about the upcoming season. In the article, I mentioned that we had a good recruiting year and that attracting quality athletes would be the key to our future success. Two weeks later, a photocopy of the article was sent to me in the mail with the following message written in the margin:

Coach,
Good to see you realize what needs to be done at the university level.
Keep up the good work!
Regards
Jack Donohue.

I had never met the man, but I had watched his Power and Holy Cross College teams on several occasions, and it was uplifting to receive a positive note from the national team coach in my first month on the job. It was a *modus operandi* that he would use for many other coaches – a note here, a phone call there, to touch base, and always included was a motivating message.

I benefited directly from Donohue's ability in 1988 when I briefly retired from coaching to open a restaurant in downtown Ottawa and moved to Kanata within blocks of the Donohue residence. Jack would come into the restaurant often and tried to promote the eatery in his weekly column in the *Ottawa Sun*. But regardless of our own hard work and Jack's promotions, the restaurant was a victim of a time-honored maxim – location, location, and location. We had planned to close the doors for good the Monday following Jack's retirement dinner. Jack insisted that everyone from out of town have at least one meal at the restaurant during the weekend, allowing us to build a small nest egg for the upcoming bankruptcy fight. In the ensuing year, Donohue played a pivotal role in helping me get back in the coaching profession and was always ready to provide a word of encouragement or a small loan to help cover monthly rent.

A decade later, I was living in Sherbrooke, Quebec and although my life was on the upswing, I was going through a tough time as Christmas approached. Out of the blue, Donohue called and said he needed to send something to me and wanted to make sure he had the right address. As I supplied the information, I figured I was about to receive Mary Jane's annual Christmas card. A few days later, I received a package containing a print of Mount Everest signed by Bernard Voyer, a famous Canadian mountain climber who had scaled Everest numerous times. Enclosed in a letter was a hand-written note that said:

> *Michael,*
> *Heard this guy talk about conquering a mountain. Though it was in French I followed his 90 min. talk because of his gestures, movements and his passion.*
> *Thought of you –*
> *Your challenges are much more than his ….job, sober, food, family and eventually your life …but we can learn from him.*
> *Believe in yourself, accept help from those who you can really trust and work your plan.*
> *We are so proud of what you have done.*
> *Just keep on believing in self & keep on doing well.*
> *Best*
> *Coach D.*

Donohue's spirit and contagious enthusiasm became a part of my life and it was with disbelief that I received news in February of 2003 that he was gravely sick.

Eddie Pomykala, the head basketball coach at Bishop' University, called me into his office and asked if I had talked to Jack recently.

I replied that I had spent two days with him in December when I was in Ottawa and that he looked great.

"Well you better give him a call because he is not doing very well," Pomykala said.

As I walked back to my desk, I had mixed feelings. In the 30 years that I knew Donohue, he was sick often although he always seemed to bounce back from any mishap with more vitality. Over the years,

Donohue suffered from malaria, diabetes and more recently muscle spasms.

So Jack was sick, that was nothing new but still, I felt uneasy as I dialed the Donohue phone number. I was somewhat relieved when his wife Mary Jane answered the phone cheerfully and proclaimed that "everything was great" in answer to my question.

"I will pass you on to Jack," she said in an upbeat voice.

Donohue got on the other end of the phone and from the moment he said hello it was clear something was wrong and even his positive demeanor couldn't hide the obvious. He told me that things were "super-duper" and then proceeded to contradict that statement by saying that he had been diagnosed with cancer. A few minutes into the conversation he said that he had to hang up and asked me to call him back in an hour.

As I hung up the phone, I was overwhelmed with emotion but when I called back later, it was vintage Donohue as the coach explained in detail his illness, how and when it was discovered, and what his options were. We talked twice more that day and, as was the norm, Donohue dominated the conversation, telling me how good the doctors were and how he was proud of the way his children and Mary Jane were handling his illness. Throughout the entire conversation, there was the trademark Donohue humor.

When I finally built up enough courage to ask him how serious the cancer was, he confided that his days were numbered. He died less than two months later with his entire family at his side. He was eulogized in his native New York City and throughout Canada as a great basketball coach but to label him as simply a basketball coach would be a grave injustice to the man.

In the 30 years since he first sent me an encouraging note, I had the privilege to work with him on numerous occasions and we became good friends. I was a guest coach for several seasons with the national team and was selected as an apprentice coach with the squad that participated in the 1982 World Championships in Columbia. Due partly to Jack's strong endorsement, I spent another seven years with the Canadian Women's National Team program and in 1997, Donohue asked me to move into the family house in Kanata and assist in the training of Myong Hun Ri, a 7'9" North Korean trying to land a National Basketball Association contract. His children babysat for my family, worked at my basketball camps and later became friends. The relationships I shared with Donohue and his family was by no means unique. Jack Donohue spent a lifetime cultivating genuine friendships and passed that gift onto his family.

He was a great motivator and speaker, a man of the highest principles who passed on his positive outlook on life and strong moral principles to everyone he met. Former NCAA basketball coach and TV sports analyst Jack Armstrong aptly described Donohue's demeanor by quoting from Rudyard Kipling.

"Kipling's saying about a person who could 'walk with Kings – nor lose the common touch' was Jack Donohue," Armstrong said. "He had the ability to connect with people from different walks of life."

He dined with the highest public officials in Canada, spoke to Fortune 500 CEOs and coached some for the world's finest athletes. Yet, he was most comfortable in the most humble of settings, spending time with his family or old friends, telling stories and making his listeners laugh. He was a master storyteller and could enthrall people when telling the same story for the third or fourth time.

He took particular delight in offering a helping hand or word of encouragement to anyone whose life had taken a wrong turn. His sense of humor knew only one boundary; he refused to use profanity or off-color jokes to get a cheap laugh. Instead he would poke fun at politicians, his family or best friends and, more often than not, himself.

It was his own self-deprecating humor that made him so popular as a speaker.

In short, he was a man who truly cared about others and always seemed to have the right remedy for a person whose luck had turned sour: it could be a hug or a pat on the back, sometimes a kick in the butt or a few dollars loaned. No matter what the situation, Jack Donohue always seemed to have the right thing to say and his death left a void not only in the Canadian sports scene but among thousands of people who considered him their friend.

This is his story.

CHAPTER 1

The Early Years

Throughout his life, Jack Donohue was portrayed as a New Yorker, a description he fostered, though it was not totally accurate. While Donohue established his coaching credentials at Bronx's Tolentine High School and at Power Memorial Academy, a private Catholic boys' high school located on the outskirts of Manhattan's Hell's Kitchen, he was actually born and raised in Yonkers just north of the city line, spent seven years in Worcester, Massachusetts, and called Kanata, Ontario, his home for the final 31 years of his life. Despite living elsewhere, Donohue felt very much like a New Yorker. He loved the hustle and bustle of the Big Apple, its intensity and its diverse population.

John Patrick Donohue was born on June 4, 1931, to John Joseph Donohue and Sarah Gertrude Delaney, Irish immigrants who came to the United States separately and later met in their adopted country. When the first Irish came to New York City in the 1840s, they were destitute and willing to risk everything to escape the horrors of the infamous potato famines that ravished their island country. The majority of the new immigrants settled in the notorious Five Points slums, located in lower Manhattan, and it took a generation before they were able to establish themselves as legitimate citizens and overcome the bigotry that immigrants of all nationalities have to endure upon their arrival in North

America. At the turn of the 20th century, the majority of the Irish had left Five Points for the more upscale neighborhoods of Manhattan or the boroughs of Brooklyn, Queens and the Bronx. By the time John Donohue and Sarah Delaney arrived in the U.S., the Irish had established themselves in New York City and had found employment in the fire and the police departments, and had become politicians, lawyers and businessmen.

Sarah, a nurse, crossed the Atlantic first and resided in mid-town Manhattan with relatives. John Sr. had a promising career as a jockey in Ireland cut short when he became too big to ride professionally. Since his older brother was destined to inherit the family farm in Longford, in the central part of Ireland, John Sr. decided the best thing to do was to seek his fortune in America.

In 1926, he followed his sisters who had immigrated to the States during the prosperity of the Roaring 20s and soon found work as a lineman for Con Edison, the public utility that supplied New York City with electricity. He met his bride-to-be at an Irish get-together in Manhattan and shortly afterwards John asked Sarah to marry him. Following the wedding, the newlyweds settled into a modest family home at 142 Alexander Street in the McLean section of Yonkers, a middle-class Irish neighborhood just north of the Bronx border.

It was a close-knit neighborhood of single-family homes and small apartment buildings. Driveways big enough for one car separated the brick and clapboard residences and bordered small, but well-trimmed front lawns. McLean Street, which served as the boundary line between Yonkers and the Bronx, was lined with shops and bars catering to the predominately Irish residents of the area.

To help supplement their income, the young Donohues rented an upstairs apartment to an outside tenant for several years, but with the arrival of Jack and his sister Mary (who was born two years after Jack) the family regained the top floor to meet the needs of a growing family.

Jack and Mary were raised during the dark days of the Depression but there were no soup lines for the Donohue clan. John's work with Con Edison provided steady employment and as a result, the family enjoyed a relatively comfortable style of living. "Sunday dinners were a tradition at our house and it was no big deal if you brought someone home," Jack remembered. "My father would simply tell my mother to put some more soup on and cook a few more potatoes."

Both children attended the local parochial school, St. Barnabas, where they not only learned their ABCs but also received a solid foundation in the teachings of the Catholic Church.

The Transfiguration Church, located in the notorious Five Points section of Manhattan, was built to minister to the religious needs of the Irish immigrants and when the Irish dispersed to other areas of the city, they set up new churches that were administered by Irish clergy. In 1910, Monsignor Reilly founded St. Barnabas parish to service the area's growing Catholic community, one of mainly Irish and Italian descent. The Church was beautiful in its simplicity with eight stained windows depicting the life of Christ and an oversized organ in the church loft where the parish choir sang each Sunday. Within three years of opening the church, Reilly oversaw the construction of St. Barnabas grammar school and, in 1923 a girl's high school was built across the street.

The church became a focal point of the community and its jurisdiction included parts of Yonkers and the Bronx. When New York Irish Catholics were asked where they lived, they would name the parish to which they belonged rather than a geographic location. On Sunday, everyone went to Mass, the children attended the parish school and social events revolved around such parochial organizations as the Knights of Columbus, the Ladies Solidarity and Holy Name Society, while the Catholic Youth Organization provided sport leagues and dances for young Catholics.

The St. Barnabas parish included the McLean section of Yonkers and the Woodlawn section of the Bronx and had clearly defined boundaries that allowed it to keep its homogenous nature for over a century. To the east was the Bronx River Parkway while the western portion of St. Barnabas ended at Van Cortland Park, a vast green space that included two golf courses, baseball diamonds and the city's best cross-country course. The northern border stopped at the Yonkers reservoir that pumped water from upstate New York into New York City's homes while the Woodlawn cemetery served as the southern boundary.

By most standards, Jack was a good student who behaved himself inside the classroom. It was a different story away from the watchful eyes of the nuns as Jack loved to play practical jokes and demonstrated a keen sense of humour that would later become his trademark. He loved to tease people and his younger sister Mary was one of the first targets of his barbs. "Even then he had a good sense of humor and he was always teasing me," Mary recalled. "We used to fight like cats and dogs. It was only later in life that we got very close and I think that is normal."

Jack and Mary grew up before the advent of TV, video games and computers, but the silver screen provided a great escape for the pair. Jack enjoyed westerns and comedies and it was a love affair that would last a lifetime. When World War II broke out, Sarah Donohue went back to work to help with a nursing shortage and her absence on Friday nights provided an opportunity for the rest of the family to go to the cinema on a weekly basis. "My mother would work on Friday nights so, after supper, my father would take us to the local movie theatre and we would watch the latest releases," Mary recalled.

Because the country was involved in a war on two fronts, there were plenty of action films, although Jack preferred comedies. He would study the comedians of the era and watch how they got laughs, their timing and delivery. Years later he would accumulate a library of old films: gangster movies set in New York City and comedies featuring W.C. Fields and his personal favourite – the Three Stooges.

The other form of entertainment was family parties held at the Yonkers house where the group would inevitably end up in the kitchen swapping stories. The evening would end with the singing of Irish songs and John Sr. would be quick to stop any form of Irish music that he didn't feel was being played or sung properly, instructing the guilty parties the proper way to sing.

"My father was a beer drinker and would tell me that anyone who drank hard liquor was an alcoholic," Jack would say years later.

It was advice that Jack took to heart. Throughout his life the younger Donohue avoided alcohol of any kind. He would have an occasional beer or glass of wine but preferred sipping on a Pepsi, regardless of the occasion or setting. After all, drinking tended to interfere with his favourite Irish pastime – telling stories.

The extended Donohue family often kidded John Sr. about his strong work ethic. "My father had unbelievable work habits," Jack Donohue recalled. "My cousins would tell my father that if he missed a day of work the lights would still go on in New York City. His line was 'we are never going to find out because I'm not missing a day.' I can remember him walking 20 blocks to catch a bus for work during snowstorms."

*   *   *   *   *

Discipline was a staple of the Donohues' life but their upbringing also included valuable life lessons passed on by a father whose street smarts surpassed his formal education. Jack and Mary were expected to behave and toe the proverbial line. At school, the nuns and brothers kept everyone on the right path and the clergy were not above using corporal punishment to deliver God's message. At home, the threat of the strap was often enough to modify wayward behaviour.

Donohue would reminisce later in life that he grew up in a healthy, loving family environment but that did not stop him from attempting to run away from home on occasions to escape what he perceived at the time to be cruel and dictatorial parents. However, his attempts at flight always seemed to hit snags. His first endeavors often were a joint effort as he enlisted the family dog to accompany him for company and safety. But the canine was no dummy and was, in fact, better trained than his young master. The dog refused to cross any street, the first hurdle in any serious escape plan. Jack would pull on the dog's leash or try to push him from behind, but the family pet was too well disciplined and refused to budge. Jack would eventually give up his escape attempts just about the time his mother would call for him to come in the house for dinner. Eventually, Jack figured that if he was going to run away it would have to be a solo affair. So on one of those days when home life seemed unbearable, he would cross the forbidden streets of Yonkers and head to his Aunt's house a few blocks away. There, he could enjoy one of life's necessities that his own parents had always denied him, reading comic books!

The young Donohue also displayed a unique understanding of the world around him. When his father purchased a dog of questionable pedigree that was black and white, Jack named him Red. "Why are you calling a dog that is black and white from head to toe, Red?" his father asked him.

"Have you ever heard of a dog called Black and White?" was the youngster's curt reply. "If I go around the neighborhood yelling Black and White, here Black and White, everyone will think I am crazy," Jack explained with an air of satisfaction. "And I am not crazy!" The name Red stuck.

Father and son enjoyed fishing trips on the Hudson River, the Long Island Sound or neighboring lakes and it was during one of those trips that his father taught Jack an invaluable lesson. Just as they were heading out to the fishing site, eight-year-old Jack remarked that it was a great day. Without saying a word his father turned the car around and drove back home. When they arrived back at Alexander Street, the sun had not yet risen. Jack's father walked across the neighbor's lawn and borrowed the *New York Times*, which was lying on the front porch. Jack watched in bewilderment as his father opened the paper to the classified section and pointing to the obituaries told his son "Check this list every day and if Donohue, Jack isn't there, it's going to be a great day."

A few years later Jack told his father that he was trying out for the Mount St. Michael's Academy football team. "I was excited about playing on an organized team with uniforms, playing on grass," Donohue said. "In my neighborhood, we didn't get to play on grass much. They used to spray paint the asphalt green and call it grass – nobody knew the difference."

His father didn't understand the whole concept of trying out for a school activity; if someone wanted to do something they should just do it. But the elder Donohue supported his child's efforts. "If it is important enough to you, shoot for the moon and if you come up short you're still in the stars," John told him.

Those two beliefs would become cornerstones in Jack's life and he used both of them to encourage athletes, his family and countless other people who benefited from his motivational speeches.

* * * * *

In the late 1930s, Jack fell in love with sports the first time his father took him to Van Cortland Park so he could watch the elder Donohue compete against other grown men in a game of handball. The game, played against a concrete wall, required foot speed as well as hand-eye coordination and stamina. It was a popular pastime among older men, particularly for first-generation immigrants.

Jack and his friends, however, preferred the more American sports of baseball and football, sports John Sr. had a hard time understanding. "My father has never accepted American football," Donohue said in an article in *Sunrise* magazine in 1966, shortly before his father died. "He maintains that the Gaelic brand is more refined, because you can't tackle or touch a man from behind. Well, I've seen the Gaelic game and what they can do to you from the front is not refined. It is assault and mayhem."

Sports for children of that era were not structured the way they are today and they were void of much adult interference. The neighborhood boys simply organized themselves on a daily basis. They would play stickball on isolated streets or in a nearby park, baseball anywhere they could find an empty lot and football in the local schoolyards and parks. Van Cortland Park, one of the city's largest green spaces, afforded local youngsters a major league size baseball diamond as well as numerous fields in which to play pick-up football games. Even then, Jack's leadership qualities were evident. He would be sure everyone knew when and where they were meeting, and would help pick teams once everyone arrived.

Jack didn't just play games; he studied them as well. He knew rules, strategies and took great delight in the subtleties of each sport. He became an avid reader of the city newspapers' numerous sports pages and could rattle off his favourite players' stats at the drop of a hat. As a youngster, he played all sports, but baseball was his favourite, a game that was, to him, cerebral as well as physical. He looked forward to trips to Yankee Stadium, where, at the shrine that Babe Ruth built, he saw future Hall of Famers such as Joe DiMaggio and Bill Dickey. Jack was a keen student of the game and he appreciated the lesser-known players who would move runners over or who had the patience to work a pitcher for a walk. The days spent in Yankee Stadium and those playing in the local sandlots would prove invaluable when he became a high school baseball coach.

In his early teens, basketball was not on Jack's list of things to do. "I didn't start playing basketball until I was 16 and only then because of peer pressure," Donohue said. "All my friends were playing and if I wanted to continue being their friend I had to play too."

Despite his late start in the sport, he took to it quickly. He enjoyed the teamwork and discovered that he could make up for a lack of skill by being a smarter player than his opponent.

Donohue's world changed in his final year of high school when he obtained a driver's license and could drive legally. It was an event that expanded his immediate horizons and allowed him to go beyond the boundaries of Yonkers and the Upper Bronx.

His first experiences driving a car, however, took place much earlier during fishing excursions with his father and uncles. On more than one occasion Jack would have to drive home because the adults were under the "influence" even though the teenager was underage and unlicensed at the time.

Once he was able to legally drive, he became a chauffeur for his sister and her friends, gladly offering them rides for an opportunity to get behind the wheel of a car. Big brother Jack was also given the responsibility of teaching Mary how to drive, an exercise that did not turn out as originally planned. The Donohue family car had a manual transmission which could cause serious problems for novice drivers. On one of their first driving lessons Mary stalled the car in the intersection of a busy street in Yonkers. As she tried nervously to get the car going again, Jack's loud commands and lack of patience only made the situation worse. After a few minutes of futile attempts at starting the car, Jack stormed out of the car and walked home, leaving his sister stuck in the car in a state of panic. When Jack arrived home his father asked him what happened to Mary and the family car. When Jack explained Mary's dilemma the elder Donohue quickly sent Jack back to rescue his stranded sister.

* * * * *

The need for religious vocations was always stressed from the pulpit on Sunday and reinforced in the Catholic schools by the nuns and brothers who constantly voiced a need for more clergy. Jack developed a strong affinity with his faith at an early age and for a while it appeared that he would follow the path of many of his countrymen into a religious order. After his graduation from St. Barnabas grammar school, he attended Mount St. Michael's High School in the Bronx located a few miles to the east. There, he continued to do well in the classroom and was popular with his classmates. He also admired the work of the Marist Brothers who taught at the school and at one point he thought seriously about joining the Order.

"A Marist brother came to the house one day to talk to my parents and Jack about the possibility of his studying for the brotherhood but nothing came of it," Mary said. Jack wrestled with the idea of a religious life but eventually announced that he was going to attend nearby Fordham University and study to be a doctor. He was off to conquer new worlds but he never yielded his strong attachment to Catholicism.

Jack enrolled in the pre-med programme at Fordham at the tender age of 17 but was more interested in hanging out in the school's gymnasium on the Rose Hill campus than studying in the school's library. During freshman orientation he wandered over to the gym and soon found himself involved in a 2-on-2 pick-up game with three strangers.

Jack became mad when his teammate, another freshman, was unable to stop his man from scoring and after questioning his defensive ability, Jack decided to switch defensive assignments. The switch didn't make a difference as the taller, older player continued to score at will and it was only after the game that Donohue discovered that one of his opponents was the leading scorer of the Fordham varsity team.

After the game Jack was formally introduced to his teammate, a fellow named Arthur Goldstein whose father was one of the pioneers of professional basketball. Donohue and Goldstein were enrolled in the same pre-med classes but the pair preferred to spend any free time shooting hoops in the gym than learning about the intricacies of anatomy.

"We used to go in the gym during our spare time and we would get kicked out if there was a gym class going on," Goldstein said. "Finally in the second semester, we actually had gym class but by then the phys-ed teacher was so used to chasing us out of the gym that he wouldn't let us stay for class. We walked in for our first gym class and he kicked us out."

The two freshmen were good students but as the year progressed, they began to question if medicine was really their calling, particularly when final exams rolled around.

"Jack would tell everyone that he was the reason I passed freshman chemistry, yet I got the higher mark in the class and he was sitting behind me," Goldstein said.

In his sophomore year Jack and his neighborhood friend Walter McLaughlin, would drive to Fordham together in McLaughlin's father's 1935 Ford. McLaughlin's family lived on the corner of Katonah Avenue and E. 241st Street in the Woodlawn section of the Bronx, a few blocks south of Donohue's Alexander St. home. The two had met while teammates on St. Barnabas' Catholic Youth Organization (CYO) baseball team and soon became close friends. It was during his sophomore year that Donohue began his coaching career running CYO programs for the elementary school kids at St. Barnabas. St. Barnabas had no male athletic teams since nuns staffed the school, so Father Breen, one of the parish priests, recruited Jack to fill the void by coaching the boys' basketball and baseball teams.

"We shared a car together while commuting to Fordham for a year and Jack would race home from Fordham in the afternoon to coach the boys," McLaughlin said.

One of his better players was Walter's younger brother Jackie who would later earn a scholarship to St. Louis University. Even then, Donohue showed an ability to size up talent. "The team wasn't very good so Jack put some of the sixth graders on the team such as Jimmy (Hughie) Donohue [no relation] and Frank McArdle. In two years, Jack had built St. Barnabas into the diocese champs." Jackie McLaughlin, Hughie Donohue and Frank McArdle would all earn scholarships to Division I colleges.

* * * * *

"Allie Shies is the reason I became a coach," Jack Donohue would often say when people asked him about his decision to make coaching his life-long profession. "If it weren't for Allie I probably would have become a doctor, and maybe not a good doctor at that."

Jack was pursuing his goal as a pre-med student at Fordham when Shies, a member of the Fordham basketball team, persuaded Donohue and Walter McLaughlin to spend the summer working at an overnight camp at the eastern tip of Long Island.

Camp Momoweta was situated on a small lake with plywood cabins and dining hall, outdoor latrines and a solitary dirt basketball court. A dirt entry road gave campers an indication of the Spartan life that awaited them. There were no television sets or comfortable rooms, but the fresh air and the green spaces were an oasis to the city's kids who attended the camp. The swimming area was the camp's best feature with a wooden pier and diving board that launched swimmers into a cool lake during hot summer days.

"Jim Mulvihill advertised horse back riding at the camp but only had one horse," Walter McLaughlin recalled. "He had the horse tied up off in the distance because he didn't want the parents to see how sway-back the horse was and I don't recall any campers actually riding the horse."

"Kids would have to pick the activity they wanted to participate in each day – baseball, basketball, archery – and there were always ten or so kids that were left without an activity and Jack would take those kids,"

Shies said. "He would organize a 'pick-up paper' activity and made it so much fun that kids stopped choosing other activities because they wanted to join Jack. He would have contests and give prizes to the person who he claimed picked up the most paper."

Donohue had taken a page out of Mark Twain's *Tom Sawyer* and made it work to perfection. It wasn't long before Camp Momoweta was the cleanest camp in the Northeast.

"The kids asked how he knew who picked up the most paper and he told them he had experts come in at night and go through the whole garbage and determine which camper had collected the most refuse," Shies said. It was a preposterous story but the kids bought into it and the race to see who would win the daily prize intensified.

"Jack was a leader with the kids," McLaughlin said. "He had a knack for keeping them interested and was always thinking of games to keep them busy or telling stories. I figured the kids liked me a lot but each session the kids would pick their favorite counselor and Jack always won in a landslide."

It was back in the old neighborhood that Allie Shiels first noticed Jack's leadership qualities when he observed Donohue coaching baseball at St. Barnabas and knew that he was in his natural element. "Baseball was his first love and he was a really good coach," Allie recalled.

So, one day, when Jack talked about being a doctor, Allie made a poignant point that stuck with Donohue for the rest of his life. "The most important thing for a person is to do something that they are passionate about," Shiels said. "I don't know how good a doctor you are going to be but I know you love coaching. That is what you enjoy and that is what you are good at." Donohue was taken aback by the statement but gave it a lot of thought. Within a few days he decided that Allie was right and the medical profession's loss was basketball's gain. Jack Donohue was going to be a high school basketball coach.

CHAPTER 2

Not a Boot Shine Kind of Guy

Jack graduated from Fordham University with a degree in Economics (he switched from pre-med after his freshman year) and a desire to coach at one of New York's Catholic high schools. But those plans were put on hold due to an armed conflict halfway around the world.

World War II had not directly affected the Donohue family – Jack's father John was too old for the military and when the United States entered the fray on December 8, 1941, young Jack was just 10 years old. Still, Jack had followed the news of the war through the New York City dailies and the newsreels that were shown in the local movie theatres. And so, in 1950, when the United States introduced a United Nations (UN) resolution to send troops to South Korea in response to an attack by the communist regime of North Korea, Donohue was watching closely.

The conflict was more than just a grab for land between two long-time rivals. This was the era of the ideological Cold War between the East and the West and in the minds of patriotic Americans the lines were clearly defined between good and evil. The Soviet Bloc controlled most of Eastern Europe and half of Germany while China was flexing its muscle in Southeast Asia. When China-supported troops crossed the 38th parallel separating North and South Korea, the U.S. reacted quickly and asked the United Nations to provide military assistance to South Korea. In order to send any troops to a disputed area, the UN needed the full support of the Security Council, a five-nation committee that included the Soviet Union. Historically, the Soviets had always vetoed military action against another communist regime, but when they foolishly boycotted a Security Council meeting (they were protesting nationalist China's membership on the Council), the United States and its allies pushed though Resolution 85 demanding that North Korea stop the aggression and withdraw its troops to the 38th parallel that separated the two countries. North Korea ignored the UN request and troops were dispatched to aid the South Korean government.

The war in Korea was winding down by the time Donohue graduated from Fordham but sensing it was his duty to contribute to the peacekeeping operation, he enlisted in the Army in 1953. The Armed Forces would never be the same!

Donohue applied and was accepted to the Officer's Candidate School (OCS) at Fort Benning, Georgia, where he soon became fast friends with another candidate, Teddy Burns. It wasn't long before Donohue's leadership skills and sense of humor would become evident to his fellow candidates.

"Jack was very intelligent and he was very committed to doing his best at OCS, but he had a different attitude about certain things," Burns recalls. "For example, I and most of the other guys in our company were concerned about demerits, but not Jack."

Demerits were usually given for such infractions as sloppy dress or not taking care of equipment properly and resulted in extra work, often for an entire regiment and usually to be carried out on the weekend.

"I hated to have to do extra work, particularly for someone else's mistake but Jack took a different approach," Burns said. "He figured that the work would have to be done anyway so what difference did it make when he did it."

One of the most time-consuming jobs in the Army was to constantly spit-shine shoes in anticipation of a sudden inspection. After Jack was cited several times for unshined shoes and other uniform infractions, he decided there had to be a better way. He had several pairs of spare shoes hidden in the ducts above his sleeping quarters and whenever there was an inspection indoors, he would show off the same pair of shoes that he never actually wore.

Keeping shoes clean outside of the barracks was a different story and the problem came to a head one day when the company was out on the firing range. Donohue was busy manning a machine gun and his friend Burns was feeding ammunition into the weapon when the Commanding Officer came by for an unannounced inspection. He stopped in front of Donohue and took one look at his boots. Not only were they dirty but also the right boot had a huge hole, clearly exposing Jack's big toe. The commander was so shocked that he called the entire company over to take a look at the offending boot.

"Jack was not a boot shine type of guy," Burns says with complete conviction.

* * * * *

"Jack was always one step ahead of everyone else and he was always trying to figure out how to do things the easiest way—which wasn't always the Army way," Burns says. The rest of the company soon began to look to Jack for leadership. His ways were often unorthodox by army standards, but almost always effective.

Once, the unit was sent out on maneuvers and Jack demonstrated his ability to think ahead. One morning while awaiting orders Jack grabbed a pair of rakes and handed one to Burns and told him to start raking. "Why, no one told us to rake," Burns said surprised at Donohue's initiative at doing physical work. "Just do it and be quiet," Jack advised him as he started raking pine needles. Seconds later, the Company Commander walked by and loudly commended the two for showing such initiative. Within seconds the entire company had rakes in hand following Donohue's lead.

When he was finished raking Jack took some of the pine needles to his pup tent and started digging an 8-inch cubed hole into the ground. "What are you doing that for?" Burns inquired. "You'll see, just give me a hand". Later that day, an MP arrived at the Commanding Officer's tent looking for Jack.

"Donohue, your chariot awaits you," the CO informed him as Donohue walked out of the tent, climbed into a jeep and headed back to the base. The Fort Benning basketball team had a game that night and since Jack was one of their better players he was called in from maneuvers for the contest. After the game, he had the staff car make a detour to the Post Exchange where he loaded up on candies and other goodies. Upon his return, he stashed the contraband into the hole dug earlier and then covered it with pine needles out of the sight of the daily inspectors.

*   *   *   *   *

Daily reveille came at 0500 hours each morning and was followed by roll call and more often than not, some form of physical exercise. On one rainy day, Donohue and Burns awoke at the appointed hour and heard the overnight duty man yell into the barracks "Ponchos and helmet liners." "Jack rose from his bed and said 'You heard the man' and then proceeded to put on just his boots, followed by his poncho, helmet and helmet liner," Burns recalled. Donohue didn't bother putting on his full uniform because he realized that the rain would soak the uniform during roll call, forcing him to dig out a second dry uniform when it was time to go back for training later in the morning. By now, many of the barracks' inhabitants had learned to trust Donohue's judgment and proceeded to file out of the barracks with just their boots, helmet and a poncho over their underwear.

"The important thing was to answer roll call," Burns noted. "It was dark and rainy and Jack was gambling that the tactical officer wouldn't notice how the candidates weren't dressed underneath the ponchos."

Donohue was also playing a hunch that because of the rain they would forego any physical activity and be sent back to the barracks. So the entire barracks stood at attention and answered roll call in their underwear. "After roll call, the orders of the day were issued and then one of four things could happen," Burns stated. "We could jog to the physical training field and perform the army's daily dozen exercises; jog to the obstacle course and run through the course several times; go on a 5-mile run; or lastly, forego any exercise and head back to the barracks and prepare for the day's activities." Because of the rain, Donohue was counting on the latter, but he and his fellow candidates were dismayed when the tactical officer decided that rain or no rain, it was a perfect day for a long run. As they commenced the run, Burns and Donohue eyed each other and came up with the same thought – finish the run and get back to the barracks before the impending daylight would expose their ruse. "There would be hell to pay if we had to explain why we had bare legs showing below the ponchos," Burns said. But Irish luck prevailed as the company arrived back at the barracks undetected.

"God is good to dumb Irishmen," Donohue would assert throughout his life.

* * * * *

Part of the training at OCS was placing the prospective officers in combat situations in order to judge their ability to properly assess a particular military problem, develop a strategy and then execute that plan successfully. "There were multiple phases to the combat problems permitting several candidates an opportunity to play the commanding officer role," Burns recalled. "Simulating real combat conditions, we were issued C rations, but were not permitted to make fires to heat the food." While in the field the soldiers had nothing to eat but C rations, cold canned hamburgers covered with solid white grease on top. "It was not a very appetizing sight and it tasted just as bad as it looked,' Burns recalls.

On one such excursion, Donohue was selected as the commanding officer, with Burns serving as his radioman, and ordered to attack a hill with tank and artillery support.

"Jack ordered me to get a tank, which I did, and when it arrived he went behind the vehicle and talked on the radio to the tank commander going over their attack plans," Burns said. Donohue had devised a sound military strategy to take the hill, but had more than just war games on his mind. As he talked to the tank commander he opened his back pack, removed two cans of C rations and placed them on the tank's red-hot exhaust pipe. By the time Donohue had finished talking to the tank commander the two cans of rations were properly heated. He opened both cans, handed one can to Burns and ate from the other. When the meal was finished, Donohue's unit proceeded to capture the hill.

Shortly after completion of OCS, Donohue and Burns were assigned to Fort Jackson, where they quickly met the Regimental Adjutant, First Lieutenant Cash.

"Here we were all impressed with our bars and being second lieutenants and this first lieutenant tells us how lucky it is that we came that day," Burns says. "The whole base was having a fitness test and it was the same test we did every day at Fort Benning. Lieutenant Cash figured that the two of us would be in great shape and able to help raise the regiment's scores since everything was done on an average."

"What is the average for this regiment?" Jack asked his new superior. "224 out of 500" the first lieutenant replied. Donohue and Burns were accustomed to getting perfect scores on a course that consisted of five sections with each section worth 100 points each. "We went out and scored 100 on each of the three exercises when Jack decides that he has done enough for our new regiment," Burns says. "Let's go, we did our bit," Donohue said as he walked off the course. "We already pulled up the average so let's go check out the PX."

The pair needed shaving cream and other necessaries so they left the course and headed to the Post Exchange. "Once we got there Jack was weighed down by some heavy decisions: which candy bars to buy. Should he get the Hershey's with almonds or the plain Hershey's?" Burns recalls.

Meanwhile back on the fitness course, Lieutenant Cash was besides himself wondering what had happened to his two star newcomers. After several hours of waiting, he sent the rest of his company on a search mission. When they finally located the two wayward officers, it was too late for Donohue and Burns to finish the last two legs of the fitness test. "That little side trip to the PX cost us duty on our first weekend at Fort Jackson," Burns chuckles.

Lt. Cash figured that since the pair liked the PX so much, an appropriate discipline would be to take inventory at the base store that Sunday. Donohue was upset that he missed Sunday Mass but soon delved, literally, into the task at hand. "He was counting and I was writing down the information, but we weren't getting very far," Burns says.

That was because they made the mistake of starting in the candy section. "Jack would call out an item like Three Musketeers and say 'six.' Then he would say 'Oops, wait a second, make that five' as he put one in his mouth. Finally another guy came to help us and we got past that section."

*   *   *   *   *

Jack loved to play practical jokes and found the serious side of army life a perfect venue for his shenanigans. On selected weekends, families were allowed to visit the base and on one such occasion Donohue was given an opportunity to play a joke on Eddie Aumen, a friend in the regiment. Ed was married to a young woman who came from an Amish community in Pennsylvania. While her husband was off at a different part of the base, Patricia Aumen watched a softball game outside of the regimental officers' barracks. When the weather suddenly turned cold the ever-gallant Donohue went into the barracks where he found an army overcoat and put it on the young lady who was dressed in just shorts and a blouse.

After the game ended, everyone retreated to the barracks' day room and the playful Donohue kept an eye out the window. When he saw Eddie approach the area, he quickly ran outside and exclaimed "Boy, Eddie, what a wife you have, she's tremendous! I had no idea that she played strip poker!" Poor Eddie didn't know what to think when he walked into the building and found his wife in the middle of a room of soldiers wearing an army overcoat that covered her completely and gave the impression that she was wearing nothing underneath. Eddie was relieved and the rest of the company roared with laugher when he discovered that his wife was indeed fully clothed.

Donohue couldn't avoid trouble off the base either. One day, he and Burns decided to go to a movie in town. Donohue was at the wheel of their vehicle and as usual was not paying full attention when he realized that they had just passed the movie theatre. He quickly tried to make an illegal U-turn, but he misjudged the width of the street and ended up with the car's front wheels up against the curb. Just then a policeman pulled up and started writing a ticket for an illegal U-turn. Jack protested vehemently. He believed that his inability to make a proper U-turn cleared him of any guilt. "How can you give me a ticket for a U-turn when I didn't make one," he pleaded. "What I did was a Y turn and there are no laws against that. I'm from Yonkers and up there we make Y turns all the time." After arguing over semantics for several frustrating minutes the police officer finally gave up. He placed the ticket book into his back pocket and shook his head in disbelief as he returned to his patrol car, allowing Donohue to go on his way without a ticket.

The Columbia School for Women was situated a few miles from Fort Jackson and soon became a favourite hangout for Jack and Ted. On one occasion, Donohue convinced the head mistress of one of the dorms that he was organizing a USO show and was looking for local talent. To audition, each girl had to dance with the two officers who would then make a decision on which girls would have the pleasure of serving their country as entertainers. After the bogus audition, Donohue and Burns brought the girls downstairs to a social room that contained a soda fountain. They spent the rest of the night making ice cream sodas and charging a penny for them.

"The biggest thing about Jack was the fact that he cared so much about people," Burns remembers. "Once his mother and sister drove all the way from New York with a present – an Irish setter puppy. The only problem was that it barked all night and Jack was worried about keeping people in the barracks awake." So he moved himself and the dog into a furnace room in the basement of the barracks, out of sight and sound of the rest of the company. Or so he thought. Burns, aware of his friend's new but illegal sleeping routine, would tell the men under his command to make sure that they checked the furnace room when they had sentry duty at night. The guards annoyed the hell out of Donohue when he had to repeatedly answer their queries throughout the night. After a few weeks, the dog ran away and Jack sent the entire company out on a search and recovery mission. "I don't know who else would send a company of 200 men to locate his missing pet," Burns noted. "As they marched through the fields they could hear the dog barking in the distance but they never found him."

"Jack had great respect for the military and he enjoyed his tour of duty very much," Burns goes on to say. "He was very serious about the army and about his leadership ability. His engaging personality and jovial attitude made our time in the service more bearable."

CHAPTER 3

High School Coach

After his two-year stint with the Army, Jack entered NYU's master's program in physical education. It was a degree that would come in handy when he would apply for high school coaching jobs. Jack's first coaching experience, with the fourth grade students at St. Barnabas, had been a labor of love and in those days he gave little thought of coaching for a living.

"I was coaching the older kids at St. Barnabas when I first met Jack," Frank Shiels recalled. "He really loved what he was doing and it was obvious that the kids liked playing for him."

It was Frank's younger brother, Allie Shiels, whose talk convinced Donohue that coaching was his true calling. Once Donohue decided that he would indeed make coaching his livelihood, he dedicated himself to perfecting his craft. He attended games, practices, read books on coaching and picked the minds of the coaches he meet through his travels to local gymnasiums. Coaching, which started out as a Saturday morning pastime, soon became an obsession for Donohue and he set two goals for himself.

"I wanted to be a varsity high school coach by the time I was 30 and I wanted to own my own summer camp by the time I was 38," Donohue said years later.

Donohue began to coach part-time while attending NYU although success on the hard court was fleeting at first. Jack was beside himself, sensing the players weren't responding to his coaching techniques.

"I remember he was really depressed over the team's play," Allie Shiels said. "We used to go for these long walks in the winter, discussing the problems he was having with the team."

The depression didn't last long; the following year Donohue heard that St. Nicolas of Tolentine High School was looking for a head coach and armed with nothing more than a year's experience as a JV coach and a world of confidence, Donohue applied for the job. The school's principal Brother Victor Christopher Dardis recalls how one August day in 1954 the school's current basketball coach, Tom Birch, came into his office and said he had taken a job with General Motors but wanted to continue coaching.

"I told him that it was school policy that coaches had to be full-time teachers and so we began looking for a new coach. Someone mentioned Jack and although he didn't have any varsity experience, I was impressed that he was a Ranger in the Army. I always believed that you have to give people an opportunity to gain experience, so I hired Jack. It was the best hiring of my life."

Just a year out of the Army, Donohue was now a head coach in a New York City high school, and he was going to make the most of the opportunity.

* * * * *

The Cathedral of St. Nicholas of Tolentine, located on the southwest corner of Fordham and University Roads, is a commanding edifice whose steeples tower over the adjacent apartment buildings that make up the Bronx parish. The church's dominance over the neighborhood extended beyond its physical appearance.

"The Church dominated our lives and respect for authority was unquestioned," said Jimmy Boyle, a member of Donohue's first two Tolentine teams. "You went to grammar and high school at the parish schools and if you got married it usually was to someone who lived within the neighborhood."

Tolentine was located in a blue-collar neighborhood where the men were employed in occupations that had a hierarchical structure such as policeman, fireman, construction workers and union-related jobs.

"Security was the rule of the day," Boyle explained.

The parish inclusiveness may have indeed generated a sense of safety but it was not always conducive to fielding winning athletic teams.

"We only had about 38 students in my graduating class," Boyle recalled.

Despite the low numbers, the Tolentine players were looking forward to making their mark in the 1954-55 basketball season. The only problem was that when school started they didn't have a coach.

"It was September and we still didn't know who was coaching us," Boyle said. "The season wasn't starting for another two months but we knew that we were going to be a pretty good team and we wanted to know who the coach was. We were afraid that one of the brothers, who really wasn't a coach, would have to take the job."

One day, a school announcement instructed all prospective players for the varsity basketball team to report to the boys' locker room to meet the new coach and the players' fears were quickly put to rest. The team and the rest of the school soon found out that Jack Donohue was interested in more than just the game of basketball.

"He was very demanding of course, but easy to play for," Boyle recalled. "He took an interest not only in basketball but in your academic, personal and family lives."

Jack was only 23 when he took over the reins of the Tolentine basketball program at a time when the Catholic High School Athletic Association (CHSAA) was coming into its own. Prior to the mid-1950s, its rival, the Public School Athletic League, was considered to be the stronger of the two leagues, although the CHSAA had a reputation for more disciplined play and better coaching. The talent level began to sway in favor of the Catholic league when Tom and Sam Stith entered Brooklyn's St. Francis Prep and led them to three consecutive CHSAA titles from 1955-1958.

Suddenly, many of the city's better players were enrolled in Catholic schools and moving on to successful college and professional careers.

*   *   *   *   *

Donohue wasted little time in turning the program into one of the best in the city and began to establish a reputation as one of the up and coming young coaches in the metropolitan area. Tom Konchalski started following high school basketball in the Big Apple when his younger brother Steve was a player with the Archbishop Molloy High School freshman team. His interest in basketball soon became an obsession and then an occupation. His passion for the game, commitment to fundamentals and team play and insistence on total effort and team play in practices and games paid off huge dividends on the court.

Today, Tom Konchalski heads the High School Basketball Insider Report, one of the leading scouting services in the United States, and Steve Konchalski coaches the men's basketball team at St. Francis Xavier University in Nova Scotia. Over the years, Tom has befriended such basketball greats as Ernie Grunfeld and Bernard King and is considered one of the foremost experts on the American high school basketball scene with particular emphasis on New York City cagers. Konchalski has an encyclopedic mind when it comes to recalling players or teams and one of the things he remembers vividly is the impact Donohue had on the city's basketball scene.

"He was a great coach," Konchalski said. "What he did at Tolentine was really amazing because it was a parochial school with a small enrollment from the neighborhood. Unlike many of the other Catholic schools that attracted students from the entire metropolitan area, Tolentine's enrollment was restricted to the parish's boundaries."

Despite those restrictions Donohue posted one of the best records in the city, compiling an incredible 80-16 win-loss mark over a four-year span.

* * * * *

Donohue always considered his players and students 'his boys' and while he was not above riding them when they failed to meet his expectations, there was nothing he wouldn't do for any of them. On the basketball court, baseball diamond or in the classroom he taught and encouraged, often using unconventional methods to motivate his students and athletes to exceed their own expectations. The same message—to dream big dreams—that his father had imparted on him years earlier, he passed on to his boys.

Donohue didn't accept anything but all-out effort and, at times, his criticisms would drip with sarcasm. His car became a taxi service for his high school players and his parents' home a refuge for a student-athlete who was having trouble at home or needed a place to stay after a late practice or game. Above all, he preached the value of teamwork and the notion that no one was above the team. His players knew the importance of being able to depend on each other and most important of all they knew they could count on their coach in times of need.

At one point Brother Victor became concerned that Donohue was spending too much time on basketball.

"I called him into my office to have a heart-to-heart talk and explained that basketball wasn't everything, that he needed some time off and perhaps go out on a date with a girl," Dardis recalled.

"No problem," Donohue said with enthusiasm. "In fact I might have a date this Saturday night. I told her that if there were no basketball games this weekend we could go out."

Brother Victor just shook his head in disbelief.

Within a year of taking the Tolentine job, Donohue's attention to detail, his demands for perfection and his belief that team effort could often overcome superior individual talent was paying off dividends. In his first season at Tolentine, the school advanced to the CHSAA playoffs, the first of four consecutive playoff appearances the club would make under Donohue's direction. In that initial year, Joe "Doc" Dougherty and Bob "Rip" Cleary led the Tolentine squad and the team was known as the Doc and Rip show. They faced the Chaminade High School Flyers in the quarter-finals of the city playoffs and jumped out to an 11-point lead. But the Flyers rebounded with a 6-0 run to end the first half and went on to record a 72-63 win.

Tolentine was back in the playoffs in 1957 but a great individual performance by a future pro star did them in. Tom Stith racked up 27 points to lead the St. Francis Terriers to a convincing 69-51 win. Stith then led the Terriers to wins over St. Ann's and LaSalle High Schools to capture the city championship, their third consecutive title. Making the playoffs that year was an impressive feat for Tolentine since the school was forced to play the second half of the season without their all-city star, Jimmy Boyle.

"My brother developed mono and was forced to sit out the second half of the season," Brian Boyle said. "Jack would come over to the house to bring the school work that he had missed and helped him with it. One Friday night he brought the whole team over, 15 guys crammed into a small living room and Jack had us all laughing with his stories."

Tolentine was ousted in the first round of the playoffs two years running but they were gaining confidence—confidence that paid off by the end of the '58 season. They were matched up against Chaminade in the opening round of the playoffs for the second time in three years, but this time Tolentine's Paul Mahoney exploded for 30 points as the Wildcats downed the Flyers, 73-55. Tolentine's run ended in the semis when they went up against All Hollows and fell 79-70. The Wildcats had nothing left in the third place game as they were trounced 76-41 by Manhattan Prep ending the school's most successful season on a disappointing note. While Tolentine was winning on the court, the members of the basketball team were also learning valuable lessons about life.

"Jack had the ability to make people feel good about themselves, and for teenage boys that was important," Brian Boyle said. "He gave the same attention to the 15th player on his team as he did the star. It was great because no matter where you stood on the team you would have time with the coach, moments alone when you could get personal advice."

* * * * *

When Donohue accepted the job at Tolentine, his duties also included coaching the varsity baseball team, a position he relished as much as the basketball post. But while he was an astute student of the game, he didn't have any experience conducting a baseball practice. On the basketball side he had several mentors and regularly conversed with other high school coaches about strategies and drills. That wasn't the case in baseball where many of the schools did not approach their national pastime with the same fervor or commitment. Donohue was not prepared to just follow others' mediocrity, so he enlisted the help of his friend and rival Jack Curran. Curran, a star baseball player at All Hollows and St. John's University who was drafted by the Brooklyn Dodgers and played three years in the Pittsburgh Pirates' farm system, provided Donohue with drills and practice plans.

"Jack called me and asked for some help so I gave him drills to run in practice," Curran said. "He was always trying to learn and improve himself."

The Tolentine baseball program didn't capture any championship banners under Donohue's tutelage, but it did produce some outstanding people. Steve Ryan, one of the team's starting pitchers, enjoyed a successful career as a sports executive, serving first as a vice-president with the National Hockey League before being appointed CEO of the Major Indoor Soccer League.

"I made the team in my freshman year," Ryan recalled. "We didn't have a lot of talent but Coach Donohue was an excellent coach. He would practice situational baseball and taught us how to play the game properly. During the basketball season, he would have Buck Freedman, an assistant coach at St. John's University, come in and work with the players. Jack was one of the first coaches to be involved with mentors."

The 1958 junior varsity baseball roster also included a skinny sophomore named Jack Mulqueen.

"I grew up playing stickball in the streets and if you could hit in stickball you could hit a baseball," Mulqueen said.

The youngster's batting ability earned him a spot on the team although he soon learned that you needed more than skill to play for Donohue.

"We were down by a run in the final inning, had the bases loaded with two outs and I knew Jack was going to need a pinch-hitter. I looked around the bench and saw I was the best hitter available so I started warming up, swinging a few bats and moving out to the on-deck circle. I was confident that he was going to send me up to bat."

But Donohue selected another, less-skilled hitter to pinch hit. The batter made out and Tolentine went down to defeat.

"I couldn't understand why he didn't put me in," Mulqueen said. "I came to him and said 'Mr. Donohue you should have put me in.'"

For Donohue it was a no-brainer; Mulqueen had received a detention from one of the brothers earlier in the day and that had sealed his fate.

"He explained to me that because of the detention there was no way that I was going to play that afternoon," Mulqueen recalled. "I didn't understand it at the time but he was teaching me that I had to be responsible not just on the baseball field but in the classroom as well. Winning or losing a baseball game was secondary to building character."

It was a lesson Mulqueen took to heart and stayed with him when he became a leading fashion designer in New York City.

Donohue also had a huge impact on the life of John McSherry, an overweight kid who liked to hang around the gym and baseball diamond after school. Jack employed him as the team manager and encouraged him to make a career out of the one thing he loved—sports,

"Jack told me that I should look into refereeing basketball and umpiring baseball games," John McSherry said. "When he moved to Power, he used to have me come down there and officiate basketball and baseball scrimmages. That's how I got started and that's the main reason why I became a National League umpire."

*   *   *   *   *

In 1957, Donohue received a call from one of the priests from St. Barnabas, soliciting his help in reviving the parish's CYO program. Two parishioners had offered to coach the grammar school team and Jack agreed to act as a consultant to the volunteers One of Donohue's suggestions was to bring up a fifth-grader, Frankie McLaughlin, to play with the eighth-graders.

"Frank was already a gym rat but he was the smallest player on the team," his brother Walter said. "I remember sitting with Jack during one of the varsity games. It looked like it was a challenge for Frank to get the ball to the basket but he was heaving shots from the outside. I was embarrassed and apologized to Jack for Frank's shots but Jack assured me that he wanted Frank to shoot the ball."

"The team is not that good and they might get shutout if Frank doesn't score," Jack said to his friend.

Donohue was able to persuade Tom Murray, a student at Iona Prep, to coach the team the next three years and St. Barnabas once again became one of the better teams in the city. Jack would take Murray to Yeshiva practices to watch Red Sarachek's coaching style and was always willing to lend a helping hand to the young coach.

"Jack is the reason I became a high school coach," Murray said. "When I graduated from Iona Prep, I wasn't planning on going to college but Jack told me that I needed a college degree if I wanted to coach."

Murray took the advice to heart and attended St. Mary's of the Plains before returning to New York when he started a successful career at Archbishop Stepinac High School. He moved to Cardinal Hayes in 1968 where he directed the school to two city titles and three second-place finishes. Donohue had taken the Tolentine basketball program to new heights but things at the school were changing. The parish decided to build a new school and expand its enrollment but after a dispute with the Christian Brothers, the parish chose to bring in the St. Augustine order to take over the administrative and teaching responsibilities for the new school. Brother Dardis was reassigned to St. Joseph's High School in West New York while Donohue pondered his future.

"Jack had received some offers from colleges and other schools," Dardis said. "He told me that if I was leaving he didn't want to stay and began exploring other possibilities."

A chance conversation landed Donohue his next coaching job, a job that would make him a household name in North American sporting circles. He had arranged a scrimmage with Power Memorial High School that winter when the head coach told Jack that he was thinking of stepping down as the school's basketball coach and Jack should apply for the job. Donohue applied and was appointed the school's athletic director and varsity basketball coach and, in 1958, he began to weave his magic in the heart of the Big Apple. Power offered a lot of things that Jack didn't have at Tolentine. It was an all-boys school located in Manhattan, within walking distance of the old Madison Square Garden, the home of the NBA's New York Knicks. Power had recently built the Gold Star Gym and had a strong nucleus returning for the 1958-59 campaign. Donohue now had access to some of the best high school players in the United States; could offer tuition scholarships and recruit from anywhere in the city.

"Jack got all the publicity when he went to Power and coached (Lew) Alcindor, but he did a great job coaching at Tolentine," Dardis said. "In 1960, three of the five starters at Manhattan College were from Tolentine and it was Jack who developed them as players. I'll tell you what kind of person Jack Donohue was. In his first year at Power, the baseball coach at St. Joseph's High School developed a case of TB and couldn't coach. Jack volunteered his services and coached the St. Joe's team that year even though he was teaching at Power."

CHAPTER 4

Usual Suspects

In the coaching fraternity, Jack Donohue looked up to two men he referred to as his adopted fathers, Bernie (Red) Sarachek and Joe Lapchick. He learned valuable lessons not only about basketball, but also about life itself from both of them, although their delivery couldn't have been more different.

"Red and Joe were both mentors of Jack," Hall of Fame Coach Lou Carnesecca said. Carnesecca's famed coaching career began as St Ann's High School in midtown Manhattan. He later became Lapchick's assistant at St. John's University and assumed the head coaching job at St. John's when Lapchick retired in 1965. In the 1980s, Carnesecca coaxed Sarachek out of retirement to be his assistant at St. John's.

"Jack was very close to Joe and would spend a lot of time at the Lapchick house in Yonkers," Carnesecca related. "Red was very helpful to Jack, in fact Red helped me out a lot as well."

Sarachek was one of the great fundamental coaches of all time, his genius often overlooked by the fact that he coached at Yeshiva College, a rabbinical college where the Torah assumed greater importance than the proper execution of the pick-and-roll. Sarachek had a rough manner, but was a superb teacher who didn't always believe in positive reinforcement.

Yeshiva was often in need of a gym for practice or a game and Donohue would arrange for the team to use the Gold Star Gym at Power. There, he could watch first hand the coaching methods employed by Sarachek while soaking up the man's knowledge of the game.

"I remember Jack would get a bunch of guys from St. Barnabas together to scrimmage against Yeshiva," Tom Murray recalled.

On other occasions, he would take Murray and other young coaches to Yeshiva's practices where they could observe Sarachek's unique ability to teach and motivate. Donohue respected Sarachek's court savvy, but more importantly, he admired Red's passion for the game and his determination to do things the right way. He was a straight shooter who never worried about hurting someone's feelings.

Soon after the State of Israel was established, an Israeli basketball team was sent on a goodwill tour of the United States with the marquee event a fundraising game against Yeshiva University at Madison Square Garden. The organizers mentioned to Sarachek that a win for Israel in front of a sold-out crowd would be a tremendous boost to the morale of the new nation.

Those same organizers were very upset, however, when Yeshiva went out and beat the Israelis. When Donohue suggested to his mentor that he got a lot of powerful people in the Jewish community mad at him, Sarachek had a simple reply.

"How many times in my life do you think I will have a chance to beat a country?"

* * * * *

Joe Lapchick was one of the first big names in professional basketball, a 6'5 center with the Original Celtics who later became a successful coach at both the collegiate and professional levels. He possessed outstanding motivational skills and a keen understanding of the human psyche, traits he inherited from his father.

"My father told me that his own father was a master at being able to motivate his six children, not only to do what they were supposed to do, but to do extra things as well," Richard Lapchick said about his father Joe, and his paternal grandfather.

Joe Lapchick taught Donohue the importance of motivation and the need to care for people. Lapchick spent endless hours with his disciple teaching him to respect his profession and the importance of loyalty; lessons that Donohue employed at the high school, collegiate and international level.

He gave Donohue tapes of the St. John's games that Jack would show his Power team, making them one of the first high schools to watch game film on a regular basis.

"Joe Lapchick was a saintly man who understood the psychology of coaching and the importance of dealing with individuals differently," commented Danny Buckley, coach of the powerful Lasalle High School team. "He wasn't an educated man, but one of the most intelligent men I've ever met."

As a professional player Joe Lapchick displayed a sense of compassion and acceptance rarely seen in the 1920s. The Celtics' biggest rivals at the time were the Harlem Rens, an all-black team led by a center named Tarzan Cooper. Prior to the opening tip-off of each game, Lapchick would approach Cooper and instead of offering the traditional handshake, he would hug his black opponent. The message was clear, the star player of the Celtics considered the black man his friend and equal.

"My father's actions were unpopular with a lot of fans, but he was telling everyone that this is more than just a game," the younger Lapchick said.

Joe began his coaching career at New York's St. John's University, and then moved on to the New York Knicks with the advent of the National Basketball Association. There, he instilled a team-first strategy that was unique among professional teams of that era.

"Lapchick had a rule that we couldn't shoot on our first possession until all five players had touched the ball," point guard and league all-star Dick McGuire said in *Garden Glory*. "Unless it was a lay-up, we had to work the ball around and get everyone involved."

He also started Sweetwater Clifton, one of the first black stars in the NBA, much to the chagrin of some bigoted fans who would picket Lapchick's Yonkers home or hang an image of the coach from a tree outside their house. Lapchick led the Knicks to three Eastern Conference championships in the early 50s and never had a losing season, but a dispute with club president Ned Irish put his job in jeopardy.

Irish was a former newspaperman whose marketing skills brought college basketball to Madison Square Garden and he was also one of the founders of the NBA. However, he proved to be a better promoter than a judge of basketball talent. Lapchick wanted a greater say in the team's personnel and felt the club's performance was being compromised by Irish's handling of the college draft. Fearing that he was being set up as the fall guy after the team faltered in the mid-50s, Lapchick resigned as coach before Irish had a chance to fire him.

He returned to St. John's in 1954, replacing the legendary Frank McGuire, and continued to produce winning teams for the Redmen for another 10 years. He did so with class and style, characteristics he passed on to many young coaches he would mentor over the next decade.

When Lapchick discovered that some of his players at St. John's were receiving passing grades without doing the required academic work, he was shocked that a Catholic institution would condone such a practice. To combat a lackadaisical attitude towards an education of which he was deprived, Lapchick became the first college coach to institute mandatory study hall for his players. He compensated for his lack of formal learning by reading voraciously, particularly books on history and politics that sharpened his social consciousness, a consciousness that he shared with his son Richard.

"In 1965, we read the *Autobiography of Malcolm X* and Bill Russell's *Go for the Glory* and it raised our awareness of racial problems in the United States," the younger Lapchick said.

Those books, and a visit to the German concentration camp at Dachau when he was 14, changed Richard Lapchick's outlook on life. He dedicated his life to causes of social justice and played an integral role in the sports boycott of South Africa during the apartheid era.

In turn, Donohue took a fatherly interest in Richard just as the elder Lapchick had mentored him.

"I became a big fan of Jack Donohue when he offered me a scholarship to Power," Richard said.

Even though he decided to attend nearby Manhattan Prep, Richard remained close to Donohue.

"Jack Donohue was the most giving person I ever met. When I was studying in London, England, he just showed up one day at my door to see how I was doing. He asked me if I needed anything. Before he left, he mentioned that it might be a good idea to shave my beard before I returned home to visit my father."

Lapchick took the advice to heart and was clean-shaven when he returned to New York to visit his parents.

46

"The beard was part of life during the Vietnam War era and I started growing it again as soon as I left New York."

Donohue followed Richard Lapchick's career as he developed into the foremost expert in North America on sport ethics. Lapchick accompanied the first group of NBA stars that toured South Africa following the elimination of apartheid in 1991, founded the Center for the Study of Sport in Society in Northeastern University and later chaired the DeVos Sports Business Managment / Institute for Diversity and Ethics in Sport.

"After my father died, Jack would call up and say 'I know that your father is looking down at you right now and is real proud of what you are doing'. It always meant a lot to me."

Although New York was full of characters that helped mold Donohue's own character, no two people had a greater influence on Jack Donohue's career and personal life than Lapchick and Sarachek.

*   *   *   *   *

"Coaching was different then," Danny Buckley commented about the high school basketball scene in the 1950s.

Buckley was the highly successful coach at LaSalle High School when Donohue started at Tolentine and the two quickly became on-court rivals and close friends off the court.

"We were all good friends and after games we would meet, have a beer or coffee and socialize. Coaches don't get along like that anymore, there's too much adversity, but in those days, we helped each other out," Buckley said.

In the coaching fraternity, Donohue was closest with Jack Sullivan and Jack Curran. Sullivan coached at Fordham Prep while Curran became the basketball and baseball coach at Archbishop Molloy in 1959 after an injury ended a promising professional baseball career.

"Donohue, Sullivan and Curran were named the Three Jacks because they spent so much time together," Tom Konchalski said.

Curran graduated from All Hollows in 1947 and although he was a member of school's basketball team that won the city championship, it was on the baseball diamond where Curran really thrived. He was a star pitcher who was drafted by the then-Brooklyn Dodgers and spent several years in the Pittsburgh Pirates farm system. He replaced Carnesecca at Archbishop Molloy High School and became the most successful basketball and baseball coach in New York City history. Donohue and Curran shared the same values, were passionate about their profession and always put the welfare of their players before their personal ambitions.

They lived at home with their parents, were devout Catholics and held strong moral values that they passed on to their players. They developed ties with college coaches from across the country that were looking to recruit blue chip players from the Metropolitan area. The recruiters knew that Curran and Donohue would not only recommend their own players, but also athletes from other schools, and their opinions were valued at the highest coaching levels.

* * * * *

Neither Jack nor Freddie Stegman could remember the first time they met but they were sure of one thing – it was in a gymnasium. Still a bachelor in his early 30s Donohue was, as Stegman often remarked, married to basketball, and most of his early coaching years were spent in gyms and schoolyards watching players or observing other coaches.

Stegman also spent countless hours watching players hone their skills in high school games, tournaments or pick-up games in the city's numerous outdoor parks but for a totally different reason.

Stegman made his "living" as an unofficial recruiter for American colleges long before the establishment of scouting services. He would contact colleges about New York City high school players and offer to "deliver" them to a school for a fee. He was nicknamed "the Spook" because he always appeared out of nowhere at a gym or outdoor playground. He also possessed the uncanny ability to disappear when the check arrived at a restaurant or when someone was looking to settle an outstanding debt.

For schools that didn't have large coaching staffs or recruiting budgets, Stegman could be very helpful. The problem was that Stegman couldn't always be trusted and made as many enemies as friends. Donohue found Stegman to be an interesting but flawed human being and took great delight in telling stories about his buddy's antics.

Not everyone approved of Stegman's tactics. In the award-winning book *Foul*, a biography of New York City High School legend Connie Hawkins, author Dan Wolf, took issue with Stegman's very existence.

"Spook is the most notorious of the freelance recruiters," Wolf said in his book. "He prowls the schoolyards, community centers, and high school gyms, lining up players for whatever college would pay him the most. If a coach in the Southwest needs a backcourt man and he has the money to spend, Spook can supply him. How long the kid stays in school is somebody else's business."

Stegman walked a very slim line between legal and illegal activities. Jack Molinas, who traded potential NBA stardom for a career as basketball's number-one point-shaver and game fixer, used Stegman to recruit teammates for money tournaments in the metropolitan area.

"Spook's job was to hook up high school players from the metropolitan area with college coaches who were looking for a playmaking guard or a rebounding center or what have you," Molinas was quoted in *The Wizard of Odds*, a book detailing the gambling and point-shaving scandals that plagued college basketball in the early 1960s.

"Spook knew everyone, everywhere, and I was very friendly with him. He would come to my office and ask me for ten or twenty bucks to buy some needy kid a meal and I would always lay it on him. Stegman could be a charming man in one moment, vulgar and crass the next, but in the late 50s and early 60s he was a player in New York City basketball."

It was Stegman who introduced Molinas to Hawkins and Roger Brown, an introduction that got the high school All-Americans banned from both the NCAA and the National Basketball Association. During the Christmas holidays of 1961, Connie Hawkins was broke and borrowed $250 from Jack Molinas with the promise to repay, a promise he kept. Although neither Hawkins nor Brown was enlisted to throw games, their association with Molinas ended Hawkins' collegiate career. Hawkins was tainted and NBA commissioner Walter Kennedy banned Hawkins for life. The ban was lifted in 1969 when Kennedy settled a lawsuit Hawkins had filed against the NBA.

The Spook's detractors also included most of New York City's high school coaches. Molloy's Jack Curran had a standing rule that no player was to talk to Stegman and Donohue made sure that Freddie was always at arm's length from his team. He didn't let him come near the Power gym except for games, and Friendship Farm was also out of bounds during summer sessions.

Still he couldn't shut himself off completely from the fast talking Stegman and he loved hearing stories of how Freddie would try to con people. When Jack moved away from New York, first to Worcester and later to Canada, he kept in touch with Stegman and was always willing to help out financially when the Spook was down on his luck, which was more often than not. When they were young, Donohue's children referred to Freddie as Mr. Collect because every time he called the Donohue residence they would hear the operator say "Phone call from Freddie Collect."

On one trip back to New York City, Jack agreed to meet Freddie in the lobby of one of the city's swankier hotels for coffee. As they sat and chatted, Freddie congratulated himself for picking such a high-class meeting place.

"You got to hand it to me, I certainly take you to the nicest places," Stegman stated as men dressed in power suits walked through the lobby.

"I would be more impressed if you picked up the check," Donohue replied "These two coffees are costing me $25."

"What's the difference, you're loaded. Here I am taking you to a classy place and you're worried about a measly $25."

On another trip, Donohue recalled going to a bar to meet some friends and invited Freddie to join them.

"Nah, that place stinks," was Freddie's reply.

"What, did you bounce a check there or something?"

"No, nothing like that, I just don't like the clientele."

When Jack arrived at the bar, he discovered why Freddie was averse to joining him.

"Hey Jack, tell that friend of yours, the Spook, not to be showing his face around here no more. We don't like people with funny money coming in here."

Jack couldn't believe his ears.

"Are you nuts?" Donohue asked Freddie the next time he saw him. "Passing counterfeit money in a bar filled with cops, judges and newspaper guys. You got to be crazy."

"Ah, it was no big deal. Those friends of yours are too sensitive. How was I to know it was counterfeit? I am not a crook."

"How much did it cost you?" Donohue asked

"I got $200 for $20!"

* * * * *

"The first person I met when I came to New York was Jack Donohue," Vince Cazzetta said. "And the second person I met was Freddie Stegman."

Cazzetta was the antithesis of Stegman, a saintly man who was not only an outstanding coach but a person of impeccable character. He was the assistant coach of Seattle University when Elgin Baylor was the team's star and coached two All-Americans, Eddie Miles and Charley Brown, during a five-year stint as Seattle's head coach.

In 1959, he visited New York City and Donohue in search of players and the two coaches hit it off right away developing a strong affection for each other. They had similar interests and traits. They were both devout Catholics, family men who would each father six children and they had success on the basketball court.

One of Cazzetta's first recruits when he was named Seattle's head coach was Waverly Davis who earned an all-city selection in Donohue's first year at Power.

Although Davis was the only player from Power that Cazzetta would recruit from Jack's teams during an eight-year span at Seattle and the University of Rhode Island, he and Donohue remained friends for life.

Donohue recommended Stegman as a person who knew all the players in the city, but cautioned Vince to be careful in his dealings with Freddie. Cazzetta never developed the same attachment to Stegman as Donohue had; he dealt with the Spook out of necessity.

"In those days, a head college coach was lucky to have a part-time assistant, let alone a recruiting coach," Cazzetta explained. "So the head coach had to do most of the recruiting and it was hard to go to high school games locally during the season. If you were coaching on the West Coast it was impossible to see players from the East Coast. People like Freddie served a purpose because they knew who the players were."

Cazzetta's coaching expertise was recognized on a national level when he led Connie Hawkins and the Pittsburgh Pipers to the American Basketball Association championship in 1968, earning Coach of the Year honors in the process.

"George Mikan (the NBA all-time great and then commissioner of the ABA) said I could have anyone I wanted to be the guest speaker at the league's awards dinner and the only one I wanted was Jack," Cazzetta said. "He agreed and did an outstanding job. Jack was always a very good friend."

* * * * *

The name McGuire has long been synonymous with New York City basketball. Frank McGuire, who grew up in an Irish working class section of Manhattan, was perhaps the most well-known and successful coach to hail from the city. He began his coaching career at St. John's University, won a NCAA championship at the University of North Carolina, spent two years as head coach of the NBA's Philadelphia Warriors and then finished his career at the University of South Carolina. The key to his collegiate success was his ability to recruit New York City players. He was revered by many of New York's high school coaches and developed an underground railroad that delivered some of the top players to whatever school he was coaching.

During his St. John's days, Frank coached Dick and Al McGuire. The two brothers from Astoria, no relation to Frank, would later carve their own niche in the history of New York basketball.

Donohue was friendly with Dick whose ball handling feats earned him the nicknamed 'Tricky Dick'. He was an outstanding playmaker who went on to enjoy a Hall of Fame professional career with the New York Knicks. When his playing days ended, he stayed involved in the game, first as head coach of the Detroit Pistons. In 1965, he renewed his relationship with the Knicks as head coach and was the team's assistant coach and scout when the club won their only two NBA titles. His younger brother Al was not as talented a player as his brother Dick but made up for that deficiency with a brash attitude. He played briefly with the Knicks before pursuing a successful coaching career at the collegiate level.

Donohue had a stronger relationship with Al, mainly because the two Irishmen were similar in so many ways. They each had a keen sense of humor, understood that players, not coaches, won games and knew how to work the media. McGuire insisted that his players graduate from college and, like Donohue, was always more concerned about the person than the athlete.

On the bench, Donohue and Al were masterful at devising winning game plans, were fiercely competitive during games, yelling at players and picking up technical fouls. But neither ever lost track of the fact that it was a game and there were more important things in life than the final score of a basketball match.

And they shared an appreciation for the dealings of one Freddie Stegman. While Donohue's relationship with Stegman was strictly personal, McGuire used the Spook's unique talents to build winning basketball teams. When Al received his first coaching job at Belmont Abbey he immediately got on the phone to Stegman looking for players.

"You select the kids who have the talent and I will convince their parents that they should be going to Belmont Abbey," McGuire told Stegman.

Freddie nabbed three players (reportedly interrupting a craps game to introduce McGuire to the prospective recruits) while McGuire visited their parents guaranteeing that each of them would graduate from Belmont Abbey. With the help of Stegman, McGuire developed a winning program at the small Catholic school, then moved to prime time when he became the head coach of Marquette University at the same time Lew Alcindor was leading the Power Panthers to a National High School Championship.

McGuire had little chance of landing the highly sought-after center, but asked Donohue for a favor. He wanted to attend a practice and have his picture taken with Alcindor.

"I knew that I didn't have a chance to recruit Alcindor but if I could get that picture in the paper, make it look like Marquette was really going after this guy, it would help my recruiting a lot. It did, too."

Years later, both McGuire and Donohue did separate TV specials featuring the elusive Stegman and they remained friends although they purposely never coached against each other. When Jack became head coach at Holy Cross College, he called Al to discuss scheduling a game between Marquette and Holy Cross. McGuire said he looked at games as personal duels with the other coach and was always looking for a psychological edge over the opposing coach.

"He told me he considered me a good friend so let's not screw that up by playing against each other," Donohue explained.

* * * * *

Jack Donohue's influence was not restricted to the players that he coached and that fact was never more evident than his association with the McLaughlin family.

Walter McLaughlin Sr. was a New York City detective who moved his family to the Bronx section of Woodlawn in 1947 and was intent on seeing his four sons receive a college education. It was an education that eluded Walter Sr. when he and his younger brother incurred the wrath of their own father, himself a high-ranking police officer, when they left college to unsuccessfully pursue professional baseball careers.

A third brother, Albert, was the captain and catcher for the Commerce high school baseball team that captured the New York City championship in 1924 and featured a first baseman named Lou Gehrig. A year later, when a New York Yankee scout signed Gehrig out of Columbia University, he also inked Albert, who was attending NYU at the time, to a professional contract.

Albert's father, the commander of the Alexander police precinct situated near Yankee Stadium, was furious that a third son was foregoing a college education for baseball and marched into Colonel Rupert's office and made the Yankee owner rip up his son's contract. While Gehrig would go on to become one of major league's baseball greatest hitters, Albert found success as a lawyer.

Donohue became close to the family when he and Walter, the oldest of four brothers, played together on CYO baseball and basketball teams for St. Barnabas. Their friendship grew when both enrolled at Fordham University and decided to commute together in a 1935 DeSoto that belonged to Walter's dad.

While Walter and Jack stayed in touch throughout their lives, it was Walter's two younger brothers, Frank and Tom, who developed a closer relationship with Donohue.

Donohue briefly coached Frank's fourth grade CYO squad and the pair would later be reunited in 1969 when Frank would initiate a successful coaching career as a volunteer coach on Donohue's Holy Cross College staff.

Tommy first developed a love for basketball while dribbling through chairs at the St. Barnabas gym under Donohue's watchful eye and later become a university coach and then one of New England's top sports agents. Donohue was now coaching at Power but opened up the St. Barnabas gym every Saturday providing the youngest McLaughlin and his friends with drills to improve their skills.

Jack would later try to recruit both brothers to Holy Cross College, but instead they chose Fordham and Tennessee respectively. But those rejections never soured the relationship that Donohue had with the family. He respected their values, work ethic and a strong friendship developed between the four men. Frank and Tom honed their playing skills in the summer at Jack's basketball camp and got their first taste of coaching as counselors at the upstate camp. Unable to convince Frank to attend Holy Cross as a student-athlete in 1965, he persuaded him to join his staff four years later as a volunteer coach.

"I was a low draft pick of the Knicks and had no real chance of making the team," McLaughlin said. "I was planning on being the junior varsity coach at Mount St. Michael's but Jack convinced me to go to Worcester. I rented a room for $8 a week and sold life insurance on the side."

While the coaching experience didn't pay, it led to a position with Digger Phelps at Fordham University the following year and subsequent stints at Notre Dame and Harvard University before he returned to his alma mater as athletic director in 1992.

When Tom's career at Tennessee hit a roadblock, he went to Donohue for help in transferring. Jack desperately tried to get him into Holy Cross, but the college was adamant about not accepting transfer students. So he brokered an arrangement that saw Tom go to University of Massachusetts to play alongside Julius Erving under Coach Jack Leaman, an old Donohue friend.

Years later, after a pro career in Europe and coaching stints at UMass and Stanford University, Tom joined Bob Wolff as a sports agent. A decade ago he founded his own sports agency, Best in Sports, and has developed a reputation as a real-life Jerry McGuire, a straight shooter who stays away from problem athletes and concentrates his efforts on clients who are solid citizens. His value system strongly echoed those of the coach who introduced him to the fundamentals of basketball 40 years earlier.

"People like Jack Donohue come along very seldom," Frank McLaughlin said. "Jack was truly an amazing man and his values couldn't help but rub off on people who met him. Jack treated everyone the same whether you were a janitor cleaning up the gym or a doctor. Every person had value and that's why Jack was always happy, because he truly loved people and that's what made him tick, interacting with all sorts of people."

CHAPTER 5

The Power and the Glory

The story of Power Memorial Academy dates to 1909, when Monsignor Power, pastor of All Saints parish in Manhattan, petitioned the Christian Brothers of Ireland to come to New York, to teach the boys in his parish in a new parochial grade school. The parish, located in the western part of Harlem, was made up of working-class Irish and so the good monsignor asked for the Christian Brothers since he felt that other teaching orders knew little about Ireland or Irish history, and he reasoned that they would be unsuitable since most of his parishioners were of Irish birth or Irish descent.

The grammar school was a success and three years later, the Brothers were asked to open a high school in the parish. Five adjoining brownstones were secured from West 124th Street and turned into one building. Attendance at the new All Hallows High School increased every year, forcing the school to expand until it occupied five more adjoining buildings.

Finally, in 1931, the Brothers moved All Hollows to a new building uptown at 164th Street and Walton Avenue. While All Hollows continued to be successful in its new location, there was a call to continue secondary education in the vacant building on 124th street. Once again, the Christian Brothers answered the call by staffing the new school, and, as a fitting tribute to the priest who had first invited the order to set up a school in his parish, called it Power Memorial Academy. Monsignor Power had died in 1926, but his name would live on through the exploits of the Power Memorial students.

On September 21st, 1931, Power Memorial opened its doors to thirty-one first year students. But it wasn't too long before Power was facing the same problem as its predecessor: the school was too small for an ever-growing enrollment.

As the brothers searched for a solution, they were told of an empty hospital located on 61st Street. In 1938, they purchased that hospital and Power Memorial Academy now had a midtown address and a date with destiny. The buildings that Power vacated would not stay empty for long. They eventually became home to another Catholic secondary school, Rice High School.

*   *   *   *   *

Like most Catholic orders, the Irish Christian Brothers felt that physical activity was an important part of the spiritual and intellectual development of young men, and the school's first varsity basketball team, nicknamed the Panthers, began playing in the late 1930s. The sport was popular among the Irish, and Power Memorial was competitive from the beginning. Martin Burns became the first of many Power players to receive individual recognition when he was named to the 1936 all-New York City team.

The school captured the Manhattan-Richmond championship in 1937 before losing to Iona Prep 22-16 in the CHSAA semi-finals. That year Tom Holohan became the second Panther to be named to an all-city team.

Two years later, Power struck gold for the first time when Connie Toomb scored a basket with 20 seconds left to play, and Tom Courtney added a foul shot to lead the Panthers to a 27-25 win over St. John's Prep to capture the city title. Power's Ed McCabe, held to just four points in the title game, was named to the *World-Tribune* all-city team.

In 1941, another all-city player, John Ezersky, led Power to the metropolitan championship, but the Power basketball program faltered after the 1941-42 campaign.

It experienced a revival during the 1950-51 season as a pair of sophomores – George Yearwood and Dick Percudani – earned spots on the varsity team and led it back to respectability.

Percudani moved on to Georgetown University after graduation where he played varsity basketball for three years before returning to Power to become the JV coach and Donohue's trusted assistant.

The Power basketball program went into another tailspin in the years following the graduation of Yearwood and Percudani, but it received a shot in the arm when Power administrators realized the need for modern athletic facilities and decided to build a gym that the school could call its own. Up to that point, Power basketball teams had used the 12th Regiment Armory on 61st Street for the majority of its games and practices.

In order to pay for the new gym the school embarked on a series of fundraising events that included selling chance books and holding "Gym Building and Fundraising" pep rallies. Finally, in the mid 1950s, ground was broken and a year later, the Gold Star Gym was opened and dedicated to Power Memorial's World War II veterans. The gym, a testament to the tenacity and loyalty of the Power students, gave the Panthers the best high school venue in the city. In addition, they were about to add an outstanding coaching staff that would build an unparalleled high school dynasty.

When Donohue arrived at Power, he found a veteran team with more talent than any of his Tolentine teams. In his inaugural season at Power, the Panther roster included two players, Waverly Davis and Jim Lawlor, who would earn all-star status under Donohue tutelage.

The Panthers advanced to the city's playoffs where they met Archbishop Molloy High School and head coach Jack Curran in the first of several playoff battles between the two friends.

Both coaches were in their first year at their respective schools and the 1959 game was the beginning of one of the best rivalries in the annals of New York City basketball. The game was not decided until the final minutes when Power broke a 53-53 tie with a 12-7 run en route to a 65-60 victory.

"Power became Molloy's nemesis for so many years," Tom Konchalski said, "It would seem like they would meet every year in the semi-finals and Power always won."

The victory over Molloy pitted the Panthers against All Hollows, a club that had finished third to Power in regular season play. The two teams had split two previous meetings, but Donohue had Power playing its best basketball of the year and the Panthers appeared headed for its first CHSAA title since 1939.

Everything changed when Jim Lawlor got sick the night before the title game and Power was forced to play without its all-city backcourt ace. All Hollows jumped to a 12-point lead early in the second half, and then held off a furious second half rally by Power to register a 59-52 win.

"Power was the best team in the city that year, but Lawlor's absence was a major factor in the final," Konchalski said.

When Davis, Lawlor and Tom Brennan graduated at the end of that year, Donohue and the Panthers underwent a rebuilding phase. The 1961 squad featured three seniors: Warren 'Joe' Issac, Bob Zuppe and Kevin Turner, who all earned athletic scholarships to college. Issac attended Iona College in New Rochelle, and in his final year of college ball he led the nation in rebounding before embarking on a successful pro career in Italy.

* * * * *

Arthur Kenney recalls walking down 10th avenue trying to make it to St. Jude's Church in time to serve 6 o'clock mass. He carried his cassock and surplice in one hand as he navigated the icy streets of Manhattan's West Side. His concentration was broken by a sudden shout from a passing car.

"Hey, Art Kenney!" the voice said.

"It awoke me from my trance and as I spun around, I slipped on the ice, but managed not to drop my cassock or surplice." Kenney recalled. "It was Coach Donohue, who was driving several of his student-athletes to school and happened to be driving by St. Jude's, just as I was about to arrive for Mass. He asked me why I had not been to the recent tryouts, and invited me to Power that afternoon."

A month earlier, Kenney attended a tryout at the Power Memorial gym along with a number of the better local grammar school players. He had gone in hopes of attaining one of two scholarships that Power annually gave to graduating grade school students who showed basketball promise.

He was tall for his age and had a pretty good tryout. But when he didn't hear back from the head coach he assumed that he hadn't made a good enough impression, and made plans to attend Xavier High School the following year.

"With over 200 eighth-graders at the tryout, I felt I had little hope of receiving a scholarship, in spite of my uniform from St. Jude's, the patron saint of hopeless cases," Kenney said.

"I had decided that I would attend Xavier High School, following the tradition set by my father and brother, until that morning encounter with Coach Donohue set me on a different course."

An excited Kenney made his way to the Power gymnasium that afternoon and was immediately put into action by Donohue.

"When I arrived, Coach Donohue had me play with the varsity team during their scrimmage game with a rival, and treated me as if I were already a member of the team. He even told Mel Kellogg that he should use the picks that I was setting for him. Well, my prayers to St. Jude were answered, and I received a scholarship."

Kenney began to make weekly trips to Power on Saturdays, where he would spend the entire day playing and practicing. One day, he asked a friend and grammar school teammate, Lew Alcindor, to join him. Alcindor (who would later change his name to Kareem Abdul-Jabbar) was a year younger, but was taller at 6'7".

Alcindor's first love was baseball. He pitched and played in the outfield, but in the winter he played basketball for St. Jude's.

"Arthur said we could play inside and inside sounded pretty good in February, so I went with him." Alcindor would later say.

Unlike Tolentine, Power attracted its students from throughout the greater New York metropolitan area, and for the first time Donohue had the ability to go out and recruit players from anywhere in the city—players that would bring Power to the upper echelons of high school basketball.

Donohue was pleased to have Kenney at Power but he also knew that the future fortunes of the Power basketball program rested on his ability to convince Kenney's grammar school friend to attend Power as well.

Alcindor was already promised a scholarship when he showed up with a hundred other eighth graders one Saturday afternoon to showcase their skills to Donohue.

Prior to the session, Donohue told the select group that there were two scholarships available and to try to do their best in the drills and scrimmages. What he didn't tell them was that one scholarship was already reserved for the tall, skinny black kid.

Among the players assembled that day was a guard from lower Manhattan named Charlie Farrugia. At just under five feet and possessing agility and basketball skills, Farrugia was the antithesis of the 6'7" Alcindor, who had the height, but whose skills were still a work in progress.

"I was an eighth grader at St. Stephan's and playing for the Madison Square club team," Farrugia recalled. "We scrimmaged against the Power freshman team, and I played well. After the game, the Power JV coach, Dick Percudani, came up to me and asked what school I played for and I told him I was still in grammar school."

Percudani encouraged Farrugia to attend a tryout at Power and to try to secure a scholarship to the school.

Farrugia showed up on the appointed Saturday, but when he looked at the bigger players he didn't think his chances of landing a scholarship were that good. So he was surprised when Donohue called him over to talk towards the end of the workout, and told the youngster of his two choices.

"He told me he was picking Alcindor and myself, and both picks surprised me," Farrugia said. "Kareem was bigger than anyone else, but he didn't have very good hands. But at the start of our freshman year he had grown to 6'9" and by the time he was a sophomore, the change was unbelievable."

Several high schools had shown interest in Alcindor while he was still attending St. Jude's, but he quickly narrowed his choices to Power and Archbishop Molloy. Both schools offered legal scholarships, although at least one other school took the recruiting process a step further.

"There was one school in our league that offered the entire St. Jude's team scholarships if Lewie went there," Curran revealed.

Alcindor took a liking to Curran, who was building his own destiny across the East River at Molloy, but Molloy was in Queen's and that meant a two-hour commute every day, while Power was just a few subway stops away.

Alcindor was impressed with Power's academic reputation, their new gym and their coach. Power had everything a young Alcindor was looking for in a high school.

"I had a good feeling about Coach Donohue almost immediately," Alcindor recounted in his first autobiography *Giant Steps*. "He knew how to talk to kids like they were really there…he was both personable and authoritative."

When Alcindor decided on Power, the 13-year-old called Curran to inform him that he had decided not to attend Molloy, a classy move by a grammar school student.

"I had a lot of respect for Coach Curran and felt that I had to call him and tell him of my decision. I said it was too far to travel everyday," Alcindor explained.

"Lew, it is too far to travel and I can't see you coming here either," Curran responded with complete honesty.

Years later, Curran, the winningest coach in New York High School basketball history, would wonder if perhaps he should have done things differently.

"We lost a lot of games to Power with Lew in the line-up," Curran remembered. "Sometimes, I think maybe I should have offered to drive him to school, but it was out of the way."

The offer probably wouldn't have made a difference. Donohue had sold Alcindor on the benefits of a Power education in the classroom and on the courts.

"Coach Donohue knew what he was doing. No way I was going anywhere but Power."

There was also another upside to going to Power – Donohue's ability to get tickets to watch the New York Knicks play in Madison Square Garden. He later took Alcindor to his first two pro games, where the future NBA star was mesmerized by the world champion Boston Celtics.

"When you are 14 years old and you are sitting in Madison Square Garden watching the Celtics playing, it just didn't get any better than that," Alcindor said.

With Alcindor on board and Donohue at the helm, the Power Panthers were about to make basketball history.

* * * * *

When Alcindor arrived at Power in the fall of 1962 he entered an entirely different world, but he soon made the necessary adjustments.

He began his first year at Power practicing with the freshman team under Percudani, and by his own admission was scared the first few weeks of practice. He wasn't sure just how effective he was going to be against stronger, tougher freshmen from others schools.

Both Percudani and Donohue knew that Alcindor would initially struggle no matter what level he played that year, but they also knew that as he developed physically and mentally, he had the potential to be very, very good. The two men then discussed having him learn at the highest level under Donohue's watchful eye. So one morning, Donohue called a startled Alcindor into his office and handed him a varsity uniform and informed him that he would be playing with the varsity team that afternoon in a scrimmage against Erasmus Hall.

"That wasn't the plan," Jabbar recalled forty years later.

As the Power team rode the subway to Brooklyn for the game, Alcindor felt proud at being brought up to the varsity team and at the same time apprehensive of what lay ahead. It was a different story after the game as Alcindor cried in the locker room after losing to Erasmus. As he sat there, tears running down his face, he suddenly looked at his teammates who were staring at him in disbelief

"It was a defining moment in my life," Jabbar said. "I was with the big boys now. I was 13 years old but I had to learn to compete like an adult. Up until that time I was acting more like a 12-year-old and now I had to act like a 15-year-old, I had no other choice."

In another scrimmage, Lincoln High School's 7' center Dave Newmark proved to be too physical and experienced for Alcindor, who fouled out in the third quarter of yet another loss.

The basketball education of Lew Alcindor was proving to be a painful experience. But he began to flourish under Donohue's combination of stingy barbs, occasional praise and commitment to fundamentals. In *Giant Steps*, Alcindor recounted Donohue's psychological approach with players.

"Mr. Donohue coached through benign humiliation. He challenged your pride, knowing the worst thing that can happen to an adolescent is to look bad in front of the guys. He took the game seriously and insisted that we do the same, that we make ourselves proud by winning and playing well. We had to play our absolute hardest, nothing else was acceptable...what he was ultimately after was for every one of us to learn to light our own fires and glow our brightest. He was a basketball coach and he knew what he was doing."

Alcindor also learned early that his coach would battle for his players. During a scrimmage with Boys High, Alcindor was bitten on the arm. When Donohue discovered the red mark on Lew's arm, he immediately confronted the Boys head coach, Micky Fisher.

"You better get whoever did that out of here," Donohue yelled. The game was stopped and the guilty party was dispatched to the locker room.

Things got better as the regular season began. Alcindor would start each quarter, win the jump ball, and play at least half the game, a rare feat for a 13-year old boy. In one game, a televised encounter with Fordham Prep, Alcindor gave Metropolitan New York a glimpse of what was to come, when he snatched a game-high 21 rebounds. After the game, Donohue quipped to Alcindor that perhaps they should have all their games televised.

The basketball education of Lew Alcindor continued throughout his freshman year and the team finished second in the Manhattan section to Danny Buckley's LaSalle High School team, led by an all-city center named Val Reid. Their second-place finish earned them a berth in the city playoffs and the Panthers met a more experienced St. John's Prep in the first round of the playoffs.

St. John's held a one-point lead with just seconds left on the scoreboard clock, when Johnny Hayes, Power's all-city guard, stole the ball and launched a desperation shot from just over mid-court as the buzzer sounded.

The basket swished in and the Power players mobbed Hayes, while the St. John's Prep coach, Herb Hess, protested the play, claiming the shot came after the horn sounded.

The protest was denied and Power advanced to the semi-finals, where their opponent was the undefeated Holy Cross High School Knights.

Holy Cross was led by Bobby MacIntyre, a two-time all-city player, and Mike Riordan, both of whom would later play professional basketball. MacIntyre would later star at New York City's St. John's University, while Riordan would play at Providence College before moving on to an NBA all-star career with the New York Knicks and Baltimore Bullets.

At 6'6" MacIntyre gave up several inches to Alcindor but was stronger and more experienced inside. But it was his ability to shoot from the outside that caused problems for the Power squad.

Donohue and Percudani set up a defense that was geared towards stopping the high school All-American and the strategy worked well. What the coaches had not counted on was McIntyre's teammates picking up the slack.

The Panthers held the high scoring forward to just 11 points before he fouled out with just over five minutes to play in the game. However, Joe Heather and Mike Riordan, at the time two unheralded juniors, scored 16 and 15 points respectively for the Knights, who jumped out to an early lead and maintained it throughout the game.

George Barbezat, a hard-nosed two-way player, engineered a late rally that cut the Knights' lead to 55-51 but Holy Cross point guard Paul Sullivan responded with six straight points to seal Power's fate. MacIntyre and Riordan alternated guarding Alcindor and held the freshman to nine points.

The Crusaders came up short in the finals against Power's main rival, Danny Buckley's LaSalle Academy and center Val Reid. LaSalle prevailed in the championship game with a 47-43 win.

The Holy Cross loss didn't end the season for the Panthers. Donohue placed the team in the Iona College post-season tournament, where they captured the tournament championship with five consecutive victories.

When school ended, Alcindor and Kenney and the rest of the Power squad spent most of the summer upstate at Donohue's Friendship Farm, constructing cabins and playing a lot of basketball. When they returned to Manhattan in August, they were ready to take on LaSalle, Val Reid and anyone else that got in their way.

CHAPTER 6

Friendship Farm

Donohue was now sitting on top of his own little world: coaching basketball during the school year and baseball in the summer, living at home with his parents and establishing a name for himself in New York City as an excellent tactician and motivator.

He had realized one of his goals, to be a head coach by the age of 30, but it wasn't enough. He wanted to achieve his second goal and began to think about setting up his own summer camp. After searching for a suitable spot, he purchased land in Saugerties, New York, about 100 miles north of New York City. He called the site Friendship Farm and decided that it was an ideal spot for an all-sports camp, similar to Camp Momoweta where he had worked as a college student.

The Saugerties property was a 30-acre lot, set off from the main road by a long, winding dirt road, with a trail in the back that led to the Hudson River. When Donohue saw the property he envisioned modern cabins, baseball fields, basketball courts and swimming in the Hudson River for future campers, but anyone else saw a dilapidated property that was in desperate need of work. Few people, who visited the property in the late 1950s, would ever imagine that it would one day become the destination point for some of the top basketball players and coaches in the country.

To get to the main property, one had to pass over a railroad crossing that had no warning signals. Right after the railroad tracks, there was a drop so steep in the dirt road that a driver couldn't see the road in front of him once he crossed the tracks. When Jack purchased the property, it came with a colonial era house and an old red barn. With his father supplying the know-how and a few friends and high school players providing the brawn, the property was slowly converted into a primitive camp.

Donohue's first sessions were all-sport camps that even offered archery and rifle. But Donohue soon realized that the future of Friendship Farm was as a specialized basketball camp. Not only could he attract players and coaches from the city, but it was also an excellent way to ensure that his Power players were spending the summer working on their game. That first group of Power Memorial basketball players constructed a cabin that housed approximately 40 campers. They put down a floor in the barn from old discarded railroad ties, which now became the dining hall and kitchen.

"There was this old barn that Coach Donohue wanted to turn into a dining hall for the campers, but it had a dirt floor," former Power player Jackie Bonner remembers. "So he had us 'snaking railway ties' which was his way of saying gathering discarded railway ties and putting them on the barn floor."

The railroad company was constantly replacing the existing ties on the tracks that ran through the property. Donohue instructed the players to put the used ones in his father's car and drive them back to the barn.

"None of us had a license but we were allowed to drive Coach's father's car to transport the ties," Bonner said. "The car was a 1949 Studebaker and so old that it had a starter pedal you had to push to get it started. Arthur Kenney did most of the driving."

Once Jack had the first cabin built, he needed to furnish it with beds and even with the camp's primitive atmosphere, bedding for 40 people could be an expensive proposition. Donohue discovered a solution to his problem, when he found out that the army was selling surplus supplies at an auction. He took his old Fordham buddy, Art Goldstein, down to the armory on the day of the sale.

"Everything was sight unseen but that didn't stop us from bidding on a number of items," Goldstein recalled.

Donohue was so impressed with the prices that he decided to bid on additional items and before he knew it he had purchased a scaffold. He hadn't even thought about a scaffold before he arrived at the armory that morning, but there was one being auctioned so why not bid on it. *Doesn't everyone need a scaffold?*

"Jack knew what to expect with the mattresses and the bedding," Goldstein said. "The mattresses were in pretty bad shape. They were clean but really worn. If you put three of them on top of each other they made a fairly comfortable bed and with the prices that we quoted, were excellent."

To their surprise, Donohue and Goldstein had the winning bid on each of the items, including the scaffold. "We rented a truck and I drove to three different warehouses to pick up everything," Goldstein said. "At the time I was living in a gardens apartment that had old empty garages in the back and we rented them to store everything until the summer."

Well almost everything. While the two friends decided that a scaffold would come in handy for painting and construction, they were expecting a wooden scaffold that you adjusted by hand. Instead, they had bought a monstrous iron scaffold with a mechanical lift. "What are we going to do with this, Goldy?" Donohue asked his old college buddy. They loaded the rest of the merchandise first and put the scaffold in last before heading for Flushing Bay. There, the scaffolding mysteriously fell off the truck and sank to the bottom of the East River.

*   *   *   *   *

The boys who attended the camp worked hard and played hard, but Donohue made the experience an enjoyable one. Frank McLaughlin was amongst the campers in Jack's first year of operating a basketball camp and was present as the camp developed over the years.

"There were 14 of us the first year and all we had to play on was a half court made of dirt," McLaughlin said. "Friendship Farm was the first real camp just for basketball and I think Jack had grand plans of turning it into a state-of-the-art camp. He would wake up every morning and tell everyone what a great day it was."

McLaughlin was a rarity in that first year – he and Richie Lapchick were the only non-Power players among the 14 campers. "Jack was my first coach: a Grade 4 CYO team at St. Barnabas that he coached briefly while he was attending Fordham. He talked to me about going to Power, but Fordham was closer."

Frank earned all-city honors in his final year at Fordham Prep and despite turning down Jack's scholarship offer to Power, the two remained close friends.

Part of Donohue's success at Power was due to the fact that he surrounded himself with good people: hard working, success-orientated men with strong values. At Power it was Jack Kuhnert and Dick Percudani and at Friendship Farm it was Jimmy Herrion and Richie Tricario.

Herrion, who later became Jack's assistant coach at Holy Cross College, acted as Donohue's second in command, while Tricario started as the camp trainer and increased his responsibilities each summer. "I graduated from Mount St. Michael's and then earned my training certification at college," Tricario said. "Jack started to twist my arm about being the camp's trainer, but I resisted as long as I could." Tricario finally agreed to take on the job and soon proved indispensable.

"Jack was away more with recruiting once he took the job at Holy Cross and Richie ran the camp in his absence," Donohue's wife Mary Jane recalls. "Joyce Herrion and I would be in the main house looking after our kids, when campers would show up at the front door.

"Mr. Tricario said that we had to come here to get some TLC," the youngsters would announce.

"They had no idea what TLC was but we sat them down, gave them milk and cookies and after a little while they would say they were ready to go back to camp," Mary Jane recalled.

Friendship Farm was a drop-in center for high school and college coaches, and not surprisingly many of the campers later became successful coaches. Frank McLaughlin, Danny Nee, Tommy Sullivan, Bobby Gregory and Tom McLaughlin came in the early years as campers and later became counselors. That quintet not only became outstanding collegiate players, but also went on to become Division I coaches. Jimmy Herrion's sons, Tommy and Billy, also worked at the camp before establishing successful coaching careers in their own right.

As the camp grew, its reputation brought in more and more campers, counselors and guest coaches. It wasn't long before Friendship Farm attracted established coaches who came to give lectures, and ended up staying late into the night to discuss the finer points of basketball and to socialize with Donohue and his staff. Bobby Knight and Tates Locke were regular visitors as were Jack Leaman of the University of Massachusetts, Jack Curran and Howie Garfinkle.

Garfinkle, who started and still runs the famed Five Star Basketball camp, and Curran once locked horns in the camp championship game. "Howie's first camp experience was at Friendship Farm and one year his team went undefeated throughout the week with three of my players: Kevin Joyce, Brian Winters and Bobby Carver," Curran said. "I had to play him in the championship game and coach against my own high school players."

Curran did have 6'10" Tom Riker on his team and used the big man to perfection as he upset the undefeated Garfinkle squad in the title game. Riker would later become a college teammate of Joyce, Winters and Carver at the University of South Carolina, and was a first round draft pick of the New York Knicks.

"The camp would always have interesting people stop by and give lectures. Both Bobby Knight and Coach Leaman were regulars," Tom McLaughlin recalled. "It was funny to see Lew Alcindor at the camp, because here was the number-one high school player in the world and he was living in these rustic conditions."

Bobby Knight would arrive from West Point every Monday and give a defensive lecture. Often he would stay the rest of the day and talk basketball with the camp coaches. "He was a great guy," Tricario said. "At the end of each lecture he used to throw a basketball at mid-court and then have 100 campers fight for it. We were lucky that no one ever sued us."

Tom McLaughlin had graduated from camper to junior counselor when he first met a future teammate and NBA Hall of Famer. "Julius Erving would come down to the camp with his college coach, Jack Leaman," McLaughlin said. "That was interesting because Julius and I eventually ended up as teammates at UMass, but we first met at Friendship Farm."

Late one night, a car pulled into the driveway and two big black guys got out of the car and walked past surprised campers to the main house where Donohue greeted them. The pair was Tom Hoover of the New York Knicks and the Knicks' heralded first round draft pick from Grambling University, Willis Reed. Hoover was set to lecture the following morning and brought Reed along for the ride.

During his lecture, Hoover explained that Wilt Chamberlain would put himself in a bad position by constantly taking fade away shots, shots that were low percentage and left the big man in poor rebounding position. To prove his point he brought a camper up to take a few fade away jumpers from the post area. Unfortunately, he chose Alcindor who had spent part of the summer practicing the very shot that Hoover had been preaching against. As Alcindor calmly hit shot after fall away shot, Hoover became more upset and finally moved on to another subject.

After the lecture, Hoover and Reed joined the camp's all-stars in a game against the staff. Such contests are normal at summer camps with the pros exerting a minimum amount of effort to record a resounding victory in front of the entire camp. But the counselors at Friendship Farm were no ordinary players and quickly their team which included Alcindor, Frank McArdle and Frank McLaughlin had a comfortable lead over the team led by the two pros.

"All of sudden Reed called time-out and walked to the sidelines," McLaughlin recalled. "He was wearing sweat pants, not expecting much of a game, and he took off the pants which meant that he was now taking the game seriously."

Hoover and Reed rallied their squad for the win and that impromptu game marked the first time that Alcindor, who later changed his name to Kareem Abdul-Jabbar, and Reed, two future Hall of Fame players, would battle against each other.

* * * * *

The Camp eventually expanded to include two full outdoor courts and a half court for shooting behind the renovated barn. Whenever it rained the campers were shipped to a local school to spend the day.

Each year, Jack would add to the camp buildings, another cabin, more outdoor courts and finally a swimming pool, but even after all the additions the camp was still quite primitive.

Tommy McLaughlin recalled that despite the conditions Donohue and Herrion always made the time enjoyable with their sense of humor and small rewards. "Coach Donohue and Jim Herrion would reward you for making the best bed by taking you off grounds to the local ice cream parlor and the opportunity to make your own sundae."

In his autobiography *Giant Steps*, Kareem Abdul-Jabbar expressed displeasure with having to spend his summers at Friendship Farm, away from the hustle and bustle of New York City in the summer.

"My idea was to go up there for one or two weeks and work on my game, not spend the entire summer there," Jabbar said. "I wanted to spend most of the time in Harlem. I mean there was a big difference between Saugerties, New York, and Harlem.

But for other Power players, summer at the camp was something they looked forward to with much anticipation. "It was a great adventure," Jackie Bonner said. "Power was very strict and a lot of hard work, but being able to get away and spend the summer at Friendship Farm was our reward and that made everything worthwhile." Donohue made the work a fun experience and granted the high school players freedoms that they didn't possess back home.

Years later, when McLaughlin read Kareem's account of his camp days and of being forced to spend the summer there and the problems associated with being the only black kid at the camp, he called his old friend to apologize. "I told him that I never thought of him as being the only black at camp, to me he was just one of 14 guys there," McLaughlin said. "We were having so much fun that it never occurred to me that someone wouldn't want to be there."

Alcindor made the most of his time at Friendship Farm, even though he would have preferred roaming the streets of Harlem during the summer. Each year he improved as a player and when given an opportunity displayed his artistic side as well.

Donohue had installed a loudspeaker for announcements and liked to wake up the camp with a rendition of Alan Sherman's camp song – *Hello Mudda, Hello Fadda, Here I am at Camp Grenada*. One year, he decided to hold a talent night and instructed Art Kenney and Alcindor to come up with two skits. Both players originally balked at the idea but when push came to shove, Alcindor proved to be quite creative.

"The camp was broken up into two groups, and we were to come up with a camp song and do a skit," Kenney said. "Our group was more autistic than artistic, and so we only did a song that was sung to the tune of *On Wisconsin*.

"Kareem's group did a skit, and partitioned off half the dining room with a rope running across the ceiling and sheets hung on them so you could not see the kids," Kenney recalled. "They then backlit that section, and pretended they were doctors in an operating room, operating on a patient, using a saw from the barn next door. We could only see silhouettes and hear the dialogue which was very clever and very funny!

Kareem was Chief of Surgery, and Kevin Turner's brother (Kevin played at Power) was Kareem's assistant. They removed a ball ("Coach always said that we should eat, drink and sleep basketball, but this patient has taken this too far...!"), Converse sneakers and other basketball items. It was a lot of fun for those participating and those observing."

Donohue continued running the camp until the mid-1970s when his commitment with the Canadian National Team put an end to the camp. Digger Phelps came back one year and ran an all-star camp on the site, and then vandalism began to take its toll on the property. A fire destroyed the main house when the volunteer fire department could not navigate their trucks through the deep snow that had blocked the only entrance to the camp area. Mr. Marx, the camp's handyman and a member of the volunteer brigade watched from a distance with tears in his eyes as the building burned to the ground. Two years later, the Donohues sold the remains of the property and the first great basketball camp became a distant memory for those who played, coached or just dropped by to pay a visit.

"It really hurt Jack when the fire destroyed the main building," said Billy Kirsch, the head coach at Siena College and a camp regular. "He put so much effort and time there."

"He loved being there out in the fresh air with the kids, his family and friends," Frank McLaughlin said. "For Jack Donohue, every day was camp."

CHAPTER 7

City Champions

The Power Panthers finished the 1961-62 season on a high note, winning the Iona College Invitational tournament, and the buzz among basketball people in New York City was the improvement that Alcindor had shown during the season.

When Alcindor returned to school in the fall of 1962 after spending the summer at Friendship Farm, he noticed himself how much his game had improved.

"I found out just how much I had improved when I got back to Harlem" Alcindor recalls, "and saw right away that nobody on the court could stop me. It dawned on me then, that nobody could stop me."

Alcindor also noticed a big difference in the way the Power Panthers attacked opponents in pre-season scrimmages.

"Power was now wearing teams down. The games were played in quarters – you'd go maybe eight quarters in an afternoon against various teams – and we started to dominate. We went up against Erasmus Hall and Bishop Loughlin and rarely lost a period and never a game."

Alcindor's improved play was the talk of his teammates and his opponents.

"The transformation between freshman year and sophomore year was the biggest transformation I have ever seen by any player," said classmate Mike Parfett. "When he returned he was the best player in the city; could have starred in college; and probably gone pro (in those days that option did not exist). He developed the now famous Sky Hook, put on a little weight and the rest is history. I think Kareem owes a lot to his early training and that was Coach."

Frank McLaughlin, who not only played against Alcindor when Fordham Prep and Power hooked up but also befriended him during the summers at Friendship Farm, also witnessed a drastic change in Alcindor's play.

"He was good as a freshman player; he was unbelievable from sophomore year on," McLaughlin said. "I remember in the beginning watching him try to do the Mikan Drill and really struggling. Kareem Abdul-Jabbar deserves a lot of credit for everything he has accomplished, but Jack Donohue was a major force in helping him reach that level."

The Mikan Drill, named after basketball's first big man George Mikan, was a continuous lay-up drill from both sides of the basket that developed footwork and a player's ability to score inside. Jabbar mastered the drill in grammar school but had difficulty in games.

"I learnt the Mikan Drill when I was in fifth grade at St. Jude's but I had trouble taking the drill and being able to execute the skill during games," Jabbar says.

Alcindor's rapid development, according to Molloy's Curran, was the result of several factors.

"He made great strides between his freshman and sophomore year, and that was strictly from doing big man drills, working hard and just good coaching. But all the coaching in the world wouldn't do anything if you didn't have the capacity to work at it, and he did."

* * * * *

LaSalle Academy entered the 1962-63 season as the CHSAA defending champions and they were led by their all-city center Val Reid—the same Reid who had schooled Alcindor in the post the year before. As fate would have it, the two teams and centers were scheduled to meet in the opening game of the season at Madison Square Garden. The game may have only been the first game of the regular season, but bragging rights were on the line. A week prior to the game, Donohue was at the Garden watching a Knicks' game with several Power players when Reid approached him.

"Coach, next week we're playing you," Reid said with a confident smile. "You tell Loooiee that I am going to eat him up". Without batting an eyelash Donohue replied, "Hey Val, make sure you don't get indigestion."

It was Reid who ended up eating his words as Power won 56-44 and established themselves as the team to beat in the city. In the post, it was no contest as Alcindor outplayed the more experienced Reid.

"Reid had dominated Alcindor the year before when Lew was still learning the game," Tom Konchalski said. "But this time it was no contest, as Alcindor was the best player on the court."

The Power game was a preliminary to an NBA game featuring the Philadelphia Warriors and the New York Knicks, and after his domineering performance Alcindor had an opportunity to see Wilt Chamberlain score 73 points as the Warriors crushed the Knicks. For New York basketball fans the evening presented an opportunity to see the game's top center and his heir apparent.

* * * * *

Illness prevented Arthur Kenney from playing in his sophomore year, but when he was given medical clearance by the doctors to resume competitive basketball in the fall of 1962, Donohue made sure that he made up for lost time by having him work out in the gym with Alcindor several mornings a week, in addition to daily practices.

"In my junior year, I would come to school early with Coach (he often picked me and Kareem up on his way to work), and on certain days I would do early morning work-outs to get in shape, and then practice in the afternoon," Kenney recalled. Kenney and Danny Nee, another 6'7" forward, gave Power plenty of height, but Donohue preferred a smaller starting five and surrounded his 6'11" sophomore center with guards Oscar Sanchez and Bob Erickson, while Jack Bettridge and George Barbezat, both 6'2", played at the forward spots.

Sanchez was the team's quarterback, who also was responsible for defending the opposition's top backcourt scorer—a responsibility he handled with great adeptness.

Erickson possessed an accurate jump shot, his quickness forced numerous turnovers and he was often at the scoring end of a Sanchez pass, when the Panthers' vaunted running game was in high gear. Bettridge was a natural scorer, possessing a deadly outside shot, coupled with the ability to score inside against taller defenders.

Finally, there was Barbezat, the team captain who would cap a solid high school playing career by being named to the all-city team in his senior year.

Nee was the first player off the bench, and would have started on just about any other high school team. Kenney, whose main role on the team was to guard Alcindor in practice, came on the court whenever Alcindor got into foul trouble, needed a quick breather or on the rare occasions when he wasn't playing well.

That last incident didn't happen often, but one day, in a game against Cardinal Hayes, Alcindor had trouble getting untracked and watched from the bench as Kenney scored 15 points, emphasizing Donohue's belief that no one was above the team. "It didn't matter who you were, no one was above criticism from Coach Donohue," Alcindor said in *Giant Steps*.

Of course, it helped that Nee and Kenney were always ready and willing to step in when called upon.

"I spent the entire season trying to cover Kareem in practice," Kenney said. "Playing against Kareem was a baptism by fire for me, as I was constantly getting my shot blocked."

Kenney did hold his own in a drill called War, where the two big men would go one-on-one. There were no fouls, no violations, and no boundaries in the drill that resembled wrestling or rugby more than basketball.

* * * * *

Alcindor had received some early recognition when he was named as a pre-season All-American by several basketball magazines, but the accolades didn't register with the sophomore who felt being named all-city was the ultimate goal.

"I didn't know about players from the rest of the country, I only knew New York City players," Jabbar said years later. "My goal was to be the best in New York City."

Power didn't let up after the LaSalle victory and by Christmas they had compiled an impressive 8-0 record and were scheduled to play in two holiday tournaments. The first was hosted by Marti Christi High School and presented Donohue an opportunity to display his altruistic side. Stephen Fitzgerald, a star player with Rice High School, suffered an ankle sprain and was carried downstairs to the locker room where a mis-informed student manager applied hot water to the injury instead of cold. The heat caused Fitzgerald's ankle to swell even more, and the skin turned to a hideous blue color. When Donohue saw Fitzgerald's plight he insisted on helping out.

"Coach Donohue knew me because I had tried out for a scholarship to Power a few years earlier," Fitzgerald explained. "He gave me the name of a good trainer and said that I could come by and use the whirlpool at Power anytime I wanted, because Rice didn't have a whirlpool."

On other occasions, Donohue would drive Fitzgerald back home to the Bronx after a whirlpool treatment. The Rice basketball team was not surprised by Donohue's generosity and concern.

"Coach Donohue was a good friend of our coach Mike Browne,' Fitzgerald said. "We had a really small gym at Rice and it was difficult for us when we had to play on bigger courts, so coach Donohue would let us practice at Power when there was free time."

"I always said that Coach D went above and beyond for his players, and you see that his caring for people had no limits," Kenney said when he heard Fitzgerald's story.

The Panthers captured the Marti Christi tournament and then headed to Jersey City to compete in a Christmas tournament hosted by St. Peter's College. Power opened the tourney by knocking off a tough St. Francis Prep squad that featured Lloyd "Sonny" Dove, who would later star at St. John's University and play in both the NBA and ABA.

In the semis, Power was pitted against Trenton Cathedral, who was ranked in the top ten nationally and featured a high school All-American named Danny Hice. That game belonged to Barbezat who not only held Hice to 15 points, but exploded for 33 points to lead all scorers in an 85-63 rout. Power finished off St. Peter's Prep in the finals 58-40 as Alcindor was named the tourney's Most Valuable Player and Barbezat joined him on the all-star team. Suddenly, the Power Memorial Panthers and their super sophomore were not only the talk of the city, but the country as well.

The team clinched the Manhattan Division by beating LaSalle in their home gym and entered the CHSAA playoffs undefeated and as the heavy favorites. During the course of the season, the Panthers faced various tactics to try and slow the team down and contain Alcindor's production. Without a shot clock, teams would take the air out of the ball and work for a perfect shot, while on defence they would employ combination defenses and double teams on Alcindor, but Power had too much scoring potential throughout their line-up. Xaverian High School recorded a moral victory in the opening round of the playoffs, when they held the ball and managed to lose by a respectable score of 23-14.

"They were still holding the ball with one minute left, and Coach was disappointed that they did not try to win the game and appeared to be happy to lose by less than 10 points," Kenney recalled. "Coach never wanted to embarrass another team or coach, but he did not have respect for people who did not give a 100% effort."

In a more fast-paced game in the quarterfinals, the Panthers outlasted Molloy 53-45, and then knocked off the defending city champs in the CHSAA semi-finals, 65-45. In that game, Val Reid gave Alcindor an elbow to the mouth that drew blood, but by now the star center was getting used to being roughed up by the opposition and was able to shake off such tactics. He handled whatever the opposition threw at him – double teams, elbows – it didn't matter, Alcindor was the best player on the court.

He scored 13 points and was a factor on defense, as he blocked six shots and took away the Cardinals' inside game. Erickson led the Panthers in scoring with 18 points, 14 in the first half that saw Power jump to a 15-point lead after eight minutes of play, and his play earned praise from the head coach after the game.

"This was Erickson's best all-round game for us," Donohue told the media assembled outside of the winners' dressing room. "He's had better scoring games – he has the best shot in the school – but he did everything in this game."

Donohue's praise of Erickson had a two-point effect. The first was to publicly announce that Power's success was a team achievement and not the result of one player. Secondly he was complimenting a player who was more often on the receiving end of criticism.

"I was often in his doghouse because he didn't think I was working hard enough in practice and not fulfilling my potential; oddly enough that's the same gripe I had with my sons twenty years later," Erickson would recall forty years after the fact. "On the court, it was Coach's way or you got to sit; I got to sit a lot."

Power met St. Francis Prep in the finals; the same team they beat earlier in the season in the St. Peter's Christmas tournament. Dove, who was named to the all-city team, had a sensational game as he led all scorers with 29 points, but it was Alcindor and Power's commitment to team play that ruled the day. The 15-year-old sophomore had 15 points, 14 rebounds and eight blocked shots and earned the tournament's first-ever Most Valuable Player Award. It wasn't a one-man show; however, as Erickson scored 14 points, Bettridge added 10 and Barbezat, who joined Alcindor on the all-city team, chipped in with nine. After the game, Donohue once again stressed the importance of the team, when the media asked him if he thought Alcindor was a worthy recipient of the MVP award.

"Yeah, I'd say he deserved it. Yet I wish everyone on the team could have won it. But Lew is a big threat. Lew started to score in the Iona tournament," Donohue added, referring to the post season tourney a year before when the Panthers began their winning streak that was now at 29 and counting. "He was only a kid before that. Now he's a basketball player."

The win in the finals gave the Panthers a perfect 23-0 season. Pretty impressive stats, but the powerful Panther basketball machine was just starting to roll. The Power dynasty that began in 1963 included not only outstanding players, but arguably the best coaching staff in high school history. Joe Lapchick once advised Donohue to select assistant coaches that he could trust, while his other mentor, Red Sarachek, suggested that he surround himself with teachers, for the players' sake, as well as for that of the head coach.

Donohue fulfilled both requirements by selecting Dick Percudani as his assistant and JV coach and Jack Kuhnert as the freshman coach. All three coaches would eventually be inducted into various coaching halls of fame, and each provided not only coaching expertise, but also a strong commitment to the well-being of the athletes under their charge.

Percudani spent most of his coaching career as an assistant coach, but success followed him wherever he went: in the European Pro Leagues, as an assistant coach at Sacred Heart and Fairfield Universities and finally as an NBA scout. Percudani served as Director of Scouting for the Phoenix Suns of the NBA for 18 years until his untimely passing in 2001. His contributions to New York's basketball scene were recognized in June 1997 when he was inducted into the New York Catholic High School Basketball Hall of Fame.

Kuhnert joined the mathematics department of Power Memorial following his 1961 graduation from Manhattan College, and his first contribution to the Power basketball program was not on the court, but as Lew Alcindor's homeroom teacher.

"My homeroom teacher was Mr. Kuhnert, a genuinely caring adult who, if you were polite and respectful toward him, could be the nicest man in the world," Kareem said in his autobiography, *Giant Steps.*

Kuhnert became as "much of a friend as a high school teacher was going to be" to the shy freshman, and was a teacher that the budding superstar could confide in. He had an easy going nature, but students who mistook that temperament as a sign of weakness, soon found themselves in trouble.

Jabbar recalled how Kuhnert once handled the problem of a rude classmate by picking up the offending six-foot freshman by his jacket lapels and pinning him against the wall of the classroom. The student's legs were dangling in the air until the wayward lad apologized profusely. The story quickly spread throughout the school, and Kuhnert would never experience any further problems with unruly students in the class or on the basketball court.

Kuhnert took over the head coaching reins in 1965 when Donohue departed for Holy Cross College and took the team to the city finals in his first season. He compiled an incredible 89-18 record in five seasons, and continued Power's dominance of basketball in New York City, coaching the Panthers to four division titles, and to the 1970 city championship victory over Archbishop Molloy. Curran's Molloy team, led by future college All-Americans Kevin Joyce and Brian Winters, had knocked off Power the year before, but Kuhnert's squad returned the favour the following season, as they completed an undefeated (22-0) season and became the third Power team to be ranked number one in the country with the high school All-America trio of Len Elmore, Jap Trimble and Ed Searcy.

Kuhnert continued to achieve success after leaving Power for New Jersey's Freehold High School where his teams won a state championship, seven division titles and a record 10 Freehold Regional Holiday

Tournament crowns. The Freehold Holiday Tournament was aptly renamed in Kuhnert's honor following his sudden passing on October 6, 1997.

In his eulogy at a Memorial Mass in New York City following Donohue's death, Art Kenney had this to say about the coaching trio.

"The best thing about Power Memorial was the wonderful people it attracted, and the academic and athletic standards it set. Coach Donohue had an assistant, Richard Percudani, who had played for Power, and was 'cut from the same cloth.' That tandem became the best coaching trio ever to coach high school when Jack Kuhnert came to Power and joined the staff. In 1963, Power won the freshman, junior varsity, and varsity CHSAA Championships – the only time that has ever been done! The following year, in spite of replacing three starting players, our team continued through a second undefeated season, and a few years ago, was named 'The High School Team of The Century.' It was a testament to the teaching, developing and coaching ability of those three special men."

CHAPTER 8

The Courtship of Mary Jane

Mary Jane Choffin and her friend Winnie had arrived at the CYO sponsored dance in a downtown New York hotel on April 15th, 1962 hoping to meet some eligible young men, but had spent most of the night ducking in and out of the washroom trying to avoid two guys who had latched onto them shortly after they had arrived.

The evening had held such promise! The two women, friends since grammar school, had spent most of the afternoon preparing for the evening and discussing their plans for the dance and the 25-minute train ride into New York City and back. Despite growing up in nearby Westchester County, Mary Jane rarely ventured into the city, and she was looking forward to her big night out. Neither of the men was in sight when Mary Jane and Winnie cautiously left the safety of the restroom near the end of the evening, but within a minute they spotted the not-so-dandy duo that were putting on their overcoats and heading towards the exit. Feeling relieved, Mary Jane and Winnie returned to the dance floor area, but by that time all the interesting men were taken and the two decided it was time to catch a train back home. As they headed for the cloak room, a bespectacled man stopped them in their tracks.

"You two ladies aren't leaving already?" he queried.

They replied, yes, in unison.

"But there are two men inside who have been dying to meet you all night."

Without waiting for a reply, he gallantly took each one by an arm, and whisked them back to the ballroom where he introduced Winnie to his friend, Frank Shiels.

The quartet talked for a few minutes, exchanging names and home-towns when Jack Donohue, the bespectacled one, suggested that Frank take Winnie onto the dance floor. That invitation prompted a protest from Mary Jane.

"Wait a minute! You said there were two gentlemen dying to meet us!"

With that, Donohue whirled her onto the dance floor and began pouring on the Irish charm. During the dance, he discovered that the girls were planning to take the train home, and insisted on driving them to their intended destination. Not that he had a car, but in typical Donohue fashion, he told Mary Jane that his good friend Frank would be only too happy to provide transportation home. When the music stopped, Mary Jane and Winnie made one more stop at the ladies' room to discuss strategy. Winnie wanted to know if it would be safe driving home with these strangers. Mary Jane said everything was fine and added that she would feel safe driving across America with these men.

During the drive home, Frank was behind the wheel while another friend, George, sat in the front seat, leaving Donohue alone in the back between the two women, where he regaled them with story after story. Mary Jane broke a life-long rule by allowing her new beau to kiss her on a first meeting, and then went to bed wondering if she would see him again. She would later discover that Donohue hated going to dances and that on that fateful night his friends George and Frank went to the dance while Jack took in a movie. He had just happened to meet the two girls on his way in to get a ride home with his two buddies.

* * * * *

Mary Jane was the daughter of Leon Choffin and Mary Doyle. Her parents met when they were both working for Equitable Life Assurance, and after they were married they set up house in Westchester County. When Mary gave birth to Mary Jane, she became a full-time mother and housekeeper, while Leon rapidly rose in the company.

He first made a name for himself as an aggressive claims adjustor, whose specialty was catching fraudulent claimants—sometimes using unorthodox methods.

"Once there was man who was collecting unemployment benefits, claiming he couldn't work because of a bad back," Leon recalled. "I learned that he was working construction off the books, so I climbed a tree near the construction site and filmed him in action, lifting heavy materials."

Leon eventually became vice-president of the company, a position he held until his retirement. Like the Donohues, the Choffins were strict Roman Catholics and Mary Jane attended parochial school until she left home to attend the College of the Notre Dame in Baltimore. After receiving a degree in 1952, she returned to the family home in Mamaroneck, and was working for the New York State Welfare Department when she first met Donohue.

Mary Jane was smitten but did not hear from Donohue for several weeks following their initial meeting when, finally, he called to invite her to a Sportsman Dinner honoring his longtime friend and mentor, Red Sarachek. They would be sitting next to another Donohue friend, Jack Curran. Mary Jane quickly said yes, and then began to panic. She knew he was very involved in sports, coaching baseball and basketball at Power Memorial, and was full of stories about his players. She, on the other hand, was not a sports fan, and she wondered what they would talk about.

On the drive to the dinner, however, there were few pauses in the conversation. Mary Jane soon realized that not only was Donohue able to converse on a variety of subjects, he enjoyed talking and entertaining and putting his Irish wit to good use.

When they arrived at the dinner, the place cards were made out to Mr. and Mrs. Jack Donohue and Mr. and Mrs. Jack Curran, although both couples were on their first date. In the case of Mary Jane and Jack, the place cards proved to be a good omen, although the road to the altar was a rocky one.

From the beginning, Donohue stated that he did not think coaches should get involved with women because they were so totally wrapped up in their sports and it wasn't fair to the girl. Almost to prove a point, Jack would not call or come around for weeks at a time. She promised to herself on several occasions that she would not go out with him again, but neither one seemed to be able to stay away from the other for a long period of time. Once, after a three-week silence Donohue called and convinced Mary Jane to meet him at their favorite restaurant. She agreed, but in her mind she was going to fix him. He had a habit of setting a time to pick her up and then calling 15 minutes before and asking what time the date was and would eventually show up an hour late. This time she was going to turn the tables. At the designated time they were to meet, she was visiting an aunt and when she finally walked to the meeting place, she stopped at a local church to say a few prayers.

Let's see how he likes waiting! After tonight he will start showing up on time.

She arrived at the restaurant almost an hour late only to discover that Donohue had yet to arrive. The maitre d' met her at the door with the news that the gentleman in question had yet to arrive. Seeing how livid she was, he escorted her to a table.

"Sit down, sit down and have a drink," he said trying to calm her down. "He will be right here."

Mary Jane sat with a drink in one hand and a cigarette in another, both hands shaking. *As soon as I am finished my drink, I am leaving and we are through! There is no way I should be humiliated this way.* She was on the verge of tears when he walked in, very much out of breath and shame-faced.

"I am sorry, Honey – I know I am late – thanks for waiting," Donohue said. "I tried to take a shortcut and got lost."

Only Jack Donohue could come up with such a lame excuse and make it sound believable. Once again he was forgiven.

*   *   *   *   *

That September, Jack asked Mary Jane to attend the wedding of Jimmy Boyle who played for Donohue at Tolentine. The reception was in Manhattan and the couple planned to stay in the city after the wedding to see a show. Mary Jane was staying with her aunt and uncle, while her parents were out of town attending a convention. Both of her parents thought that Jack could do no wrong, mainly because he was Irish, and agreed to the weekend trip. At the wedding, the father of the groom pulled Mary Jane aside and said, "You should try to land this guy. He is really great."

Mary Jane replied she was certainly trying and made sure Jack heard her reply.

"My father was a reserved man, who normally wouldn't say something like that to someone he had just met," Jimmy Boyle said.

The evening was progressing well and the couple was on the dance floor when Jack whispered in her ear.

"I have to take you home right after the wedding, because there is an emergency at the camp and I have to go up there now."

So much for the romantic weekend that Mary Jane was expecting and she showed her displeasure by giving her beau the silent treatment. She wanted to deliver a great put down, but words escaped her as she tried to figure out if he had another woman on the side. Realizing he was in trouble, Donohue apologized profusely, but that just made Mary Jane more upset. When she returned to her aunt's and uncle's she complained bitterly about Jack's behaviour, but then blurted out, "Damn it, if he asked me to marry him tomorrow, I would."

While they had discussed marriage on several occasions, Donohue maintained his stance that coaches should not be married. It was true that Donohue's good friend Jack Curran preached the same gospel, but Mary Jane couldn't help noticing that most of the coaches she met were married, including Donohue's mentors: Red Sarachek and Joe Lapchick. Sensing the seriousness of the relationship and the frustration it was causing her daughter, Mary Jane's mother decided it was time for a woman-to-woman talk. The basic crux of the conversation was that Mary Jane had to be naive to think she had any hope of marrying a man in his 30s who was set in his ways and lived at home with his parents. Mary Jane's reply was typical of a woman in love: of course he will marry me – in time. Outwardly she put up a brave front, but inside, she was uncertain and confused. Would she be able to change his mind or was she just wasting both their time?

New Year's Eve 1963 came and Mary Jane looked stunning in her new dress as she left the house with Jack to attend a party in Queens hosted by Dick and Marie Percudani. Mary Jane was looking forward to the party even though she knew no one since Jack refused to take her to any of the Power games. Whenever the subject came up he would say that if his team lost the game he would have to stay with the boys and he would not be able to get her home.

87

The Percudanis lived in an old remodeled home filled with Italian provincial furniture. While the females gathered in the kitchen, the males congregated downstairs at the bar. When Mary Jane eventually made her way downstairs, she was introduced to everyone and a great fuss was made over Donohue, who was always invited to such parties, but rarely attended.

"As usual at most parties, the women were gathered in one area of the room to discuss babies and homemaking, while the men were on the other side talking about whatever they talk about," Mary Jane recalled. "After awhile I noticed that Jack had disappeared."

Jack reappeared just in time for the midnight champagne toast, although he insisted on ringing in the New Year with a Pepsi. When Mary Jane asked where he had been the whole time, Donohue explained that he was discussing business with Dick.

Guy Lombardo played *Auld Lang Syne* on the television as the giant ball descended on Times Square and 1964 was ushered in, in the appropriate manner. Everyone toasted, kissed and as the women began to prepare the food table, Jack grabbed Mary Jane's arm and said, "Let's go."

After the mandatory thank-yous and good-byes, the couple was back in Jack's car headed for Westchester. The atmosphere in the car was tense to say the least. Mary Jane tried several times to strike up a conversation on numerous topics, but her usually garrulous date limited his remarks to yes and no answers. Mary Jane began to realize that something was wrong and that it was over between them.

When they got back to her house she declared, "I can't keep going on like this!"

"Well there is one way to take care of it," Donohue said.

Mary Jane's mind was spinning with negative thoughts but she simply asked "How?" and was floored by his response.

"Let's get married."

"Are you kidding?'

He assured her that he wasn't, and explained how the evening had unfolded. Before picking up Mary Jane, he had visited his father, who was recuperating at a local hospital following a heart attack.

"Tonight's the night, Dad. I am going to ask Mary Jane to marry me."

"What do you think she is going to say?" his father responded.

"I hope she says yes."

"Well if she does, run like hell, because she is crazier than you are," was his father's sanguine advice. Jack had also spent part of the evening with Dick Percudani, discussing the pros and cons of married life. As he and Mary Jane sat on the couch, Jack suddenly reached into his pocket. Any other man would have emerged with an engagement ring, instead Donohue pulled out a pocket calendar! With all the confidence in the world, he stated that now was the time to pick a date.

"The way I figure it, we have to get married within the next six or seven weeks," Donohue said matter-of-factly. "What's the rush?" Mary Jane wondered aloud.

"Well, we both want to get married with a Mass, and you can't have a Mass during Lent which begins in 6 weeks," Donohue explained. "After Lent, there is baseball season, and then I have camp, so those are not good times to get married. Once camp is over, it is baseball season again and then basketball season starts, so really the only good time is in the next six weeks."

Mary Jane understood fully that good timing meant whatever was convenient to Jack. She had learned early in the courtship what his priorities were and that he was one man, for all of his good qualities, who was not going to change.

"Now, February 9 is probably the best time for the wedding. I have a game that day, but it is against Danny Buckley's LaSalle team and I'm sure I can get the game changed to Monday."

"February 9 sounds fine to me," Mary Jane replied, as she saw her now fiancé to the door.

*   *   *   *   *

Mary Jane woke up on New Year's Day with a lot on her mind, but the most pressing issue was how to break the news to her parents, that not only was she getting married, but also the wedding was going to take place in six weeks.

"I was the only child, but I was not spoiled by my parents, that job went to my aunt and uncles," Mary Jane would say later.

"I was close to my parents and I was worried about telling them I was leaving them – and in a short period of time. I was positively frightened to say anything to my dad – besides he had woken up with a headache and was like a bear."

So she went to the bathroom, where her mother was brushing her teeth and caught her completely by surprise when she said.

"Mom … Jack asked me to marry him last night and I said yes!"

Laughing and crying followed, intermixed with the obvious questions –How…When…Where??

"She took the fact that it would be happening soon very well, in fact eagerly, as if she was glad to get rid of me! What a comedown."

One parent down, one more to go.

Mary Jane walked down the stairs to the living room, where her father was lying on the couch still trying to rid himself of his pounding headache. Realizing that the direct approach had worked well with her mother, she employed that same strategy one more time. When she recalled the events of the previous evening, he simply opened an eye and said "Oh…that's nice," and went back to sleep. He admitted later to his daughter that the shock of the news instantly cleared up his aching head.

The majority of the planning fell on the shoulders of Mary Jane and her mother, and that suited them just fine. The bride-to-be returned to work on Monday to find the pipes frozen in the renovated school that served as the home for the regional Welfare office. Mary Jane and her co-workers were told to go home.

Perfect – she would get a head start on what needed to be done for the wedding.

On the way home, she stopped at the local church and was able to secure a February 9 date, despite the fact that the Catholic Church normally insisted on a six-month waiting period for prospective brides and grooms. The priest did ask if she was sure about this and with all the confidence in the world, she answered yes. When she arrived home, she and her mother decided to take advantage of the unscheduled day off and headed to the shops. The day was a huge success as Mary Jane picked out a wedding gown, a veil, and shoes, as well as dresses for the other women in the bridal party. She and her mother returned to the house and began telling a few select people the good news. The first to be told were her aunt and uncle; both of whom adored Jack. It was now time to inform Winnie, the friend who had accompanied Mary Jane the night when she first met Jack.

"How would you like to be a maid of honor in February?" Mary Jane asked over the phone.

"Great," her friend replied. "Uh…who is getting married?"

"Me, you nut, why else would I be asking you."

"Fantastic, that's great! I am so happy for you and would be honored to be your maid of honor."

Winnie had just one final question before she hung up the phone,

"To whom are you getting married?"

Jack had a few responsibilities – select a best man and two ushers, change a scheduled basketball game with his friend Danny Buckley, and, of course, get an engagement ring for his fiancée. So one night he picked Mary Jane up at her house and drove into Manhattan to the home of a friend, who Jack said could help them find the right ring. They entered the living room and were met by a man who had a selection of rings and settings laid out for their inspection. After a few minutes, they found a diamond and a setting to Mary Jane's liking and within Jack's price range. The gentleman took the ring off her hand, gave it to Jack and said,

"You should put this on her finger in privacy," and left the room.

He returned a few minutes later with coffee and cake.

"We spent the rest of the evening talking …about basketball," Mary Jane recalled. "It turned out that the man was a basketball fan who worked with his father in a jewelry store during the day and went to basketball games at night!"

* * * * *

Jack's mother doted on her only son, but didn't understand why he spent so much time on basketball and his players. She thought that it would all change once he was married and had a family to support.

"Now that you are getting married you can stop playing basketball and just be a teacher," she told him.

Sarah Delaney knew that coaches were always getting fired and figured her son would be wiser to concentrate on his more noble profession of teaching in the classroom.

Little did she realize that Jack taught so he could coach, and in his eyes, coaching was the most noble of all professions.

A blizzard was forecast for the wedding day but Donohue, in his typical nothing-can-go-wrong demeanor, assured everyone that the weather would be fine and he was right. It was a cold, clear day and Mary Jane was surprisingly cool and calm throughout the morning as the wedding party prepared for the church ceremony at her house. The maid of honor's responsibilities went to Winnie, while another friend, Nancy Castelli, and Mary Jane's future sister-in-law, Mary, served as bridesmaids. When time came to leave for church, the bridesmaids left in one limousine while Mary Jane and her father followed in a second vehicle.

"When I first got in the limo I wished we had curtains or tinted glass so people wouldn't be able to look in," Mary Jane said. "But as we began to take the half-hour drive to the church, I was enjoying being the centre of attention, as everyone tried to look in every time we had to stop for a light."

* * * * *

While Mary Jane was getting ready for Church, Jack was playing the role of chauffeur, giving rides to relatives and friends. As well, there were chores at home that needed to be finished, all the time concentrating on others rather than his own wedding just a few hours away. Jack also enlisted Art Goldstein to help drive some of the players from Manhattan up to New Rochelle.

"I had Art Kenney and Lew Alcindor in the car and all you could see were arms and legs," Goldstein recalled. "It was a funny sight to see these guys in my car for an hour as we drove to the church."

The ceremony went off without a hitch and the groom shocked a few friends by not only being on time, but actually arriving at the church earlier than expected.

The bride, wearing a full-length white silk gown, was radiant as she walked down the aisle. Frank McLaughlin and Kenney served as altar boys, while the rest of the Power team watched from pews as their coach began a new chapter in his life.

Because Jack had a game to play on Monday night, the newlyweds decided on an abbreviated honeymoon in New York City. Sunday was a day of rest, although Jack managed to take Mary Jane to the Power Memorial gym during an afternoon stroll. The team was practicing under the watchful eye of Dick Percudani and Jack wanted to make sure everything went okay. By the time they got to the gym, all the Power players were gone, but the New York Knicks were on the court practicing, and Jack discovered just how little Mary Jane knew about basketball.

As the Knicks concluded their practice, a man came up to Jack and offered the newlyweds a ride back to their hotel. When they reached the hotel, the driver told Mary Jane that he was rooting for her husband's team, so in return she would have to root for his team.

"Sure, I'll root for your team," Mary Jane said, laughing as she exited the car.

As the car pulled away from the curb she turned to Jack and asked who the man was and what team was he connected with. "That's Eddie Donovan, the coach of the New York Knicks," Jack replied in disbelief.

On Monday, Mary Jane got a taste of what married life with Jack Donohue would entail.

"Monday morning, we decided to go over to the Art Museum where the Mona Lisa was on exhibit," Mary Jane said. "After all, we were staying downtown close to the museum and it seemed a shame to miss such an opportunity. The only trouble was that we had to wait in line, which Jack detested, because the museum wasn't opened yet."

After a monumental wait of 10 minutes (there were two people in front of the couple) Jack and Mary Jane were ushered into the viewing area. They walked past the famous painting, out a side door and went out to have breakfast. As they headed back downtown they passed some movie theatres that were showing new releases. Jack pointed to one picture in particular that had received good reviews, and Mary Jane agreed that it looked interesting.

"Why don't you go and see it?" Donohue asked. "I will go back to the room and sleep – I have to sleep on the day of the game."

Mary Jane couldn't believe what she had just heard.

We have a two-day honeymoon and I am going to spend part of it in a movie theatre by myself, while you are back in the hotel sleeping. I don't think so!

After a brief but intense discussion the couple agreed to go back to the hotel together, where Mary Jane would write letters, while Jack had his pre-game sleep.

"It took Jack about 10 years to understand why I was so upset that day!"

The honeymoon continued as Mary Jane made her first appearance at a Power Memorial home game on Monday night. She began the night by having dinner with Joyce Kuhnert, while the two coaches went to the gym early to prepare for the game. The ladies took a cab to the game, but when they reached the school the cab driver became alarmed.

"He saw all the high school kids hanging outside and he didn't want to let us out. Even though it was a Monday night, the next day was a school holiday as it was Lincoln's Birthday and the gym was packed, with a long line of kids extending past the front door waiting to get in."

Power was the defending city champions and drew capacity crowds everywhere they went. Serious basketball fans also wanted every opportunity to watch Alcindor play and see if he was really as good as the hype that compared him to Wilt Chamberlain.

"Ladies, are you sure this is where you are going?" the worried driver asked. "Look at all the kids. What's going on here anyway?"

Mary Jane assured him they would be fine but when they got out of the cab, they saw the entrance was packed solid with students trying to get into the game. Suddenly, the school's principal appeared, took them by the arm and escorted them to the back of the building. They got the last seats in the gym, and Mary Jane watched her husband coach Power to a victory over LaSalle.

The couple moved to a small apartment a few blocks from Jack's parents and within the boundaries of St. Barnabas Parish. Mary Jane knew that she had married a coach who was committed to his team and whose life revolved around sports. But she did not realize how much she would be incorporated into that world until after she said 'I do'.

Jack and his coaching buddies—Curran, Buckley, Sullivan, and others—would normally meet in a restaurant or bar in the Bronx Friday nights after their games. They would discuss the games, the referees, the latest sports gossip, and of course, swap stories. Before long they started to congregate at Jack and Mary Jane's apartment.

Mary Jane soon got used to people dropping in to the apartment after games and on the weekends. They were always invited by her husband, who more often than not, forgot to tell her that company was coming. Mary Jane smiles as she remembers those days. "He has called me his bride for 40 years, not because he is romantic, but because he can't always remember my name."

CHAPTER 9

Team of the Century

Donohue and his coaching staff had some big holes to fill but the Power Panthers were still the team to beat when the 1963-64 campaign began. Point guard Oscar Sanchez, all-city forward George Barbezat, and Bobby Erickson had all graduated while sixth man Danny Nee had transferred to Fort Hamilton High School in Brooklyn.

It was a given that Alcindor was the best high school player in the city and possibly the country, but followers of the game underestimated his supporting cast and the Power coaching staff. Donohue was intent on repeating as CHSAA champs but he did not allow his players to think that far ahead. It was always the next game, the next practice, the next drill that counted and no one was allowed to give less than his best. What made the Power team so good was their unrelenting drive and commitment, their focus on being the best, as individual players and as a team.

Not even the head coach's budding romance with Mary Jane Choffin could distract the team from its immediate and long-term goals: win every game in convincing fashion and successfully defend their CHSAA title. To challenge his team, Donohue arranged an ambitious exhibition slate that would augment an already taxing league schedule. There were Christmas tournaments in Providence, Rhode Island, and upstate New York, but the highlight of the year would come on January

31st, when Power was scheduled to play DeMatha High School, a game scheduled to be played at Maryland's spacious Cole Field House in College Park. *High School Basketball Interscholastic* stated in its season preview that the Panthers might struggle with their "tough tourney grind but should learn their lessons in time for the CHSAA playoffs."

Donohue was the master of keeping distractions from his players, and the Gold Star Gym became an oasis for the team, a place where they could be isolated several hours a day from the problems of the world. Those problems included overzealous recruiters who wanted a piece of Donohue's prized center. Alcindor, fresh off another summer at Friendship Farm, had grown to 7 feet and had refined his offensive and defensive talents. There are only so many 7-footers who graduate from high school every year and if they can walk and chew gum at the same time, they can obtain a Division I scholarship. But Alcindor was the real deal, a big skilled athlete who seemingly got better every time he took to the court. Every Division I school was vying for his attention, knowing that his presence alone could turn a good team into a national contender and a bad team into a winning team. Donohue found himself spending more and more time keeping college suitors at bay, allowing his star player to concentrate on school and basketball. When Donohue first came to Power he set up a system whereby all college recruiters had to go through him before talking to any players. He set up a similar system for the media, allowing restricted access to Alcindor and the rest of the team

"No reporters, no coaches bothered Lew Alcindor," Donohue said. "We have a great team, we got a lot of publicity and he was the greatest player."

Finally, he isolated the Power players from the sharks, gamblers and leeches that had nearly destroyed basketball during the 1951 and 1960 point-shaving scandals and that included keeping his old buddy Freddie "Spook" Stegman away from his players. The system worked in part because of the unequivocal support from Alcindor's parents, Al and Cora Alcindor.

"Letters from colleges and universities began arriving in ninth grade and by junior year there was a deluge, all correspondence handled by Mr. Donohue," Jabbar recalled in his autobiography *Giant Steps*. "He received everything that came to me at school, and all mail on academic letterhead that showed up at my house was forwarded to him unopened."

When questioned about the unusual arrangement, Cora Alcindor explained that Donohue had complete control.

"We know what getting lots of publicity has done to other boys," she told a reporter. "When any of the cuckoos call here, we tell them they will have to talk to Mr. Donohue."

When Alcindor started to speculate about where he could go to play his college basketball, he asked Donohue what schools were interested in him. The coach simply answered that he could go to any school he wanted.

"Kareem was always an intellectual, but shy, and Coach shielded him from the press and the headhunters," said Mike Parfett, Jabbar's teammate on the 1963–1964 team. "He did that for all of us, but Kareem of course was the one they wanted to talk to. It gave him time to grow. There was a lot of speculation that Donohue and Alcindor would be recruited together, but that was never Coach's intent," Parfett said. "He wanted what was best for Lewis."

For his part, Alcindor appreciated the roadblocks that Donohue had set up.

"Coach Donohue wanted me to be able to focus on high school as much as possible," Jabbar said. "The things he did were for my benefit and I trusted him completely. I thought he walked on water."

Donohue extended the same rules to all his players giving them a sanctuary from the harassing phone calls from Division I recruiters and their well-meaning alumni. At Madison Square Garden, Donohue would point to his players the people they had to avoid, people who would offer them money and gifts and, in doing so, could ruin their careers. He reminded them that former New York high school stars Connie Hawkins and Roger Brown were banned from the NCAA and NBA for taking loans from Jack Molinas.

"Coach would warn us about people who would try to befriend us and then use us," Kenney said. "He told us that Freddie the Spook was his friend but that we weren't to talk to him or have any dealings with him. Coach said Freddie would steal our lunch money if we gave him a chance. Coach Donohue let it be known that the Gold Star Gym was off limits to any outside influences, and that rule allowed us to concentrate on being student-athletes and enjoy the experience. He told us that we were to be 'tigers on the court, but gentlemen off the court.'"

* * * * *

Jackie Bonner was one of the better all-round athletes at Power during the Donohue era, a two-sport man who excelled at the plate and in the backcourt. But he lived in Brooklyn which meant taking three subway lines to and from school every day, a commute that took close to an hour and a half each way. To alleviate some of that travel time, Donohue would take Bonner home to his parents' house during the baseball season and then drive him to school in the morning. When Mary Jane and Jack tied the knot in February, the Coach continued the practice of providing Bonner a place to stay after practices and games, this time in the Donohue's new apartment in Yonkers.

"Jackie Bonner spent so much time at our place, Jack used to call him my boyfriend," Mary Jane said.

In his first year at Power, he played freshman and junior varsity basketball and earned a berth on the varsity baseball team as a sophomore, a rare feat.

"In tryouts I had a lot of success hitting against Bobby Erickson and that got me a spot on the team as a sophomore," Bonner said. "We didn't have a lot of talent on the team but Jack was a great coach. He taught us fundamentals and he really understood how to play the game."

Bonner was selected to the CHSAA all-city baseball team, an accomplishment that he credits to Donohue's stats.

"I was a good hitter but Donohue had my batting average at .410 and that seemed a little high," Bonner said. "He really pushed those stats and that is why I was named to the all-city team."

He tried out and made the varsity basketball team as a junior but was forced to quit when he needed to work. It was a decision he regretted later on that year.

"We had a very good team and when we beat LaSalle at the Garden in the first game, I realized how much I missed playing."

Donohue liked the competitiveness and personality of his shortstop and was delighted when Bonner decided to spend the summer at Friendship Farm, helping to build cabins as well as to play a little basketball. Donohue became worried however when Bonner told him that he wanted to try out for the basketball team as well as the baseball team. When Jack informed Mary Jane that her "boyfriend" was trying out for the basketball team, Mary Jane responded with a simple "That's nice."

"We have most of our players back from a team that won the city championships," Donohue patiently explained to his wife, who he realized still knew so little about sports. "He is a great baseball player and person, but he hasn't played in over a year and there is no way he can make this team."

If there was one thing Donohue hated throughout his coaching career, it was cutting players. The fact that so many people he did cut would later become close friends demonstrated the humane and caring way with which he wielded the axe. Still, cutting one of his star baseball players and a kid he truly respected weighed on him. Yet he couldn't discourage him from trying out because it was Donohue himself who constantly urged his students and athletes to dream big dreams.

One day, he came home after tryouts and announced to Mary Jane that her boyfriend had indeed made the team, although he was destined to spend most of the season on the bench. The Panthers opened the regular season with an easy victory and after the game Mary Jane had a question for her husband.

"Don't you start your best players at the beginning of the game?" she queried innocently.

"Of course we do," Jack answered in a patronizing tone.

"Well then, I guess my boyfriend must be one of your better players," Mary Jane stated smugly. "He started and played more than half the game,"

"Yeah, he is starting for us," Jack said with a smile. His wife, who knew nothing about basketball, had forced her husband to admit that he had underestimated both Bonner's ability and tenacity.

* * * * *

If Jackie Bonner had been a long shot to make the Power varsity basketball team, Mike Parfett was a near impossibility. As a sophomore, Parfett was cut from the junior varsity squad, yet with unbridled resolve he showed up at the varsity tryouts the following October.

"There were several players returning from the previous year's championship team, as well as guys from the JV team that also won the city championships," Parfett recalled.

"I didn't think I had much of a chance, but one of my friends was trying out and I knew I was a better team player than he was, so I went to tryouts. The coach treated me like everyone else and after a little while he asked me my name, so it seemed there was hope."

There was hope because Parfett was exactly what a defending championship team needed – a hard-nosed player who understood how to play the game and knew his role on the team. Parfett earned a spot on the squad and although he saw limited court time, the experience paid off huge dividends.

"I played as hard as anyone else on the team, diving on the floor for loose balls, mixing it up (despite the fact that he was only 6' 0" and 165 lbs). I could shoot; I understood the game fairly well; and I was a team player and did whatever I was asked – which was mostly to get the first string ready for the game."

"I didn't have as close a relationship with Coach as Arthur or Jack Bonner but playing on that team was special for a poor kid in the city," Parfett said. His father had died when he was eight years old and his mother struggled to send him to a private Catholic school.

"The team had blue blazers that we wore to games and Coach knew I couldn't afford to buy a jacket so he gave one to me. Although I was pretty far down the bench he always made me feel important. I got hurt in one game and Coach drove me home."

Of course being treated like everyone else had its occasional downfalls.

"We were playing in the Garden and Coach Donohue yelled at me for taking a bad shot even though I made it and we were winning by over 20 points," Parfett said.

What impressed Parfett most about Donohue was how much he cared even after an injury forced the over-achieving player to the sidelines.

"I got hurt in my senior year and didn't play, but Coach Donohue went out of his way to make sure I got a scholarship to college. I went to Farleigh Dickinson and played for Bill Raftery who is now a TV analyst for ESPN and ABC."

Thirty-five years after graduating from Power, a special on Power Memorial broadcast on a New York television station prompted Parfett to send an e-mail of thanks to Donohue.

"As an educator, coach and motivator I am sure you know you touch many lives in a positive way. I'm not sure you hear it directly, hence this note. . . Basketball has helped give me the confidence to be successful. You taught me how to win with class and style. Losing with elegance followed at a later time. The decisions you made a long time ago might have

seemed small at the time, but they helped shape much of my life and for that I am most grateful. God Bless you, Mike Parfett"

* * * * *

In the sporting world, as in the real world, talent is often accorded its own set of rules and values. The superstar athlete, temperamental artist, rock star or successful financier is given leeway and discretion by an adoring public or superiors who will turn a blind eye to improper behavior or lifestyle. From grammar school to the professional ranks, many star athletes are allowed to circumvent team rules and training practices. In high school and college they sometimes receive unwarranted passing grades simply because they can throw a football or dunk a basketball. They are inundated with offers of cars, money and women for choosing a particular college where they will play sports first and possibly receive an education second. As a result, the athlete develops an attitude of me first and often overlooks the sacrifice and preparation needed to be successful in college and in the pros. Such behavior was not acceptable at Power Memorial, on their sports teams or in the classroom. Jug – after-school detention – was handed out for being late for class, talking out of turn in the classroom, smoking, having long hair or not being dressed properly.

Alcindor was once given detention because his pants were not long enough.

"Everyone at school was laughing when Kareem received 'jug' for his pants being too short since he was still growing," Kenney said. "We were saying that his pants were at an acceptable length at first period, but he had a growth spurt after lunch, and they were too short by sixth period!"

Kareem dutifully did his time after school and that night his mother, a seamstress, hemmed the pants to the proper length.

"At Power you didn't want to be noticed because that usually meant you were in trouble," Jabbar said years later.

In the Gold Star Gym the coaching staff stuck to the same rules. It didn't matter who you were or how talented you were, everyone was held accountable for their own actions.

"I remember Mr. Donohue being fairly strict with everyone," Ed Gowrie said. "I don't remember him cutting Jabbar any slack. He drove him just as hard as he drove the other players."

While Donohue's policy about restricting access to his players bothered recruiters and the media alike, *New York Post* columnist Phil Pepe appeared to understand the coach's rationale.

"The good that this man (Donohue) does is apparent," Pepe said in the *Post*. "It is why ... as Lapchick explained, 'his head is not out to here.' It is why Lewis accepted the responsibility of picking up the basketballs after practice and why he was yanked from a game earlier in the season for not raising his hand after a foul."

"Coach Donohue treated every player as an individual," Jabbar would say years later in a TV interview. "He dealt with everyone and helped them to get as close to their potential as possible. No one suffered because one player was getting too much attention."

It was that drive from Donohue, Percudani and Kuhnert that enabled Power to deliver the goods game after game. Power experienced little trouble within their league as the team extended its winning streak to 50 games by Christmas. They would be facing their biggest test in the school's history when they traveled to Maryland to face the nationally ranked DeMatha High School in January, but Donohue tried to keep their focus on immediate tasks: working hard in practice and playing well against CHSAA competition.

Keeping the players mentally and physically ready for league games became harder and harder as the DeMatha game loomed on the horizon. In Power's final game before the DeMatha showdown, the team struggled against St. Helena's High School. It was obvious that the players' minds were elsewhere and that was not acceptable to the head coach.

"I had two pairs of sneakers, a good pair of Converse and a $2.99 pair of Keds," Kenney said afterwards. "I packed the good pair and was saving it for DeMatha and was playing in the Keds, something I never did. That shows where my focus was, certainly not on St. Helena's."

Kenney wasn't the only one whose mind was elsewhere. Power held a slim six-point halftime lead when Donohue exploded at the halftime meeting held in an office below the St. Helena's gym. And then he used the n-word to describe Alcindor's play and the word stuck in the young athlete like a dagger in the back.

"I said 'there are people up in the stands saying that you are playing like a nigger' and he thought I was calling him a nigger," Donohue said recalling the painful experience.

Regardless of his intention, the coach's choice of words was a mistake and left a still young Alcindor stunned. Suddenly Donohue no longer walked on water.

"He was a person I totally trusted and now there was this element of doubt, like I didn't know this person who just said that."

Alcindor was beside himself when Donohue used the word, but he returned to the gym with his team and led a second half rally that buried St. Helena's.

"St. Helena's was one team that we hated," Jackie Bonner said. "It is hard to explain, but they had a small gym and no locker rooms and we didn't like playing there. The only thing I remember about that game was that we weren't playing very well and Coach Donohue let us have it at halftime."

After the game, the team left by train for Maryland for the much-awaited game with DeMatha, but the strong bond between the superstar high school player and his coach was broken by a misguided attempt to motivate. It would take decades before the two would come to grips with the issue.

Power arrived at their hotel late Friday night and the following morning they went to the University of Maryland's Cole Field House for a shoot around. Power played several games a year at Madison Square Garden and was used to playing in big arenas and in front of large crowds, but the Cole Field House appeared more spacious than anything they had seen or played in. The seats were set back from the court and presented a different shooting perspective, and it lacked the mystique of Madison Square Garden.

"It was such a spacious arena and cold," Bonner said, "It took a while to get used to."

Their opponent, DeMatha High School, was coached by Morgan Wooten, the master of the run and jump, a pressing defence that often caused havoc for teams trying to advance the ball up the court and into a set offence. Wooten's success at DeMatha would eventually earn him election into the Naismith Basketball Hall of Fame in Springfield, Massachusetts. This particular game attracted media frenzy and Donohue, who had always managed to protect his players in the media capital of the world, was working full-time to keep Alcindor and his teammates from the press. Now they were on a new turf, playing a game before the biggest crowd in high school history with an over abundance of media and college scouts in attendance.

"We are here to play a basketball game," Donohue reminded the Panthers after the morning shooting practice. "If you have free time, open a book and get some studying done. Make sure you rest before the game."

As the Power players left the locker room for pre-game warm-ups the capacity crowd of over 13,000 erupted into cheers. The game itself lived up to its billing as the two teams battled tooth and nail for 36 minutes.

"It was a great game, there must have been seven or eight lead changes and it wasn't decided until the final seconds of the game," Kenney said.

Offensively, Alcindor dominated, with a spectacular 35-point, 17-rebound performance. At the other end of the court, DeMatha's Bernie Williams (who would go on to enjoy a professional career in the NBA and ABA) scorched the Panthers for 18 points, most of them in the first half.

"We gave him too much room in the first half, but Charlie and I did a better job in the second half," Bonner said.

While Alcindor proved that he was the best high school player in the country that night, it was the Power backcourt that came up with the game winning plays in the final minute of the game. DeMatha held a 62-61 lead when Charlie Farrugia canned a 15' jump shot to give Power a one-point lead. On the ensuing possession Sid Catlett drove to the basket but had the ball stripped by Farrugia who calmly moved the ball down the opposite end of the court and drained another 15' shot with seven seconds remaining in the game to give Power its winning margin, 65-62.

"Thinking back on it I probably should have just run out the clock but for some reason I took a shot and luckily it went in," Farrugia said.

"It was a tough game," Alcindor said in a television special commemorating the Power dynasty. "They were a very well coached team. That was a great night. I personally felt that we had proven ourselves in the toughest possible situation going away to play a nationally ranked team."

The Panthers were now the toast of New York City, having defended the city's claim to being the home of the best high school basketball in the country, but their season was far from over. When

Donohue returned to New York, he talked about the DeMatha win and how he changed his pre-game demeanor.

"I thought our kids would be scared to death when they walked out on the floor before that crowd of over 13,000 fans," Donohue told the *New York Post's* Jack Lynn. "We don't fool around before our games but we were joking and kidding around before they went out on the court down there. I wanted to relax them as much as possible."

They still had their CHSAA title to defend and Donohue was not going to allow anyone to let their guard down.

"I don't want to be coy but we have to worry about all of them," Donohue said in response to which league team he was most concerned about. "Right now we have to worry about Stepinac. We play them next Friday."

The Panthers had little trouble with Stepinac and met Holy Cross in the semi-finals. The Panthers cruised to a 70-51 victory as the undersized Knights couldn't match-up against Power's talented front line. Alcindor was dominant inside, scoring 26 points before Donohue took him out with nearly seven minutes remaining in the game while Bettridge pumped in 20.

Power finished the dream season a week later when they easily disposed of Molloy 65-41. Prior to the game, Molloy head coach Jack Curran talked about his team's chances of upsetting the defending champs. The Molloy fans were thinking upset when their all-city center Rudy Bogad scored six points in the early going to give Molloy a temporary 8-6 lead. Alcindor held Bogad to just 10 points the rest of the way while the big center and Bettridge supplied the offensive firepower. Alcindor led all scorers with 22 points, but that stat only told half the story as he pulled down 27 rebounds and blocked six shots. Bettridge had trouble finding his range in the early going but still managed to pour in 15 points. Kenney and Bonner combined for another 15 points in their final game in Power uniforms.

The season ended but the accolades continued for Power Memorial Academy as they were voted the number-one Catholic High School team in the country. Thirty-five years later, *USA Today* would select that same Power team as the "Team of the Century."

CHAPTER 10

Trifecta

As Power's basketball reputation grew, more and more students from outside Manhattan took an interest in attending the school. Not all of them, though, came for the athletics. One of those students was Brian McCann, a Queens resident whose father encouraged him to consider Power despite its location on Manhattan's West Side.

"My father thought that Power would be a great school for me because of the Irish Christian Brothers, but I wanted to go to Mater Christi, which was just a few blocks away from our house," McCann said.

However, a neighbor who was in his first year at Power suggested that McCann accompany him to a Power basketball game to get a feel for the school.

"I remember walking into the gym and it was like I had entered a different world," McCann recalled. "The place was packed with people cheering and the players were running up and down the court. What an atmosphere! And it was only the junior varsity game!"

McCann stayed for the varsity game and decided Power was the school for him.

Although he never played basketball, Donohue left a lasting impression on the youngster.

"Mr. Donohue taught social studies and he told the most interesting stories," McCann said. "In class you would learn things because he could tell a story and relate it to what we were studying. He could tell a basketball story and relate it to Aristotle. A lot of high school students can't remember years later what their teachers said in class, but that wasn't the case with Mr. Donohue's classes."

Another Queens resident who decided to make the long trek from Queens to the West Side was a talented two-sport athlete named Ed Klimkowski.

"I grew up in a poor section of Jamaica, Queens, and was all set to go to Molloy and play baseball and basketball for Jack Curran," Klimkowski said. "Dennis Galebraith, the student manager at Power, saw me play in a grammar school tournament and suggested that I consider going to Power."

"I am just a few subway stops from Molloy, why would I want to travel all the way to Manhattan for high school?" Klimkowski asked Galbraith.

"Just come and give it a look," Galbraith responded.

Reluctantly Klimkowski made his way to Power one Saturday morning and as he walked through the doors of the Gold Star Gym he saw Lew Alcindor shooting on a side basket.

"Right then and there I decided I was going to Power," Klimkowski said. "It was the best decision I ever made in my life, I never regretted it for a moment."

As a freshman, Klimowski played JV basketball and varsity baseball. On the court he flourished under Percudani's direction while on the baseball diamond he proved to be one of the best hitters in the city despite his age. In his sophomore year, he made the jump to varsity basketball. He joined a team which had high hopes to continue their winning streak, which was currently at 56 games, when they began the 1964-65 season. The Panthers still had Alcindor and its talented floor general, Charley Farrugia, but three of the starters from the previous year had graduated.

Klimowski and a pair of talented juniors named Norwood Todmann and Eric Brown joined seniors Paul Houghton, Farrugia and Alcindor to provide Donohue with a potent line-up. The freshman and junior varsity teams coached by Kuhnert and Percudani had continued to provide the varsity team with quality players and the Panthers set their sights on a third consecutive CHSAA championship and a repeat as National Catholic High School Champions.

But before the Panthers could make a run for the championship, Jack Donohue had other things to worry about. He and Mary Jane were expecting their first child, right in the middle of the basketball season.

"It was an uneventful pregnancy….I had no aches, pains or morning sickness usually associated with being pregnant," Mary Jane said.

She did though experience problems with her doctor, a middle-aged crusty Irishman who swore like a trooper and was not known for his warm and fuzzy bedside manner.

When the big day finally came, Donohue accompanied his wife to the delivery room fully expecting to participate in the momentous occasion, though it was not yet common practice for the fathers to do so.

The doctor came into the delivery room periodically to yell at Mary Jane to hurry up and get started, but the baby was taking its time. With the lack of any visible progress the doctor left the room and after awhile Jack went out to look for him and found him sitting on a hallway floor smoking a cigarette under a NO SMOKING sign.

Upset that the doctor appeared indifferent to his wife's condition Jack asked him if there wasn't something he should be doing.

"How many babies have you delivered?" was the doctor's calm reply.

"This is my first," Jack answered.

"This is my thousandth and I ought to know more than you," the doctor responded, but nonetheless he returned with Jack to check on the mother-to-be. In the room, Mary Jane was wondering if all the pain was worth it.

"I was in agony and wondering why I ever got myself into this," she would later say. "Suddenly I was hit with a different pain and yelled 'It's coming!'"

"Nah, you are not far enough along," the doctor said unmoved by his patient's cries.

"Well damn it, I'm doing something I wasn't doing before," Mary Jane replied.

With that, the nurse in attendance took a look and told the doctor that he had better start moving because there was a little girl trying to get out. Jack, who had agreed to help during the labor but wanted nothing to do with the delivery, suddenly found himself caught in the middle of a breached delivery.

As the once calm doctor frantically washed his hands, he told Donohue that the baby was not in the normal position and may not make it.

"Mary Jane will be fine and you can have 20 other children, but this one is in trouble."

Mary Jane was rolled across the hall and literally thrown on the delivery table, while student nurses were called into the room to witness their first breach delivery.

In the end, the baby arrived safely and as the nurses attended to the mother and the child, the doctor turned to the students and said "Don't think of this as a breach – she had it much too easy!"

"You should get up here," Mary Jane said defiantly as she gave the doctor one last parting shot.

"Well, we can put it back and try again," the doctor offered, ending the conversation once and for all.

Mary Jane was a bit worried that Jack, who had been telling everyone about "my son," would be disappointed that the newborn was a girl.

"I needn't have worried," Mary Jane said later. "Carol had her Dad wrapped around her tiny finger two minutes after she was born."

*   *   *   *   *

Donohue turned his attention back to his team and, as expected, Power experienced little trouble in league play. They were not as big as they were in the previous two seasons but they were more athletic, and Donohue had the team playing at a high intensity throughout the season. They headed up to Providence for a Christmas tourney and an expected showdown with Boston's Catholic Memorial High School. Memorial was coached by former Holy Cross great Ronnie Perry and led by 6' 10" Ron Teixeria, one of the top high school players in New England. The draw was set up so that the two powerhouses would meet in the final, although Power had a tougher than expected semi-final game against CHSAA opponent Chaminade High School. The Chaminade Flyers were well coached by Jim Schwartz whose brother Danny handled the point position, while a young Bob Kissane provided scoring from the forward position. Kissane remembers giving the Panthers a scare.

"We played Power in the semis, and they were looking ahead to playing Catholic Memorial, with Teixeria, in the finals," Kissane said.

"Chaminade was a lot better than Power realized, and we were leading after three quarters. Then they turned on the jets and won the game. I was guarding Lew Alcindor who was in his last year while I was a 170 lb. sophomore. I did OK driving on him a few times but he also took one of my jumpers right out of the air from about 10' away from me! People who never saw him play in high school will never know how well he could run. He really filled the lane on the break."

After the hard-fought victory against Chaminade, the Panthers rebounded with a solid win over Catholic Memorial and Teixeria. Once again, all eyes turned to the Washington area and the rematch against DeMatha High School. DeMatha was gunning for revenge after losing to Power by three points the year before and featured a potent line-up led by Bob Whitmore, Bernie Williams and Sid Catlett. Both Whitmore and Catlett would later star at Notre Dame University, while Williams would play professional basketball after a stellar collegiate career at LaSalle. Williams would average close to ten points a game during a five-year pro career in the NBA and ABA.

Coach Wootten's famed trapping defense proved to be ineffective against Power the year before, so he devised a game plan that involved slowing the game down. DeMatha walked the ball up the court on offense and then double and triple-teamed Alcindor at the defensive end, challenging Power to shoot from the outside. Williams and Catlett were responsible for sandwiching Alcindor whenever he touched the ball while Bernie Williams controlled the offense at the point guard position.

The game, listed as one of basketball's Top 50 Magical Moments in *Total Basketball*, was once again a closely-played affair but this time it was DeMatha that escape with a three-point victory.

"We didn't want the same person to beat us twice," Wooten said. "Our strategy in the 1964 game was to let Kareem score whatever he could, while we stopped everyone else. In 1965, we would try and stop Kareem and force the other players to pick up the slack, if they could. He always had a player in front of Kareem and behind him depending on where the ball was. When he received the ball we sent a third player to cover him."

The strategy worked as Alcindor was held to 12 points, well below his average, while his teammates were unable to hit open shots. In the second half, Donohue inserted Klimowski who responded with an 11-point performance, but it wasn't enough.

DeMatha hit two clutch shots in the final minute to record a well-deserved 46-43 victory. Power's 71-game winning streak was over and in the locker room afterwards Donohue refused to allow Alcindor to take the blame for the loss.

"This is a team game; we win games as a team and we lose as a team," he said in the subdued locker room.

Farrugia, who made the winning shots the year before, sat in the locker room in disbelief.

"The entire team shot the ball poorly," he recounted. "It was just one of those games where nobody got hot and we lost."

The Panthers were disappointed in the loss and the end of the streak. Few of them realized the impact that the Power-DeMatha series had on high school basketball.

"The two Power games brought high school basketball to the national level," Wootten said. "Both games were decided by three points and the media attention sparked interest throughout the country. After the first game, it would have been easy for Jack to say that they had beaten us and not play again. But right away he said he would come back to Maryland and play us the next year because he knew how important these games were to high school basketball. I always had the highest respect for Jack."

Power returned to New York and met little resistance in the league playoffs. In the semi-finals they met Holy Cross, and while Holy Cross's head coach Bill O'Meara had his team practice shooting over tennis rackets, the Knights didn't have the talent to stay with Power and lost the game 74-56. It was a different story in the finals where they met Rice, a team loaded with talent. Bob Leinhard and Louie LaSalle provided the Rice Raiders with scoring punch while a sophomore sensation named Dean "the Dream" Meminger handled the point guard position with precision. Despite his youth, Meminger was already establishing a reputation as one of the great high school players to ever come out of New York City. That season, he became only the second player in CHSAA history to be selected to the all-city team as a sophomore. He was the key to the Rice offense and Farrugia was given the assignment of stopping him.

"Charley, get in his jock and don't worry about him beating you,' Donohue instructed his point guard. "Even if he drives past you, he still has to deal with Lewis."

Farrugia understood the instructions – he had spent two years applying pressure against the opposition's top guards, secure in the knowledge that Alcindor was behind him with his shot blocking ability. Rice triple-teamed Alcindor in the first quarter and trailed by just two points, 12-10, after eight minutes of play. It appeared to the capacity crowd that the talented Rice team might spoil Alcindor's going away party.

But Farrugia's defense and Alcindor's offense proved too much for Rice.

"I was able to steal the ball from Meminger earlier in the game and that got to him," Farrugia recalled. "After that he wasn't playing with the same confidence."

Meminger had scored 17 points against Power earlier in the season, but Farrugia held him to just one point as Power dominated the final three quarters en route to a convincing 71-46 win. Alcindor led a second quarter explosion that saw Power take a 34-19 halftime lead. The domination continued in the second half despite the fact that Donohue used his bench liberally with 14 different players seeing floor time.

The story as always was Alcindor, who finished his storied high school career in typical fashion scoring 32 points, pulling down 22 rebounds and blocking eight opposition shots. He finished his four-year career with 2,067 points, at the time a New York City school record.

Meminger would go on to lead Rice to city titles in his junior and senior years, and would become a two-time All American at Marquette University and enjoy a professional career that included a championship ring with the New York Knicks. Thirty years later, when the Power Memorial team was inducted into the New York City High School Hall of Fame, Meminger attended the ceremony and re-introduced himself to Farrugia.

"He shook my hand and said he wanted to meet the guy who held him to one point," Farrugia said. "He was a real class act."

In the locker room following the championship win over Rice, the Power players engaged in a strawberry cream pie fight while Donohue discussed his own future with the press. He assured them that he would return to coach Power and that any talk of a Donohue-Alcindor package deal was simply unfounded rumours.

But those rumours wouldn't go away, in part because Donohue was controlling those trying to recruit his star center. Cynics believed that the coach was restricting access to his star player because he secretly wanted to work out a package deal. The reality was that if Donohue was guilty of anything it was of being overly protective of his players—but more often than not the players benefited from that protection. Players never questioned Donohue's ways nor did their parents and other high school coaches adopted similar rules.

"Coach D was a great story teller and his stories always had a message that either motivated us or warned us of the dangers that could happen in our environment," Bobby Erickson said. "We heard about the CCNY players that where in on basketball fixes and he was a little paranoid that unsavory people could harm his players. So the rule was not to speak to anyone about basketball. This resulted in all scholarship offers going through him, which was his way of protecting us."

Donohue took the same interest with all of his graduating players, limiting access, providing advice and then finally letting the player make the final decision. Marquette was talking to Farrugia and the flashy point guard was leaning towards the Jesuit school when Donohue made some keen observations.

"Coach suggested that perhaps I should look at some smaller schools, that I might not get a lot of playing time at Marquette because of my size," Farrugia said.

The advice made sense and Farrugia eventually accepted a scholarship offer to a junior college in Texas.

"I came down there and played two years of junior college ball. I spent another two years playing college ball and then spent my two years of military service playing for the base team," Farrugia said. "Coach was right because Marquette recruited Dean Meminger two years later and I would not have gotten a lot of playing time there in my final year."

"In fact, when I started in Texas it wasn't because I was better than the other guys but because I was a better fundamental player. I remember my college coach asking me how I knew so much about playing the game and I told him the reason was the coaching staff at Power."

* * * * *

Alcindor narrowed his college choices to four schools: Michigan, St. John's, UCLA and Columbia. He liked the idea of attending an Ivy League school (his father had studied music at Columbia's Julliard

School), but the Columbia basketball program was in decline and success on the court was as important to him as a quality education. He wanted a place that would offer both. He liked Michigan, but after awhile he ruled it out.

That left St. John's and UCLA. St. John's main attraction was their coach, Joe Lapchick, who Alcindor took a liking to when he was a freshman at Power. An added bonus was Lapchick's son Richard who had befriended Alcindor during two summers at Friendship Farm. But St. John's was eliminated when it forced its legendary coach into mandatory retirement following the 1964-65 season. If Lapchick wasn't going to be on the sidelines, Alcindor was going to look elsewhere. Shortly after the announcement of Lapchick's retirement became public, Alcindor visited the UCLA campus and met their coach, John Wooden. The visit erased any doubts Alcindor may have had and he returned to New York with his mind made up – he was going to UCLA!

The icing on the cake came when the high school senior received a phone call and letter from two of UCLA's most well known African-American graduates, Jackie Robinson and statesman Ralph Bunch.

Power's prized center wasn't the only member of the team being courted by major colleges. After the Rice game, Donohue had said that he was staying at Power but the truth of the matter was that Donohue was seriously considering several college offers that had come his way and he knew that it was time to move on.

Brother Kilelea, who had hired Donohue back in 1959 and had given him free reign in running the basketball program, had left in 1964. In his absence, Donohue suddenly found himself answering to the brothers about the way he was running one of the most successful basketball programs in the country. While not personally close to each other, Kilelea and Donohue respected each other.

"I never regretted that decision to hire Jack Donohue because he lived up to all the good reports that I had received about him," Kilelea would say years later. "He was a fine Catholic gentleman who always treated everyone respectfully; an excellent coach who enhanced the reputation of Power Memorial Academy through the extremely successful record of victories of all of the Power basketball teams during his coaching career; a classy person who always represented the school well. I was very proud of him and of his overall performance at Power Memorial Academy. I respected his expertise and gave him a free rein to do his job according to the regulations of the New York City Catholic Basketball League. I never received any complaint about Jack. From my point of view Jack Donohue had a good influence on the students at Power Memorial Academy."

With Kilelea gone, Donohue began to pursue college offers with more enthusiasm. He finally accepted an offer from Holy Cross College in Worcester, Massachusetts, a job he earned on his own merits despite the fact the people suggested that he used Alcindor as a bargaining chip.

Donohue was now commuting back and forth from Worcester to New York and during a chance meeting with Walter McLaughlin he informed his old friend that he told Holy Cross that Alcindor would not be joining him. Alcindor made an official visit to Holy Cross, out of respect for all that Donohue did for him, and that trip refueled the rumours of a package deal and the accusations that Donohue was pressing his superstar to join him at Holy Cross.

"Coach Donohue was totally above board in his dealing with me and allowed me freedom in choosing a college," Jabbar said. "He always did things with my best interests at heart."

The high school senior was still upset about the halftime incident in his junior year but he also respected the man who helped him grow during his four years at Power. At a press conference held at the Gold Star Gym, Alcindor announced that he would be attending UCLA in the fall. The two catalysts for Power's incredible three-year run were leaving New York City but the Power legacy they helped build would continue. The Panthers won four more city titles and finished second on another five occasions before the school closed its doors in 1984, making way for luxury apartments and condominiums.

* * * * *

It was while her husband was away recruiting for his new school that Mary Jane discovered she was pregnant for the second time. Getting pregnant was one thing, finding time to tell her husband she was with child was a much bigger task. "Jack was never home at that time. He was meeting the Holy Cross people, recruiting and finishing his job at Power. We never had any time alone."

The two were scheduled to meet in Worcester to look at houses while Mary Jane's parents looked after Carol. *What a perfect time to spring the news*. Mary Jane drove up to Worcester and met Jack at a realtor's office, who then proceeded to show them several two bedroom houses.

"Dennis Galbrieth, Jack's student manager at Power, was going to attend a school at Worcester and was going to live with us," Mary Jane said. "Jack had asked the agent to show us two-bedroom houses, but I kept saying we needed something bigger. This was going to be the first house we bought and we were both a little anxious about making the right decision."

Jack had his eye on a particular home, a Cape Cod with two bed-rooms and an alcove that could serve as Dennis' bedroom. Mary Jane tried to steer her husband alone into a room so she could break the news about her pregnancy to him in private, but was unsuccessful in her attempts. When he pressed Mary Jane to make a decision she insisted that they needed a three-bedroom house. Jack began to lose patience and demanded to know why she was so set on a three-bedroom house when a two-bedroom would do just fine. Finally, the tension became too great for Mary Jane, and she blurted out: "We need a three-bedroom house because I am pregnant, and I haven't been able to get you alone to tell you."

"I think you need some time alone," the realtor said as she quietly slipped into another room and began checking her listings for bigger homes.

As Jack hugged his pregnant wife, he whispered the words that Mary Jane wanted to hear, "You know, I think we should be looking at three-bedroom homes."

CHAPTER 11

New England Chill

The College of the Holy Cross is located in Worcester, Massachusetts, the economic and social centre of central Massachusetts. The Jesuit-run school is noted for its quality of education and is ranked among the top liberal arts colleges in the United States. The Jesuits have always preached and practiced a total approach to a person's development, and the college's mission statement talks of promoting the "intellectual, physical and social development of students."

In 1947, the Holy Cross Crusaders made basketball history when they captured the NCAA National Championship, one of the smallest schools to ever accomplish the feat and the first New England school to claim the title. The club, coached by the legendary Doggie Julian, defeated Navy, City College of New York and Oklahoma to win the national title. That same year, the football team played in the Orange Bowl and four years later Holy Cross won the NCAA Division I Baseball Championship. In the ensuing decade, the basketball Crusaders would make four more NCAA appearances, and in 1954, they captured the prestigious National Invitational Tournament (NIT) in Madison Square Garden, the site of their 1947 NCAA victory.

The basketball program during that era sent six players to the NBA, including Bob Cousy, Tom Heinsohn, Togo Palazzi and George Kaftan.

Seven players eventually went on to coach in the college ranks, while other graduates became successful educators and businessmen. Earle Markey, a fourth-round draft pick of the Boston Celtics, joined the Jesuits and spent several years as a missionary in the Philippines before returning to Worcester to become the dean of students at his alma mater. Holy Cross was proud of its athletic and academic traditions, and the powers-that-be at the college expected their coaches to produce winning teams without jeopardizing the school's academic integrity.

The basketball teams continued to post winning records in the late 50s and early 60s, but were no longer able to compete with the elite Division I teams on a consistent basis. While other colleges started to lower admission standards for athletes and entice blue-chip players with illegal financial enticements, Holy Cross maintained its rigid policies and pursuit of academic excellence.

When Frank Oftring (a member of the '47 championship team) resigned as the Crusaders' head coach in 1965 after four winning seasons, the school looked for a new coach to lead the Crusaders back into post-season play that had eluded the school for the past three seasons.

In early March, Holy Cross named Jack Donohue as the school's tenth head coach. Instantly there was speculation that the coach had used his relationship with Alcindor to help secure a college job. Although the rumors were untrue, it didn't stop skeptics from questioning Donohue's credentials.

His first public appearance at Holy Cross was at the Varsity Club Dinner in the spring of 1965, where he addressed the Alcindor situation and at the same time gave New Englanders a taste of his legendary sense of humor. "I know that you are all waiting to hear what news I have about Lew Alcindor," he said. "Frankly, I don't have any. But I can tell you this much at least. We have enrolled his father and mother."

With or without Alcindor, there were plenty of other basketball observers convinced that Donohue would have nothing but success in Massachusetts. One New York writer confidently predicted that Donohue would restore Holy Cross as a national power in a few years. "With Alcindor, it'll take Donohue two years to make Holy Cross into a national power. Without him, it may take three. He is a great coach with a tremendous basketball mind. He knows where the high school basketball talent is hidden, and he's got recruiting warmth that will flood Holy Cross with superstars."

Donohue did know where the talent was hidden, and his personality was a plus when talking to young players, but the coach and the scribe were soon to find out that getting superstars into Holy Cross was a difficult chore.

*   *   *   *   *

The first high school player that Donohue tried to recruit to Holy Cross was not Alcindor, but the former star of his St. Barnabas CYO team, Frankie McLaughlin.

"I knew before anyone else that Jack had gotten the Holy Cross job because he walked to my house the night he accepted and told me that he wanted me to play for him," McLaughlin said. "And I would have loved to have played for him."

The problem was that McLaughlin, an all-city player in his senior year at Fordham Prep, had verbally agreed to attend Fordham University and he didn't want to go back on his word. The pair did take a trip to Lapchick's house a few nights later where Jack sought his mentor's advice as to whom he should choose as an assistant coach.

"Jack had a list of 17 coaches and he explained in detail the pros and cons of each candidate," McLaughlin recalled. "Lapchick sat back and listened patiently until Jack was finished and then asked one question."

"Of the 17 coaches whom would you go to for help with a personal problem?"

"Well, I guess Jimmy Herrion," Jack said, mentioning the name of the head coach of Sacred Heart High School in Yonkers. "Then that is the person you should hire," Lapchick said. "Everyone you named has basketball credentials. You need more than that," Lapchick stated.

A phone call later and Herrion agreed to move to Worcester as Donohue's assistant. McLaughlin, on the other hand, was staying home and had a solid collegiate career at Fordham.

*   *   *   *   *

When Donohue took over the team at Holy Cross, he inherited a team that was 13-10 with six of those wins coming against Division II schools. As the team began practicing on October 15, it was obvious that his first year in Worcester would be a struggle. He was shell-shocked when the Crusaders were upset 76-67, by Harvard in their season opener. "What the hell are we are doing here? We are out of our league!" Donohue said to Herrion after the game.

Herrion tried to reassure his boss that it was just one game, and that they did know what they were doing, but it would take some time. The college game was proving to be a much greater challenge than Donohue had first imagined.

"To be honest, I think we suffered on the court from a tactical standpoint in the beginning of the season," said Richie Murphy. Murphy was Donohue's first captain at Holy Cross, a sharp shooting 6'4" forward whose older brother John had played for Donohue at Power Memorial. Richie was a high school all-star while playing at All Hollows and was in his final year at Holy Cross when Donohue took over the reins. "It wasn't from a lack of effort from the coaches," Murphy continued, "but in high school you didn't see as many defenses as you did in college. Harvard played a 3-2 zone, something that we hadn't practiced against, and we had trouble scoring in that game. But Coach was a very good game coach, and he made the necessary adjustments as the season progressed."

The Crusaders didn't look much better the next time out as they pulled out a four-point win over St. Michael's College, a Division II school from Vermont. Consecutive losses to Yale and Massachusetts left the Crusaders with an unfamiliar 1-3 record and a coaching staff scrambling for answers. The season hit a low point in January when Holy Cross dropped back-to-back games to two Division II schools: St. Anselm's and Springfield College.

In less than a year, Donohue had gone from coaching the best high school team in the country, surrounded by players who would make their living playing basketball, to a team that was battling to keep their heads above water. Another problem the new coach experienced was learning how to handle college players.

"Jack had to go through a transition period in dealing with college players," Murphy said. "Jack couldn't treat the Holy Cross players the same way he did with his teams at Power and Tolentine, they just didn't respond the same way."

In New York City, Catholic high school teachers and coaches possessed absolute authority and concerned parents at home supported this strict discipline. So Donohue made adjustments, and eventually proved to be an effective motivator at the college level.

Ralph Willard was a junior when he was on Donohue's first Holy Cross team and he knew that the new coach was the right choice for a team whose roster was full of players from the New York metropolitan area. "He came to Holy Cross with a good reputation and we all knew about his success at Power Memorial," Willard said. "He was a good fit because there were a lot of players from New York and New Jersey, and he could relate to us."

As the season evolved, the Crusaders began to come together and pulled out some memorable wins in the second half of the season. The first was a trip back to Donohue's old haunt, Madison Square Garden, where Holy Cross beat a very good Manhattan College team 68-66. The next opponent was Connecticut at home; a contest in which Donohue demonstrated that he was literally willing to fight for his players. The game was closely contested, when a scuffle broke out between University of Connecticut's Wes Bialosuknia and Holy Cross's Al Stazinski.

Bialosuknia, an outstanding shooter who later played in the ABA, took exception to the tight defense employed by Stazinski, and they ended up on the floor battling for a loose ball. Push led to shove and suddenly both benches emptied as Bialosuknia and Stazinski began to fight. The melee left freshman manager Jim Maloney in a quandary. "The last thing I wanted to do was to go out on the court, but I had no choice," Maloney said. "Everyone else was there, so I had to go."

As he made his way towards the melee, he was accosted by UConn's Tom Penders. Penders, who would later become head coach at Fordham, Texas and Houston, grabbed Maloney by his tie with his left hand, and reared back to deliver a punch with his right hand. As Maloney prepared for the worse, Murphy came to his rescue and blindsided Penders with a body block that sent the would-be assailant to the floor. Maloney also fell to the floor and when he got up he saw two Worcester policemen trying to drag Donohue off an UConn player. After the floor was cleared, the two teams got back to playing basketball and Holy Cross prevailed 73-70.

Losses to Rhode Island, UMass and Providence ensured that the Crusaders would suffer their first losing season since World War II, but the team refused to throw in the towel and came up with their best effort of the season when they returned to New York.

"Trips to New York were always special," Maloney said. "Coach would always have us stay in a hotel across from Madison Square Garden where all the NBA players stayed. Then he would send me over to the Garden to pick up tickets he had waiting for him. When we went over to the game it seemed everyone in the Garden knew Coach Donohue."

Holy Cross's opponents on the final trip to New York were the St. John's University Redmen, a team ranked in the Top 20 in the country and headed for post-season play. Though the Redmen line-up included future pro Sonny Dove, Holy Cross controlled the tempo of the game and came away with a 63-60 victory. When the team bus rolled onto the Holy Cross campus at two o'clock in the morning following the win, a crowd of nearly 1,200 students was on hand to greet the team. "We want Jack," they chanted. "We want Jack."

"The Manhattan win was big because it was in Madison Square Garden," Murphy said. "But nothing could compare to beating St. John's on the road and then having over 1,000 fans greet us when we got back to campus. It was an experience that I will never forget."

The Crusaders finished the season with a hard-fought loss to Boston College, a team coached by former Holy Cross great Bob Cousy. Before the contest, Murphy and his teammates received another show of support from the student body. "We were in Kimball Dining Hall finishing our pre-game meal when the rest of the students began to file in," Murphy recalled. "As we stood up to leave, a few students started to clap and by the time we reached the doors, everyone had risen to give us a standing ovation. It was quite a feeling."

Murphy entered his final college game needing 27 points to reach the coveted 1,000 career point milestone and had 21 points by halftime.

"As we were leaving the floor at the half, the announcer gave the half time scorers and said that Richie Murphy has 21 points and needs just six more points to reach the 1,000-mark for his career. I couldn't believe he said that."

With less than six minutes remaining in the game Murphy, one of the best foul shooters in the school's history, walked to the line for a one-and-one, needing just a single point to reach the 1,000-point plateau. He missed the first shot, however, and Boston College called a time out after grabbing the defensive rebound.

"During the time out, BC changed defenses to a box-and-one on me," Murphy said. "I didn't get a shot the rest of the game and finished the game at 999 points." In doing so, the popular Murphy earned the nickname 999. "Years after my playing days were over, we were celebrating a family Christmas and after we finished opening the presents my wife said there was another present for me outside," Murphy said. "I walked out to the driveway and there was a new license plate on the car, RJM999. No respect!"

The team finished with a 10-13 record, the first losing record since 1944-45, but Murphy ended his career with positive feelings, feelings shared by some of his teammates.

"The night when I was inducted into the Varsity Club Hall of Fame, Keith Hochstein came up to me and said that of all the teams he ever played for, the 1965-66 squad was a team in the truest sense of the word, and I included that in my speech that night."

Hochstein, who was a sophomore in Donohue's initial season at Holy Cross, remembers the year was a great deal of fun despite a losing record. "There was tremendous rapport and unselfishness on that team," Hochstein said. "There were no stars on that team, and Jack Donohue fostered that principle. He had guys who understood the game, there were no prima donnas."

Murphy finished his three-year varsity career by being invited to several all-star games at the conclusion of the season. Long before the advent of NBA combines, such events were a reward for deserving seniors, and also gave pro scouts a look at prospective NBA players. After one such game, Donohue was driving Murphy and Mike Riordan back to New York City. Riordan had just finished his junior year at Providence College and the two collegians began discussing their futures. "I've been accepted to Fordham Law," Murphy told Riordan. "What about the NBA," Riordan queried. "Mike, I am not a pro player, I am going to be a lawyer," Murphy said with his usual candor. "What about you, what are you going do after you graduate from Providence next year?"

"I am going to play pro basketball," was Riordan's equally candid reply. Murphy didn't say anything, but the answer floored him. "I remembered we played Providence a few weeks earlier and I scored 28 points and Mike scored 4, and he is talking about playing in the NBA," Murphy said. "I couldn't believe it."

A year later Riordan became a 12th round draft pick of the New York Knicks and pursued his dream of playing professional basketball. He toiled in the Eastern League before becoming a member of the Knicks championship team of 1969-70 as the team's designated fouler. His career received a big break when he was part of the trade with the

Baltimore Bullets that sent Earl "The Pearl" Monroe to the Knicks. Riordan's hard work and perseverance paid off in Baltimore, where he earned a starting spot as a shooting guard and was named to the NBA all-star team.

*   *   *   *   *

It was time for Donohue and Herrion to hit the recruiting trail following their first year, and what better place to start than metropolitan New York. They listed the blue-chip players who could possibly meet the high admissions set by Holy Cross, and spent most of their time and energies enticing the young men with the benefits of going to school at the Cross. Donohue had five scholarships to give out that year, and he set his sights on players that would re-establish the Crusaders as a national power.

"Coach Donohue and Herrion recruited five outstanding high school players but none of them were accepted," Jim Maloney recalled. "All five players received scholarships from Division I schools and many of them ended up playing against Holy Cross."

In the end, they signed just two players, Jackie Lahey from nearby Shrewsbury and Tony Barclay from New York's Christ the King. Barclay was an intelligent, tough defensive player who came from a winning high school program and was the consummate team player. He had also attended Friendship Farms as a camper for two years, worked in the camp's kitchen for another summer and developed a strong bond with Donohue.

"My father died when I was young and then in my freshman year at Holy Cross my mother passed away," Barclay said. "Coach Donohue became a father figure to me and provided me with guidance during my four years in Worcester."

Both Lahey and Barclay enjoyed fine collegiate careers and served as the team's co-captains in their senior year, but they were not the blue chippers Donohue needed to compete against the likes of UCLA, North Carolina or Boston College.

Donohue was finding out first-hand that luring the nation's best high school players to Worcester, Massachusetts, would not be as easy a task as convincing high school players to go to Power Memorial. To begin with, Holy Cross had some of the highest standards in the country, and they also had limited academic programs. There were no phys-ed or recreation classes that were the popular choices of many incoming student-athletes. Finally, Holy Cross didn't cheat. There were no cars offered, no bogus summer time jobs and no under-the-table inducements to seal the deal.

While Donohue didn't have the recruiting year he had hoped for, the 1966-67 squad was bolstered by the addition of two players from the freshman team—Ed Siudut and Ron Teixeira. Siudut was a student-athlete in the truest sense of the term. His work in the classroom earned him academic all-American honors and an NCAA post-graduate scholarship in 1969. That same year, he was drafted by both the NBA's San Francisco Warriors and the ABA's New York Nets.

Despite Siudut and Keith Hochstein's presence in the line-up, the Crusaders got off to another bad start in 1966, losing four of their five games, including a 65-44 blowout by Army. But a pair of overtime wins against Western Kentucky and Pennsylvania helped turn the season around. Donohue kept his unbeaten streak in New York alive with a 73-63 win over Fordham to give the Crusaders a 15-7 record. With a NIT bid hanging on the team's three final games, Holy Cross's post-season hopes were dashed when they lost home games to Providence College and Boston College, two teams that advanced to the NCAA tournament.

For Willard, the team's captain, the NIT snub was a major disappointment as he ended his collegiate career without making a post-season appearance. The US Army and a possible trip to Vietnam were now waiting for him after graduation.

"At Holy Cross winning and academics were important, but the most important thing was the big picture," Willard said. "Not making the NIT was a disappointing way to end my college career, but Coach Donohue was good at making us see the big picture. I think a lot about the guys on those teams in my last two years at Holy Cross. We showed a lot of improvement, were very close and had the ability to communicate on the court." After his stint with the army, Willard joined the coaching fraternity and eventually returned to Holy Cross as the school's head coach in 1999, and led them to three consecutive NCAA appearances from 2000 to 2003.

Siudut distinguished himself in his rookie year, averaging 20 points and 11 rebounds a game, but the team's other sophomore sensation, Teixeira, struggled under Donohue's command. Teixeria had played for former Crusader captain Ron Perry at Catholic Memorial High School, and was considered by many as the top New England high school player in his senior year . He had good size, could shoot from the outside and was dexterous for a big man. But he didn't like playing inside, and shied away from contact, a trait that did not endear him to his head coach. He worried about maintaining high grades and played just one season at Cross before leaving the team to concentrate on school.

Bob Kissane played on the freshman team when Teixeira decided to pack it in.

"He was very fast, extremely strong and quite agile, but never played with much enthusiasm," Kissane recalled. "After basketball, he became a body builder and would be seen lifting weights while we were practicing. He was huge. He later became a martial arts instructor. I think he is a very bright guy, successful in business, but he was just not excited about being a player."

The Teixeira affair would upset many New England alumni, who felt that Donohue had ruined a gifted athlete and his absence from the basketball team would not sit well with some Holy Cross fans. The perfect match that some had predicted between Jack Donohue and Holy Cross was beginning to show signs of imperfection. As Donohue later would later joke, "You've heard of the rambling wreck from Georgia Tech? Well I was the total loss at Holy Cross."

CHAPTER 12

NIT Blues

"Worcester can be a rough place for a person like Jack to fit in," Jackie Leaman said. "He was a New Yorker and a lot of people considered him an outsider. There were people at Worcester who never accepted Jack. I know because I came from Cambridge, moved 60 miles west to Amherst, and a lot of people didn't accept me either."

Leaman was an assistant coach at University of Massachusetts when Donohue took over the reins at Holy Cross and the two quickly became fierce competitors on the court and close friends away from the gym.

"It was different then," Leaman said, echoing Danny Buckley's comments about the coaching profession. "It was a much friendlier group then. When we played games we were very competitive and wanted to beat the other team, but after the game we would socialize and sometimes laugh at how we acted during the game. In those days you did your own scouting, so if you saw a coach you knew scouting a game, you would sit next to them in the stands and spend some time together."

Leaman saw a sample of Donohue's game demeanor early in their relationship when Holy Cross was playing in Amherst. Donohue was annoyed with what he considered was bias officiating and even more frustrated with the referees' refusal to discuss the matter with him. So he literally took the matter into his own hands.

"We had Clarence Hill on the foul line to shoot a free throw when Jack came onto the court and took the ball out of his hands, startling the player, the refs and everyone else in the gym," Leaman said. "The ref demanded that Jack give the ball back but he refused to return the ball until the referee would listen to his complaints, which he eventually did. I have never seen anything like it."

Donohue's unorthodox behavior earned him a technical foul but he got his point across. Despite that run-in, Donohue insisted that opposition coaches were not bitter rivals but compatriots and always invited both groups back to his Worcester house for post-game parties after home games, parties that were hosted by Mary Jane, now the mother of a growing family. In Jack's first year at Holy Cross their second child, John Joe was born and in subsequent years Kathy, Marybeth, Bryan and Maura were added to the clan.

"It was nothing to have 10 to 30 people in your house starting at 11 p.m., plus the opposing coach and the referee." Mary Jane said.

Hosting was a role she was given early in her marriage when her husband was still coaching at Power Memorial.

"One day I fell while I had Carol in my arms and as I attempted to protect her I sprained my ankle," Mary Jane said. "It swelled up beautifully but since there was a children's birthday party in the afternoon, a game and then the grown-up party at night, no one is paying attention to my injury. Finally, at the post-game party, things begin to slow down and two nurses and one coach are across from me and noticed my oversized ankle. They say 'gee you'd better stay off it'...but they remained seated and allowed me to continue to run around on one foot."

Any time a visiting coach was in Worcester to scout or recruit, he received an invitation back to the Donohue house for dinner or a drink and it was not unusual for Donohue to bring a player or two back to the house for a home-cooked meal.

* * * * *

Things were looking up for the Crusaders as the 1967-68 season began. Keith Hochstein and Ed Siduit provided Donohue with two experienced, skilled forwards and the team's strategy was to get the ball to the pair. Hochstein was only 6'4" but a more adept post player than the taller Siduit. While Hochstein scored his points inside against taller players,

Siduit's ability to score inside or outside made him one of the most effective scorers in the Northeast. He utilized a jump hook with either hand in the post area and could move outside where he possessed uncanny shooting range.

The highlight of the schedule was a game between the UCLA Bruins and Holy Cross pitting Lew Alcindor against his former high school coach in college basketball's most sacred shrine, Madison Square Garden. On paper it was a mismatch and the game played out that way with the Bruins posting a 90-67 win over the Crusaders.

Prior to the game, Donohue, ever the optimist, saw winning the game not as an impossible task but rather as the ultimate challenge.

"Sure they'd be favored," Donohue told a New England sports magazine. "But what do we have to lose? They'd probably have a long winning streak going. They might be ready for a bad night, and we might benefit. Anyhow, think of the build-up, Alcindor against his old coach."

After the game Donohue conceded the obvious when he mentioned that it was a lot more fun coaching Alcindor than trying to defend against him. Following the loss to the Bruins, Holy Cross went on an eight-game run defeating Boston College, Boston University, Fordham, Syracuse, UMass, Assumption, Connecticut and Providence to give them a 15-6 record with two games remaining in the regular season. They dropped an 83-67 road decision to a strong St. John's team and then saw their NIT hopes disappear when the Bob Cousy–coached Boston College squad came into Worcester Auditorium and defeated them 90-87.

They finished with a 15-8 record including wins over some of the better schools in the East but it wasn't good enough to advance to either the NIT or the NCAA tournament. In the mid-1960s only 31 teams advanced to post season play, 19 to the NCAA championship and 12 to the NIT. Unlike the modern day set-up featuring 65 teams, geographical boundaries were strictly enforced, and if a team belonged to a conference the only way to advance to the NCAA tournament was to win your conference.

For years, the Atlantic Coast Conference, featuring powerhouse teams such as North Carolina, South Carolina and Maryland, would routinely see their best team upset in the conference tournament and thus eliminated from NCAA consideration. Finishing second in a strong conference often meant a trip to New York City for the still prestigious National Invitational Tournament. In the East, the Ivy League champion received an automatic bid and three at-large berths were awarded to a field of schools that included Boston College, Syracuse, Seton Hall, Providence and the Big Five schools of Philadelphia. The Donohue-coached Crusaders of 1965-1972 didn't have the same talent level as the teams they battled for an NCAA berth and a more realistic goal was being invited to the NIT. Yet that goal eluded Donohue and the Crusaders during his seven year stint at Holy Cross.

"It seemed every year Jack would have around 16 wins with three or four games left, but those games were always against teams that had a lot more talent," Frank McLaughlin said. "Teams like Boston College, St. John's Providence and Connecticut. Holy Cross would have a winning season but end it with a string of losses that meant not going to the NIT and the year would end with a bad taste."

The 1968-69 season was a perfect example as the Crusaders defeated Providence, Georgetown, Syracuse, Seton Hall, and Connecticut and had a 16-5 mark with three home games remaining. The Crusaders once again had a powerful one-two punch, this time it was sophomore Bob Kissane and Siduit. Alumni and fans were thinking a possible NCAA berth or at worse a trip to New York for the NIT when disaster struck. In the final two weeks of the season, the team dropped consecutive home games to Providence, St. John's and Boston College to finish with a 16-8 record, not good enough for post-season play.

* * * * *

Jimmy Herrion left the Holy Cross coaching staff after the 1967-68 season to coach at nearby Worcester Tech and Donohue replaced him with another New York–bred coach, Frank McArdle, who proved to be an invaluable resource for the head coach. McArdle, who first learned the game of basketball under Donohue's tutelage at St. Barnabas Grammar School, had an excellent reputation among high school coaches and spent a lot of time recruiting in the New York metropolitan area.

"Jack had the greatest respect for Frank as a person, a player and a coach," Hughie Donohue said. "Frank was a great person to play with, a very good all-round player. He first started coaching at Blessed Sacrament and developed into an outstanding coach; he was an excellent recruiter, great with the Xs and Os and could teach fundamental basket-ball."

Hughie first met McArdle when they were teammates on the St. Barnabas CYO team and the two remained close friends until McArdle's untimely death in 1974.

"Jack was ten years older than Frank but used to refer to him as his son," Hughie said. "Frank was a tremendous person, never said a bad word or used profanity and he had this great relationship with Jack Donohue."

Palazzi said that McArdle had another trait that made him invalu-able, first to Donohue and later to George Blaney.

"The players loved him," Palazzi said. "They respected him and he was able to relate to them as basketball players and as persons."

In the spring of 1969, the two-man coaching staff set out to recruit new talent and focused their attention on the CHSAA and two NYC products in particular. Molloy's Kevin Joyce was the cream of the crop, a consensus All-American who led Jack Curran's Molloy Stanners to a city championship, the first of Curran's five CHSAA titles. Oddly enough, that year Molloy defeated their old nemesis, the Power Panthers 60-54 in the championship game as future NBA all-star Brian Winters scored a game high 27 points. Donohue had a good relationship with Joyce who had spent time at Friendship Farm but the best prospect in the city was headed for bigger places. He had verbally committed to Frank McGuire and the University of South Carolina although there was a talk of pack-age deal that would send Joyce and Curran to Boston College with Curran replacing the retiring Cousy as the Eagles' head coach.

"Boston College talked to me about the coaching position and they wanted me to bring Kevin and Brian (Winters) with me," Curran said. "Not surprisingly Frank McGuire (the legendary head coach of South Carolina and a mentor of Curran's) advised me against taking the job. He didn't think it was a good career move and of course he wanted Kevin and Brian at South Carolina."

Curran stayed at Molloy, Joyce and Winters went to South Carolina in successive years and Donohue and McArdle looked elsewhere for play-ers who could make a difference. Their second prospect was Billy Schaeffer, the top gun at Holy Cross High School, but he was headed for St. John's. The well was beginning to dry up when St. Helena's Jim Powell joined Joyce at South Carolina. However, Donohue was able to entice Jim Schnurr, an all-city player from St. Francis Prep, to Worcester.

He added Gene Doyle, another all-city product from Brooklyn, and then decided to take a gamble on a lesser-known player, Kevin Stacom, who was a high school teammate of Schaeffer. As a junior at Holy Cross High School, Stacom was a bench warmer on a team that captured the city title. A year later, he was a starter on a team that was knocked out by Molloy in the semi-finals when Stanner point guard Tom Brethel's three-pointer at the buzzer enabled Molloy to record a 53-51 win that crushed the Holy Cross High School's chances of repeating as city champs. Stacom was a gangly kid who could shoot the ball and who had shown improvement in each of his four years at Holy Cross High, but he didn't garner a lot of attention from Division I schools. Donohue became sold on the kid when he heard that he had spent his nights shooting in the St. Boniface's parish school gym in Elmont.

"The parish priests couldn't figure out how I was able to sneak into the gym all the time. They didn't realize I had a key to the front door," Stacom said. "I was a real gym rat."

Stacom was signed and would eventually develop into an outstanding collegiate player and one of the country's top shooters. Unfortunately, that metamorphosis would not occur at Holy Cross but rather at rival Providence College.

* * * * *

Frank McLaughlin completed his collegiate playing days at Fordham in the spring of 1969 and then pondered his next move. He was selected in the 11th round by the New York Knicks, a veteran team that was on the verge of winning their first NBA championship. Eddie Donovan had just taken over control of the expansion Buffalo Braves and offered McLaughlin a tryout if things didn't work out in New York. But McLaughlin realized his future didn't lie in pro basketball and he enlisted in the National Guard and began to pursue a high school coaching career.

"I signed up for the National Guard and my goal was to be the JV coach at Mount St. Michael's Academy," McLaughlin said. "But I ran into Jack who asked me what I was doing. When I told him my plans he asked me to consider coming to Worcester as a volunteer coach."

To make ends meet McLaughlin tried his hand at selling insurance to help supplement his Spartan life.

"I remember renting a room for $8 a week, and although I was selling insurance I spent most of my time at the gym as a volunteer coach."

At the same time as Frank was moving to Holy Cross, his younger brother Tommy was transferring from the University of Tennessee.

"Tom had a great freshman year, was named the team's MVP, but when he got to the varsity he didn't get any playing time and was looking to transfer," Frank said. "Ray Mears was the coach at Tennessee and he was a great coach but he only played five players and as a sophomore Tommy didn't get any floor time."

The natural place for the younger McLaughlin to transfer was Holy Cross where Donohue called the shots and his brother served as an assistant. The only problem was that, at the time, the school had a stringent policy against accepting transfer students and wouldn't even consider Tom's application.

Donohue was livid. Here was a kid with exceptional high school and university grades, had a brother who was volunteering his services as a coach and the school was adamant in refusing to even look at his request. The coach's demeanor didn't improve when he learned that Tommy was now leaning towards his arch rival, the Boston College Eagles. On Donohue's advice, McLaughlin contacted Jackie Leaman at the University of Massachusetts.

"We recruited Tom out of high school but he chose Tennessee and that was the end of that," Leaman recalled. "Then Jack called and told me that he was looking to transfer and that I should take him. My first reaction was 'if he so good why don't you take him', but Holy Cross had this strict policy about transfers. Jack said he was a good guy and would help any program in New England and he was right."

"In the end I was looking at UConn because Dee Rowe was coaching there and he was a good guy," McLaughlin said. "Finally, I chose UMass because of Jack Leaman; who was not only an excellent coach but a great person. On my visit, Julius Erving (who first met McLaughlin at Friendship Farm) came up to me and said that I should come because they were going to have a good team and that clinched it for me. I never would have considered UMass if it wasn't for Coach Donohue. I ended up as captain of the 1973 UMass team and later played professionally in Europe."

Despite losing the younger McLaughlin, the 1969-70 season was one of the happiest Donohue experienced in Worcester. The chemistry between the three coaches was excellent, the Crusaders were winning and Donohue's reputation as an after dinner speaker was flourishing. Kissane remembers his former coach was at his best when he was talking to groups and once commented that Donohue liked taking recruits to such occasions.

"Jack was certainly a colorful character," Kissane said. "He was at his best speaking before a group."

Kissane did not enjoy Donohue's coaching as much as his story telling and a relationship that started on a strong note deteriorated during his four years at Holy Cross.

As a senior at Chaminade High School on Long Island, Kissane was a highly recruited forward who was 6'9" but possessed the skills of a shooting guard. His older brother Jim played for Cousy at Boston College and Donohue and other college coaches figured that Bob would follow his brother to B.C. He was surprised when the older Kissane approached him after a Holy Cross–B.C. game and told him that he should recruit Bob.

"Isn't he going to Boston College?" Donohue asked.

"Just talk to him coach, he is open and he would be good for your program."

Donohue remembered Kissane because he played well against Power and Alcindor.

"I was mainly recruited by a local Holy Cross alumnus," Kissane recalled. "I felt that Holy Cross was bringing in a great class of big guys so that I wouldn't have to play with my back to the basket and I thought that with Eddie Siudut and Teixeria the program was really taking off. I also really liked Jack at the time, and I thought Holy Cross would be a continuation of what life was like at Chaminade. I was wrong on all counts!"

Donohue asked Kissane to play in the post with his back to the basket, an unfamiliar position and one that Kissane felt hindered his development as a player. The pair had many disagreements during his three-year stint on the varsity team and Kissane believed that Donohue slowed down a talented team.

"Our teams were considered to be chokers because we always lost to BC, Providence and St. John's at the end of the season," Kissane said. "In fact, all these teams were able to sit on the ball against us, while we sat back and let them do it. We should have been pressing them and making their guards give up the ball. Jack and I had some pretty heated arguments about it. But he was immovable on the subject. But there was nothing wrong with our guys. We were playing in handcuffs."

Despite Kissane's concerns, the 1969-70 Crusaders averaged nearly 84 points a game without a shot clock or three-point line. With the graduation of Siduit, Kissane was now 'the man' and the offence ran through him. But at 6'9", the Long Island product still preferred to play the way he did at Chaminade: facing the basket. The constant debates fueled the tension between the star player and the coach.

The team had a 16-6 record and was on the bubble of a post-season invitation. Once again, they finished the season going 0-3 against Providence, St. John's and Boston College and were shut out of the NCAA and the NIT tournaments.

* * * * *

"Jack enjoyed watching the NCAA Final Four but he really loved being at the NIT, back in New York and at the Garden," Frank McLaughlin said. "He would sit in the stands with all the other coaches and have a great time comparing notes and telling stories."

He would also offer a word of encouragement to a fellow coach going through a tough time or a helping hand to a younger coach looking for a job.

"After the 1969-70 season, Jack took me to the NIT and there he ran into Tates Locke," McLaughlin said. "During one of the games Tates took Jack aside for a one-on-one talk.

Locke informed Donohue that he was just offered the head coaching job at Clemson and he wanted to talk to McLaughlin about joining his staff.

"Jack gave the OK and Tates asked me to be his third assistant," McLaughlin said. "But before I could say yes, Digger Phelps approached me about becoming his assistant at Fordham."

Suddenly, the volunteer coach who could barely afford the $8 a week he paid for lodging in a Worcester boarding house had two *bona fide* job offers.

"Clemson paid more money for their third assistant coach than Fordham paid for their first (and only) assistant," McLaughlin said. "I knew I wasn't Digger's first choice. I was sure other guys had turned the position down because the salary was so low. But I thought being a first assistant was better for my career and I was going back to my *alma mater*."

McLaughlin chose Fordham and it turned out to be a great career choice. That year, the Fordham Rams became the toast of New York City, winning 22 games and advancing to the NIT finals. The following season, Phelps and McLaughlin were at Notre Dame where they built an NCAA powerhouse. The Fighting Irish were a perennial NCAA Top 20 squad and snapped the longest winning streak in NCAA history when they defeated Bill Walton and the UCLA Bruins 71-70 in the 1973-74 season.

On the flip side Locke had initial success at Clemson but eventually was forced to resign when a *Sports Illustrated* story chronicled recruiting violations by the coaching staff.

"Sometimes money isn't the most important thing when taking a job," McLaughlin said in retrospect. "I made the right move going with Digger."

* * * * *

Stan Grayson was a standout high school player in Chicago when several members of the local Holy Cross alumni association began to talk to him about the benefits of a Holy Cross education.

"I was considering schools like Villanova, but decided on Holy Cross after a visit to the school in my junior year," Grayson said.

Grayson, a two-time all-state player for All Saints High School, was a three-year starter for Donohue and a player who was proficient at both ends of the court. He was the team's defensive stopper who was always given the assignment of covering the opposition's top scorer whether it was Julius Erving of UMass or Ole Miss' Johnny Neumann, the country's leading scorer. He could also perform at the offensive end when needed, as evidenced by his 35-point, 22-rebound performance against Georgetown University in his junior year. Grayson was different from the majority of Holy Cross students: he was from the mid-West and he was black. Yet, in so many ways he personified the image of a Holy Cross student-athlete.

"Stan Grayson was more than just an athlete," Jim Maloney recalled. "His physical stature, 6'5", 220 lbs., commanded attention, but he was a bright, articulate young man who was a campus leader during his four years at Holy Cross."

His leadership qualities were put to the test in his sophomore season. Early in the season, the team went down to New York City and got beaten by Columbia University and their All-American guard Jim McMillan, 92–68. When they returned to Holy Cross they found the campus in turmoil following an anti-Vietnam War rally. Ten students, five whites and five blacks, were suspended by the school's administration. When the black students collectively decided to protest the suspensions by boycotting classes and student activities, Grayson joined them.

"It was my first year with the varsity and I didn't want to leave the team, but I thought I had to support the boycott," Grayson said. "I went to Jack to explain my position and he was very understanding and supportive of my actions."

Donohue told the sophomore to do what he thought was right and to re-join the team when he was ready. Grayson missed two games before returning to the club and his starting forward position. A year later, Donohue paid Grayson the ultimate compliment when a friend asked him to describe Grayson.

"Jack told him that Stan Grayson is the type of person that he wanted his daughters to marry," Mary Jane recalled.

* * * * *

Donohue never liked to run up scores, so it was not surprising that he wasn't on the bench when the school recorded its most lop-sided win in school history in the second game of the 1970-71 season: a 138–68 win over St. Michael's College, a Division II school that normally had competitive games against Holy Cross. Donohue was back in New York attending his father's funeral and McArdle was in charge. The team got off to a fast start that season winning nine of their first 11 games. Midway through the season the team had 11 straight road games against the likes of St. John's, Syracuse, Boston College and the Johnny Neumann–led University of Mississippi. The Crusaders managed to win six of them.

The team was talented and deep. Up front, Kissane and super sophomores Schnurr and Doyle combined for over 35 points and 24 rebounds a game while Grayson was the team's defensive stopper. Senior co-captain Jack Adams ran the show at the point guard position while Buddy

Venne was a reliable outside scorer when given time to shoot. When Venne and his teammates were hot, the Crusaders could play with any-one in the country but the 1970-71 team was impossible to figure out. One week they went to Chestnut Hill and edged Boston College 74-73 and a week later they lost to Assumption College, a neighboring Division II school, by 23 points.

Kissane wasn't the only New Yorker unhappy in Worcester. Stacom was seeing sporadic playing time and was concerned over the direction the basketball program was taking. When he did get a chance to play he performed well. Late in the season, he came off the bench to pour in 24 points to lead Holy Cross to a 81-70 come-from-behind win over Fairfield.

"Jack experimented with a big line-up with Doyle, Schnurr and Kissane up front, Stan Grayson at one guard and me at the point," Stacom said. "But Jack was very loyal to his veterans and Jackie Adams had done a good job at the point, so he got most of the playing time."

Stacom knew his time would come but was more upset that the school administration was hindering Donohue's attempts to upgrade the basketball schedule.

"Coach had such a dynamic personality and he could have sched-uled games with anyone in the country, but the administration wouldn't OK them," Stacom said. "The school had a reputation to maintain and it appeared to me that it wanted to be a Catholic version of Williams or Amherst."

The final straw came when the school's administration cancelled a planned trip to the West Coast where the Crusaders would play USC and UCLA.

"I knew that I had to leave if I was going to have a chance at the pros," Stacom said. "The problem was that Jack and Frank gave me my chance to play college ball and I didn't want to seem ungrateful to them."

When the season ended, he went to Donohue and told him he wanted to transfer. Many coaches would make promises, usually unfulfilled, or blackball players that attempted to change schools, but that wasn't Donohue's style. He listened to Stacom's concerns and promised to help him any way he could.

"I spent the summers playing at St. John's University and became friendly with Mike Riordan," Stacom recalled. "He was impressed that I would stay late and do drills with him. When I told him I thought I had to leave Holy Cross he told me to look at Providence."

Riordan called Dave Gavitt, the Providence coach, and told him that Stacom would help the team. At the same time, Donohue had secretly contacted Gavitt and told him that Stacom was likely to end up at his school and that the young man was worth a long look. After sitting out a mandatory year, Stacom joined All-Americans Ernie DiGregorio and Marvin Barnes and helped the Friars reach the Final Four in 1973. After graduation Stacom was drafted by the Boston Celtics and enjoyed a seven-year professional career that included a World Championship with the Celtics. He later went on to become an NBA scout. Still he remembers fondly the two years he spent at Holy Cross and the support he received from McArdle and Donohue when he decided to switch schools.

"They gave me a chance to play in the colleges and while they didn't want me to leave they were very supportive," Stacom said. "They were great guys!"

"I wish the people in Worcester got to know Jack better because he was such a good man and he did a great job there," Richie Lewis said. Lewis joined the Holy Cross athletic staff as Sports Information Director in 1966 and developed a strong bond with Donohue. "He was a great person to work for, always a gentleman, and he had a great sense of humor."

Lewis's perception of Donohue was shared by former Holy Cross great Togo Palazzi.

"Jack brought this New York attitude to Holy Cross and it was refreshing," said the New Jersey native who grew up across the river from Manhattan. "He was a great guy who had a warm personality and a great sense of humor. He used to say that the Jesuits took an oath of poverty and he lived it. Another time, he said he received his paycheck and was able to cash it on the bus."

Palazzi believed that Donohue never received full credit for the job he did during his Holy Cross days.

"He was close with Bobby Knight and Knight would bring his Army team for a pre-season scrimmage and they would play all night," Palazzi said. "I think Jack was as good as many of the coaches in the country that got a lot more credit."

CHAPTER 13

I always wanted to coach a country

Kissane and Adams graduated in 1971, but Donohue had a solid nucleus returning with Grayson, Doyle and Schnurr providing plenty of offensive punch up front while Buddy Venne regained the scoring touch that had made him a sophomore sensation two years earlier.

Venne joined the team for the 1969-70 season and immediately caught everyone's attention with an outstanding display of shooting. He averaged 27 points in his first six games as a Crusader but those numbers dropped significantly when opponents realized that he was a one-dimensional player.

He finished his sophomore year averaging a very respectable 17 points per game but became a sub in his junior year as his average dipped to 7.8. Venne regained his starting spot as a senior captain and contributed 14 points per game before graduating and spending several years playing professional basketball in Europe.

Before the 1971-72 season began, Grayson came to the coach with a request from his teammates.

"It was the 70s and everyone was wearing long hair," Grayson recalled. "But Jack had this thing about hair. It had to be short and neat and no facial hair."

Donohue was definitely old-school when it came to follicles, besides he felt referees would be harsher on teams that weren't clean shaven. Grayson, who had a well trimmed mustache in high school, asked the coach if he would allow his players to wear mustaches.

"I told him, we would keep them neat and the referees wouldn't even notice," Grayson said. "He balked, but finally, I asked him if he could tell me whether or not Todd Wells had a mustache."

Wells was a classmate and friend of Grayson's, who had daily contact with Donohue. Donohue pondered the question for several minutes, and finally had to admit that he did not know if Wells had a mustache, but he recalled that Wells was always neat and well dressed. The coach relented, allowing Grayson and his teammates to wear mustaches. On the court the Crusaders jumped out to a fast start before an injury forced Grayson to the sidelines.

"I broke my kneecap that basically ended my season and career," Grayson said. "I came back, dressed the last two games and saw some action in the final game."

The Crusaders looked like they might eventually receive the elusive NIT bid as they posted wins over Seton Hall, Furman and LaSalle, but Grayson's injury took its toll as the team dropped four of its last five games. . The students were no longer chanting 'Jack! Jack! Jack!' after victories and, the team was once again passed over by the NIT committee.

.Grayson did get some satisfaction a few months later when he was named Crusader of the Year; the third basketball player to receive the prestigious award during Donohue's tenure.

"It was disappointing to play for three years and not receive a postseason bid but, on the other hand it was very satisfying to win the Crusader of the Year award after all I went through that year," Grayson said.

The scholar-athlete would have plenty of satisfying moments after graduation. He served in Mayor Koch's administration in New York City in between a successful career as an investment banker. In 1991, he was inducted into the Holy Cross Varsity Club Hall of Fame.

By mid-season, it had become apparent that Donohue was not going to return to Holy Cross after the 1971-72 campaign. The school offered him a new contract, but he kept it stuffed in a desk drawer with no intention of signing it. He had enjoyed his time in Worcester, but it had become painfully obvious to both him and the school that it was time to move on. Whatever the expectations were when he signed his original contract, there was growing dissatisfaction over the team's inability to get to the post season. His record was one of the best in New England, a .617 winning percentage, and he had earned the respect and friendship of his coaching peers and the majority of his players as he had when he coached at Power and Tolentine.

But it was not enough and Donohue began to explore job opportunities. The Donohue era at Holy Cross was near an end, and there were just a few loose ends to tie up.

One of them was a prospective recruit by the name of Tom Woodring; a star player from New Hampshire who was recruited to the Cross by McArdle.

"I was all set to sign with Holy Cross and play for Jack Donohue," Woodring recalled. "I grew up in the Bronx and attended St. Nicolas Tolentine Grammar School before my father moved the family to New Hampshire," Woodring explained. "I knew all about Jack Donohue and was looking forward to playing for him."

But before his signed a letter of commitment he got a phone call from McArdle telling him that Donohue was leaving, but not to worry, McArdle had a scholarship to another school for him.

"Frank told me that he arranged for me to get a scholarship at his alma mater, Iona College," Woodling said. "He felt that he was going to be the coach at Iona in a year or two when (Iona had coach) Jimmy McDermott retired and said the school was a good match for me."

Woodring took his advice, played three years of varsity ball at Iona before enjoying a long professional career in Europe. With Woodring set, Donohue petitioned the school to have McArdle replace him as head coach. The school was not ready to make McArdle the head coach but agreed to keep him on as an assistant. George Blaney, a member of the 1947 National Championship team, was named the school's new head coach in the spring of 1972 and McArdle remained as his assistant for two years. Assured that his assistant coach was taken care of, Donohue began to explore job opportunities. Maura, the couple's sixth child was born a year earlier and the coach needed a job to support his family, although he wasn't losing any sleep at night over the prospect of being unemployed.

Siena College, a small Catholic school close to Albany, New York, that was looking to reemphasize its basketball program, contacted Donohue but he didn't think it was a good fit. Instead he recommended another candidate, Billy Kirsch, for the position. Kirsch, a Siena alumnus and a successful junior college coach, had been interested in the Siena job for years. He had worked at Friendship Farms and had helped him recruit players to Holy Cross and over time the two developed a strong friendship. Kirsch was appointed to the dual role of athletic director and basketball coach and under his leadership the Siena basketball team successfully returned to the Division I ranks. When Kirsch resigned as basketball coach to concentrate on his athletic director duties, the school soon became a stepping stone for aspiring young coaches such as Paul Hewitt, Louis Orr, and John Griffin.

Donohue was leaning towards a job at Florida Institute of Technology when a chance conversation with a fellow coach started Jack thinking about leaving the college scene for an opportunity to coach the Canadian national team.

"Another coach came into my office one day and dropped an ad for the Canadian National Team on my desk and said that I would do a good job coaching a country," Donohue would say years later. "I put the ad in my desk drawer and didn't think of it again. Then later, I was looking for something in my desk and there was the ad. I knew then I wasn't returning to Holy Cross, so I figured I would apply and see if anything would come of it."

Jack had spent the previous summer coaching in Germany and was intrigued by the international game. The prospect of coaching a country was quite attractive. Canada was looking for a full-time Technical Director, who would also serve as the National Team coach. The person would be responsible for selecting a team that would go to the 1972 Olympic qualifying round, but the emphasis was on building a team for 1976 Summer Games in Montreal, when Canada would have an automatic bid as the host country. Donohue applied for the job, but his first contact with his prospective employees was not positive.

"Someone called up and said they wanted to interview Jack for the job and he asked them how many other people they were going to interview and he was told 20-25," Mary Jane recalled. "Jack said that they should call him back when they had cut down to four or five candidates."

After that brief conversation, Donohue figured that he wasn't going to hear from Canada and was surprised a week later when he received a second phone call informing him that he was one of five people selected for an interview.

"We interviewed four or five people and Jack was very impressive," John Hudson, a member of the selection committee, said years after.

Hudson was a former National Track Coach and successful businessman who took over the reins of the newly formed Coaching Association of Canada in 1972.

"Jack had some international experience, but that wasn't as important a factor as his attitude. I was impressed because he knew about Canada and where we stood in the international picture. He recognized that it wasn't going to be an easy job, and you could tell he possessed a lot of basketball knowledge and displayed such a positive attitude. It wasn't that he promised to do certain things with the program; he knew how much work was required to make the team competitive on the international scene. I can't speak for the other members of the committee, but in my mind he was the best choice."

Jack returned to the States without a job offer in hand and proceeded to pursue the Florida Institute position in earnest. He took Mary Jane and two-year old Bryan to meet with officials from the school, leaving the other five children with friends and Mary Jane's parents. Jack was ready to sign a contract, but Mary Jane had an uneasy feeling about Jack taking the coaching job at the Florida Institute of Technology.

"The people were great and it was a beautiful school, but it didn't seem like the right place for Jack," Mary Jane observed. "From a career standpoint I thought it was a dead end, a place that you go to before you retire, and Jack was still young."

As Jack met with school officials, his wife was escorted to housing developments with Bryan in tow. She saw several houses that were to her liking and within their price range. She returned to the hotel where they were staying to go over her findings with her husband. As she explained in detail the pros and cons of each home, she could sense that he wasn't paying attention.

"What's wrong? Why aren't your interested in what I am saying," she asked.

"I'm not taking the job here!" he replied. "We are moving to Canada."

Mary Jane was so stunned by the announcement that she said, "Canada – where is Canada?" – thinking that he was referring to some small town in the United States.

"I am going to coach the Canadian National Team," he said with an air of satisfaction and then added, "It's a country above Maine."

While Mary Jane had been house hunting, her father had phoned the hotel to inform Jack that he had been offered the job in Canada. Jack wasted little time in calling back and telling his new employers that he appreciated their confidence and he was ready to become the first full-time Canadian National Basketball Team coach. In a matter of minutes the Donohues went from a future in sunny Florida for one in the cold North.

*   *   *   *   *

The news that Donohue was going to Canada to be the national team coach surprised many of his friends but Jack had a simple explanation

"I've always wanted to coach a country."

That summer was a hectic one for the Donohue household as Jack tried to get a feeling for his new position while Mary Jane was left to sell the house and look after the family's six kids. Mary Jane did manage to meet Jack in Ottawa, their future hometown, one weekend to look for houses. However she encountered problems when her luggage was lost by the airline.

With her baggage nowhere in sight, Mary Jane reported to a customs agent who asked her if she had anything to declare.

"Like what," the unseasoned international traveler asked.

"Cigarettes, whiskey?" the customs official replied.

"No, but I could sure use a shot now," Mary Jane said.

"So could we all! Where do you want the missing bags sent, madam?"

"To the Shadow."

"The what?"

"The Shadow, the hotel where we are staying."

"You must mean the Chateau Laurier," the agent replied

The Donohues' first attempt at bilingualism was an unequivocal failure.

CHAPTER 14

New Beginnings

In 1968 John Munro, Canada's federal Minister of National Health and Welfare, commissioned a task force on sports for Canadians in the hopes of restructuring sport within the country. The task force was implemented following the disastrous 1968 Summer Games in Mexico where Canadian athletes garnered just five medals. The 1968 performance was marginally better than the four medals picked up in the 1964 Tokyo Olympics and the lone silver medal won at the Rome Games in 1960. The Canadian public was demanding better results and with the 1976 Summer Games being held on Canadian soil for the first time, there was concern that Canada's performance as the host country would be an embarrassment to a nation with an already fragile identity on the world stage. Munro's commission recommended several innovative steps including centralizing the national sport organizations, increasing the funding for amateur sport bodies and developing professional coaches. Unlike the American system where high school coaches are paid extra for coaching and have an opportunity for advancement to the college or professional ranks, the vast majority of Canadian coaches in 1972 were volunteer coaches will little chance of upward mobility. The report stated:

Few well-paid coaching jobs are available in Canada and very few men and women consider it a full time career. The Canadian weakness in coaching is most manifest at the level of play and performance of younger athletes…. Canada has almost nothing like the U.S. set-up and nothing comparable to the European practices…the immediate emphasis should be put on providing leadership and assistance to our voluntary coaches.

The report then urged the Canadian government to provide assistance to organize and develop a National Coaches Association. The government quickly began to implement many of the commission's recommendations including providing funding for the hiring of executive directors and national team coaches. The committee left no doubt about the importance of hiring qualified coaches when it earmarked $12,000 to supplement the salaries of national team coaches while only $10,000 was allotted for supplementing those of executive directors. The government was making a statement: they wanted high calibre coaches and were more willing to help fund the salaries of coaches than those of administrators. The offices of the National Sport Organizations (NSOs) were to be housed in three connecting high-raise buildings in Vanier overlooking the Rideau River, minutes from the headquarters of Sport Canada in downtown Ottawa. Armed with money and government support, NSOs went shopping for full-time coaches in Europe and Australia. The Canadian Amateur Basketball Association (CABA) advertised world-wide for their new position and chose Donohue shortly after his interview in the spring of 1972. The CABA got more than they bargained for—Donohue not only would provide the technical expertise and leadership needed, but also would change the way a country felt about itself.

*　*　*　*　*

Once hired, Donohue had very little time to prepare a team for the 1972 qualifying round that was being held in Germany. He had no coaching staff, did not know any of the players, and had very little time to build a cohesive unit. But he had a four-year contract and understood that whatever ailed the national team would not be fixed in one summer. He made that clear in his interview for the job; he was not going to sacrifice long-term goals for short team success. If nothing else, he had time on his side and that was probably his only ally. Much of the information he received about prospective players came from the CABA volunteer board of governors and he didn't like everything he heard. On different occasions, board members told him of at least two players that he did not want to invite to training camp.

While Donohue silently marveled at the board members' ability to read his mind, he made sure that both players were given a good look. From the beginning, he sent a message to everyone that he, and only he, would be the ultimate authority when selecting a team or inviting players to tryouts. Five regional tryouts were held and from those sessions 40 players received invitations to British Columbia where two teams would be selected. Donohue would take the first team to Mexico, Europe and finally the Olympic qualifying tournament in Germany while Dr. Paul Thomas, head coach at the University of Windsor, would accompany the second team to China.

Richie Spears, who played on the national team from 1965 to 1967, was one of several veterans attempting a comeback in 1972. Spears not only had been a member of the national team but also had played professionally in Belgium. He had retired as an active player but decided to give the national team one more shot when Donohue was named coach. Spears was one of the players deemed *persona non grata* by the established basketball community after he publicly blasted the national team's coaching staff following the squad's failure to qualify for the 1968 Olympics. Although he wasn't among the 40 invited to the final training camp in British Columbia, he liked what he saw at the regional camp in Montreal.

"I had just gotten the coaching job at Dawson College in Montreal and I went to the tryout looking to recruit players," Spears recalled. "When I got there I figured I might as well give it a shot because I could still shoot the ball better than most of the guys trying out."

Donohue decided to take an uncharacteristic low-key approach as he crossed the country evaluating talent, allowing other coaches in attendance to run the practices while he sat back and watched.

"I am just here to observe," he told the players.

One of the things he observed was that none of the players appeared to be enjoying the tryout experience.

"Jack would look around and see all these players with serious faces and he would say 'this is basketball, it's supposed to be fun,'" Spears said.

The players would learn in time that, among other things, playing for Donohue could indeed be fun.

*   *   *   *   *

John McKibbon was one of the members of the ill-fated team that failed to qualify for the 1968 Games. He later enrolled at Laurentian University and pursued a theology degree while continuing his basketball career at the university level. Though he had retired from international competition he began to have second thoughts when Donohue was announced as the new head coach.

"I played in the 1960 and 1964 Olympic teams and had a successful university career afterwards," McKibbon said. "Jack was inquiring about who was who in Canadian basketball and my name kept coming up, although it wasn't always positive because I was at the end of my career. But he was his own guy and wanted to give me a shot."

McKibbon played well at a regional tryout at Camp Borden in Ontario but the weekend session ended without Donohue talking to any of the players. McKibbon returned to Sudbury and a week later he received a call from Donohue.

"John, I am in an airport in Boston I would like to invite you out to B.C. to the final camp in Courtenay," Donohue said. "I like what I saw at Camp Borden and I think we can use you. You know that most of the kids I am looking at right now are 17 and 18-years-olds and I realize that you have some experience."

That was just what McKibbon wanted to hear.

"I represented the 'old school CABA' when things were done half-heartedly. Now basketball was being taken to a new level by bringing in one of the best coaches around. I saw the transition and what Jack was going to do and, wow, what a difference. I experienced first hand as a player the difference between pre-Jack and post-Jack and it was quite a change. Jack's power, of course, wasn't so much basketball, but his philosophy, his belief system that came into play."

McKibbon continued to play well in Courtenay, but a bad ankle sprain in the final days of camp left him off the A-Team roster.

"Jack needed players right away for a trip to Mexico, so I was put on the B-Team that later toured China."

McKibbon's international playing days ended with the China tour but not his involvement in the Canadian basketball scene. He was elected into the Canadian Basketball Hall of Fame in 1997 and had the pleasure of watching his son Jeff follow in his footsteps as an outstanding player at

Laurentian University. Jeff was named an All-Canadian while at Laurentian and was a member of the national team program and played for Donohue from 1986 to 1988.

* * * * *

The national team had an ambitious tune-up for the Olympic qualifying tourney that included a trip to Mexico followed by a six-week barnstorming tour through Italy before heading to Germany. Donohue's staff included a young Winnipeg native named John Restivo who served as team manager and doubled as an assistant coach while Dexter Nelson served as the team's trainer. The trio learned quickly that international games were a far cry from contests played in Worcester, New York City or Winnipeg.

To begin with most of the games in Italy were played outdoors and both practices and games had to be finished before the sun came up or after the sun went down. That meant the team would practice at 7:30 in the morning and then wait until after nine o'clock in the evening for the games to start.

"For the first few games we would arrive an hour before the scheduled starting time and nobody would be there," Donohue recalled. "Not the other team, fans, officials, just an empty stadium."

Everyone was still home eating, he was told.

We will start the game when the fans show up.

Eventually Donohue decided to keep the team in the hotel until the organizers would come and get them. But even then there were often long waits at the outdoor arenas for games to be played.

"I remember warming up for a game and suddenly there was a loud noise like an explosion," Jamie Russell said. "I turned around and there was Hawthorne Wingo holding a broken rim in his hand."

Wingo, a fan favorite at Madison Square Garden during a brief stint with the NBA's New York Knicks, had shattered the backboard during a pre-game dunk. As workers scurried to pick up the broken glass and debris from the court, tournament organizers were in a panic trying to find a replacement.

"It was a joke as they tried to find another backboard," Russell recalls. "They finally located one in another city but it was after midnight before we started the game."

Donohue used the Italian tour to try and get a feel for his team using different combinations of players. He wasn't overly concerned about results, which was a good thing considering that the team lost as many games as they won. When the tour was over, the coach had a good feeling about the team's chances, a feeling shared by Russell.

"I was only 17 years old when I made the national team and I didn't know what to expect, but we were coming together as a team" Russell remembers.

The team made its way by train to Augsburg, Germany, for the qualifying tournament and Canada shocked the basketball world by winning its first two games against Finland and Poland. The Finnish roster was bolstered by two Americans who had become naturalized citizens while Poland was a pre-tournament favourite to be one of the two teams to advance to the Munich Games. The Canadians needed just one more win to advance to the medal round, just one more win to keep their Olympic dreams alive. But the wear and tear of eight weeks on the road was taking its toll and the team dropped their next four games as Poland and Spain advanced to the Olympics. Relegated to the consolation round, Canada responded with a pair of wins over Israel and Great Britain to finish in sixth place with a respectable 4-4 record. It was an impressive showing for the new Canadian coach.

"Canada served notice in that tournament that we were on our way towards establishing ourselves as a world basketball power," Restivo said. "We weren't in the upper echelon with teams like the Soviet Union or the United States but we showed that we could play with some of the better teams in the world. It was a big improvement for the Canadian basketball program and Jack had to take a lot of the credit for the turn around."

Four players from the 1972 team—Phil Tollestrup, Jamie Russell, Derek Sankey and John Cassidy—would stay with the team and play in the Montreal Games. The rest of the roster gave way for newer players as Canada embarked on the Donohue era.

Donohue returned to Canada following their Olympic bid and began to familiarize himself with the basketball community. He had always stressed the importance of working with people you could trust but that was difficult in 1972 because he didn't know anyone. He was pleased with Restivo's work and spent the winter months trying to establish a base of coaches and adminstrators that he could depend on for advice and information

* * * * *

Donohue's next goal was to raise the status of basketball within the country. He had been dismayed in his first cross-country tour by the attitude that the players had about the sport. They didn't expect to win; they didn't think they could win; winning wasn't important enough to them. That attitude, one that was shared by many fans, had to change and Donohue knew that the impetus for change had to come from him.

"What was wrong when I took the job was the attitude in Canada," Donohue said in a newspaper interview years later. "There wasn't a bad attitude; there wasn't any attitude at all. If you like Jack Donohue, fine. If you didn't like Jack Donohue, fine. But if you don't care about Jack Donohue, that's awful."

But little did he realize that the indifference and feeling of inferiority he had encountered that summer was not restricted to the game of basketball.

"Before Jack Donohue came to Canada there was this national feeling that we were second best in everything we did," Dan Pugliese said.

Pugliese, a former basketball coach and athletic director, was appointed by Munro to set up the National Sports Federation and it was during his watch that Donohue was hired in 1972. The idea behind the federation was to hire full-time professional staff, to place them in a centralized office building and to develop an environment of cooperation and growth. Pugliese's mandate was to restructure Sport Canada in such a way that it encouraged, promoted and produced successful international athletes and teams.

"There was an excitement in the building over the new direction that sport was taking in the country," John McConnachie said.

McConnachie, an executive with the Canadian Interuniversity Athletic Union, believed that the centralization in Vanier gave the sport organizations a new feeling of empowerment.

"There were 20 to 25 NSOs in the building and a strong internal support, with a media centre and translation services. In the early days there were a lot of creative people working in the center and a feeling that the government was strongly behind us. No longer would sports in Canada be run from kitchen tables."

Pugliese and Donohue soon became good friends and working allies. Pugliese marveled at how Donohue raised the confidence of an entire nation.

"When Jack arrived, Canadian sport was undergoing reform and the people involved needed to hear Jack tell them they were better than they thought. Until that time we were just happy to compete, but that wasn't acceptable to Jack."

He convinced people to strive for excellence and not to accept mediocrity, and his message wasn't delivered just to the basketball community. In Donohue's mind Canada needed to dream big dreams!

"He was an ambassador for this country and would talk to anyone who would listen about the need to achieve," Pugliese said. "He changed the face of amateur sport in Canada."

Donohue's plan was to promote basketball any way he could, to turn the country onto to a sport invented by a Canadian. At the same time he worked hard to get Canadians to stop considering themselves second-class athletes. One of the first things he noticed when he arrived in Canada and conducted regional camps was a negative attitude towards any sport other than hockey. Hockey was Canada's game and the country psyche was boosted by Team Canada's dramatic win over the Soviet Union in the Summit Series in 1972. Donohue was in Germany during the two-week event but he was impressed with the way the series captured the hearts of an entire country. *Now if we could only get people feeling that way about basketball.* So one day, in 1973, he told an interviewer that in ten years basketball would be the most popular sport in Canada. Suddenly everyone in Canada knew who Jack Donohue was as his comments had people rushing to defend hockey's rightful place in the hearts of its citizens. Donohue was criticized from coast to coast but that didn't faze him in the least.

"A lot of people got upset with Jack but that was OK," columnist Scott Taylor said. "He wanted people to stand up and take notice of the Canadian national team and he succeeded in doing just that"

* * * * *

Charley Kitts was a high school teacher who was looking to promote an upcoming basketball tournament in the Ottawa area when he arrived in Donohue's office at 333 River Road on a cold December morning in 1972.

"I heard that we had this high-profile American basketball coach and I went to see if he would serve as honorary chairman of our tournament," Kitts said. "I was expecting a yes or no answer and then I would be on my way."

But Donohue was impressed with Kitts's enthusiasm and invited him for lunch. He then proceeded to bombard Kitts with questions about his involvement with basketball and the local basketball scene.

"We have to get out to the schools and give clinics and get people excited about basketball," Donohue told his new-found friend.

Kitts was befuddled. All he wanted was an endorsement of his basketball tournament and this guy was talking about what *we had to do*. It wasn't long before the two of them were touring Eastern Ontario running clinics in high schools and spreading the word that Canadian basketball was on the upswing. With Kitts behind the wheel of the car, Donohue would regale his new friend with stories of his buddies back home—the Spook, Red Sarachek and Joe Lapchick. After every clinic, he would dispense his philosophy on life and on basketball with an infectious optimism.

"I always felt an obligation to preach a little to young kids because I really believe in what I am talking about," Donohue would say when explaining why he spent so much time traveling to schools. The Coach was adamant about putting basketball and other sports in their proper perspective.

"I tell them basketball is not as important as a lot of things…not as important as their real friends at school…not as important as what they learn in school… not as important as their parents…it's tough for them to realize how important their parents have been to them and how much their parents have done for them."

He delivered those messages with his core belief that everyone should dream big dreams and then pursue the dreams wholeheartedly.

"You can believe the impossible dream and it can come true in sports. But dreaming is not enough. There has to be an awful lot of sweat behind it."

Before long Kitts was Donohue's unofficial chauffeur and a friendship was formed that would prove very beneficial to the promotion of Canadian basketball in the years to come.

CHAPTER 15

Building an Olympic Dream

When Harry Franklin, the CABA's Executive Director, resigned abruptly in 1973, Jack saw an opportunity to solidify his power base within the volunteer organization. On paper the head coach reported to the Executive Director but Jack was not a "report-to" type of guy. He was used to calling the shots and had become concerned about the influence that the volunteer board exercised over his budget, travel itineraries and such mundane things as expense accounts. They had hired him to coach the team, why wouldn't they allow him to do that without interference?

When the job description for executive director was posted, Jack immediately contacted John Restivo, his current team manager, and convinced him to apply for the job. He then went to work on the board members telling them that Restivo was the best person for the job and there was no need to interview anyone else. Sure enough, Restivo was given the job after a telephone interview.

With Restivo gone, Donohue needed to find an assistant coach, a manager and some new players before the start of the 1973 season. He tabbed Gib Chapman from Acadia University as his assistant and after five people turned him down, offered the manager's job to Steve Konchalski. Konchalski was a fellow New Yorker who played at

Archbishop Molloy for Jack Curran and developed into an outstanding university player at Acadia University under Stu Aberdeen.

In 1966, Konchalski was named the Most Valuable Player at the Canadian National Championships as he led Acadia to its first university title. Though Konchalski had heard of Donohue and what he had accomplished at Power Memorial, the two had never met until the national team tryouts in Montreal in 1972. Konchalski introduced himself after the workout and mentioned that he would be interested in helping with the national team program. He had just taken a job as an assistant coach at Montreal's Loyola College and Donohue thanked him for his interest and quickly forgot about him.

A year later, as he searched for someone to say yes to the manager's position, he remembered meeting the "Polish guy" in Montreal and gave Konchalski a call.

"I said I would do it under the condition that at some time, I could get involved in coaching." Konchalski replied.

By the summer, Konchalski was on board for what would be the start of a professional relationship that would span four Olympics and 16 years and a close friendship that would last nearly 30 years. Jack quickly became comfortable with the former New Yorker and would tell people that, "in 1973 I woke up in the same hotel room with Steve Konchalski more often than I woke up in the same room with my wife."

Of course sharing a bedroom with Donohue was not as easy as it may sound. Donohue had a habit of falling asleep with the lights and TV on, would wake up in the middle of the night, read a bit, watch some TV and then fall back to sleep. On some nights, he would repeat the routine several times. If Konchalski tried to turn the lights or TV off, Donohue would instantly wake up and demand that they be put back on.

"What are you doing?" Donohue would ask half in a stupor.

"You were asleep so I was turning everything off," Konchalski would reply.

"No, no leave them on, I am going to do some reading," he would say, opening up a book. In a few minutes, he would be back to sleep with the TV blaring and the lights illuminating the room.

"He couldn't sleep without the TV and lights on so I eventually learned to sleep with them on as well," Konchalski said.

Donohue exuded confidence to everyone he encountered, but during that first full season with the national team he wondered if the team was on the right track.

"Because we were breaking new ground in establishing a Canadian national team, I didn't know what we were doing." Donohue confided years later. "Nobody had a plan on how to do this."

Mistakes were made but the veteran coach was always quick to a turn a negative experience into a positive. It was his strength.

"We probably played too many games. We were together too much, but we got over that pretty fast. After two years, we began to realize that more is not necessarily better."

Donohue knew that to build towards the Montreal Games meant bringing in new players to supplement a veteran crew that included Phil Tollestrup and a young Jamie Russell.

Tollestrup was the team's leading scorer in 1972 and a starter at Brigham Young University. At 6'5", he possessed an excellent outside shot and had the savvy to score inside when needed. He was skilled and reliable, a player you could build a team around.

But as Donohue began another cross-country tour to check out new talent he decided to give a discarded veteran one more chance.

* * * * *

Billy Robinson was one of the players CABA officials had told Donohue to not consider when he first arrived in Canada. As he watched the high-scoring guard in the 1972 tryouts, Donohue could understand some of the concerns people may have had about the talented, but troubled star. Robinson had a reputation as a rebel who wore long hair, argued with officials, teammates and coaches and didn't always like passing the ball.

"There were a lot of people who didn't think I should represent Canada, it was a question of image," Robinson said

He could be a problem but Donohue saw things that others missed. He was a gifted player, perhaps the most skilled player in camp. More importantly to Donohue, Robinson possessed a passion for the game and a love of his country, ingredients missing in a lot of other players who had previously worn the Canadian jersey. Robinson came to the 1972 camp just a month after knee surgery and the injury hindered his performance. He balked when Donohue asked him to travel with the B team to China.

"I was better than some of the players that they kept on the A team so I decided that I wasn't going to China," Robinson said.

He had dedicated his life to basketball, dreamed of playing in the NBA and that dream was suddenly shattered. Sensing his playing days were over, he bummed a ride to a nearby beach where he and Brian McKenzie, another player who was cut, decided to end their basketball careers in dramatic fashion. After a few beers, they built a small raft and then placed their sneakers, sweats and jocks on the makeshift boat, lit it on fire and sent it adrift. The Viking-like pyre was Robinson's way of saying his basketball career was over. Robinson wasn't hanging up his sneakers, he was burning them. But giving up basketball was easier said than done, and during the off-season he contacted Donohue and requested another shot at making the team.

"I tried but I couldn't quit the game," Robinson said. "I called Jack and told him I wanted another tryout and he agreed to bring me into camp."

But Donohue was insistent that the flamboyant guard change his style of play as well as get a haircut.

"He told me I was a card dealer and it was my job to deal good cards to the big guys," Robinson said. "I had 7-footers on my team and they had to respect me and that wouldn't happen if I was yelling at referees or not getting the ball to them when they were open."

Once in training camp, Donohue explained that he expected his point guard to get the ball inside to the post, it was part of his job. After one such discussion Robinson explained that he didn't have the right angle to make the pass.

"Then I will find someone who can," was Donohue's pointed reply.

But Donohue had set up an organized approach to the Canadian team, an approach that the free-spirited Robinson eventually agreed with, and welcomed.

"You could see a military approach to the way he did things and it was needed," Robinson would say years later. "That's what we needed – a military approach to how the team was going to be run. We had goals and he was going to find the players that could accomplish those goals."

Slowly Robinson and his teammates began to buy into Donohue's way of coaching, but there were stormy moments. Billy wasn't always in agreement with the way Jack did things and when Billy Robinson disagreed with something, he was not afraid to voice his opinion.

"It was a love-hate relationship," Donohue said many times. "I loved him and he hated me."

That line always drew a laugh when Jack told it, but in reality the pair developed a mutual respect that allowed them to overcome their differences. At times, they became annoyed with each other but such annoyances eventually gave way to acceptance. They also learned to appreciate what each brought to the table and to understand how they complemented each other.

"Jack Donohue changed my life," Robinson would say years later. "He made me a better basketball player and a better person."

Still the pair was different in so many ways.

"Jack was conservative, a family man while Billy was anti-establishment and a little off the wall," Konchalski said. "But they shared a competitive spirit. They both hated to lose and Jack loved Billy's competitiveness and passion. Jack was always attracted to 'off the wall' types – types like Freddie the Spook and Billy."

One of their first disagreements was on the issue of the hair, and its proper length for a basketball player. Donohue was old-school, the shorter the better, while Billy preferred flowing hair complete with a beard. Jack refused to compromise and forced Robinson to lose his locks, which would grow back during the winter when Robinson played in the CIAU or overseas.

Then there was Billy's style of play. When he was hot, he tended to shoot more than Donohue cared for and they had arguments over shot selection. In one game, Robinson took an outside shot that went in the basket and then popped out. The opposition rebounded the ball and converted a fast break at the other end of the court causing Donohue to call a time-out. In the huddle, the coach stressed the need to get the ball inside, looking at Robinson as he talked. But on the ensuing possession the defense gave Robinson an excellent look at the basket and he ended up taking a short bank shot.

This time as the ball hung in the cylinder, a defensive player knocked the ball out of the rim, a legal play in international basketball. Once again, the opposing team rebounded the miss and scored in transition. Donohue had seen enough and substituted for Robinson. As Billy walked past his coach to a seat on the bench he said 'Both of those shots were in'. Donohue looked at him in disbelief and then started laughing,

"If that's the case you better go over and talk to the person keeping score," he said as he pointed to the score clock. "They haven't given us points for either shot."

The final point of contention dealt with Donohue's habit of holding team meetings *ad nauseum*. For Billy, basketball was practicing and playing; for Jack, it was a game that could be used to reinforce a proper lifestyle and prepare its players for greater challenges off the hardwood. Robinson would often complain when another team meeting was called during a trip and act disinterested as Donohue often repeated stories.

Eventually, the point guard began to see the importance of being together.

"Slowly, I began to seeing the reason for so many meetings," Robinson said. "We were 12-14 players who were becoming a team. By being around each other so much, we started to care for and support each other .'

Robinson loved playing the game and was constantly striving to improve his skills. In the 1974 training camp, the first week consisted of three-a-day practice sessions, sessions that literally tested the physical and mental limits of the elite athletes trying to stick with the team. One of those players was Paul Armstrong, a local player who had just finished his rookie season with the Carleton University Ravens. Each night he would return to his dorm room and wonder how he would find the energy to get through the next day.

"On the last day before the final cuts, Jack gave the veteran players time off for one of the three practices while the rest of us scrimmaged," Armstrong said. "The other veterans were back in their rooms resting when Billy Robinson went to the control desk at the gym, took out a ball and spent the next two hours working on his ball handling. I couldn't believe how dedicated he was but that's the reason he was so good."

As the team started on the road to the Montreal Olympics, Robinson became the heart and soul of the team.

* * * * *

Robinson was joined in the backcourt by his friend and teammate from Simon Fraser University, Alex Devlin, who was recovering from a serious knee injury, and a high school player from Winnipeg named Martin Riley. Devlin's injury prevented him from playing in 1972 but the following year he gave Canada a big, tough guard that could play against some of the better European players. While Devlin stayed with the team until the Montreal Olympics, recurring injuries limited his effectiveness and opened the door for more playing time for Riley whose on-court appearance was the opposite of the flamboyant Robinson. Riley was steady if unspectacular and his choir boy looks reminded Donohue of the CHSAA players he coached at Tolentine and Power.

Up front, Tolestrup, Russell and Sankey were joined by Ken McKenzie and Lars Hansen. Hansen played at the University of Washington and provided the Canadians with inside scoring. He was the team's tallest member at 6'10" but was more of a finesse player. The grunt work inside was left for McKenzie who gave Donohue much needed toughness at both ends of the court.

The coaching staff used the 1973 season to evaluate players and set their sights on trying to advance to the medal round of the 1974 World Championships, a feat never accomplished by Canada in previous tournaments. One of the key events in the summer of 1973 was a trip to Cuba that included a game against an athletic Cuban team.

"The game ended when the referee tossed the opening jump ball," Donohue said about one of the country's more embarrassing losses.

Cuba won by more than 30 points but that easily could have been 60 as the Cubans dominated the game from the first basket to the final whistle. Afterwards, Donohue was philosophical about the game. Rather than rant and rave at the players, he challenged them individually and collectively.

"He asked after the game if I thought we could beat Cuba and I said I didn't know, Robinson said. "Then he said he knew we could and if I didn't think we could win, then I couldn't play for him. So I said OK, we can beat them and I started to believe it."

Getting the players to believe was one thing, getting the coaching staff to believe was another.

"We came down here to see how good we are and what we need to work on," Donohue told Chapman and Konchalski. "Well, we are not very good and there is a lot we need to improve. This is a team we may have to beat in the Olympics so we better figure a way to do it."

And that's exactly what they did.

* * * * *

Most coaches and players will say that the best officials are those that are not noticed during the game, refs who let the players play and try not to steal the spotlight.

While North American officials are schooled in their profession and are constantly evaluated and take pride in their work, this was not always the case in the rest of the world.

International matches were often officiated by referees from participating countries, referees that were blatant in their favoritism. A noted exception was North American referees who tried to maintain a semblance of equilibrium in their calls and brought a professional approach to each game that was lacking by the majority of FIBA officials. A referee often accompanied Canadian teams on international trips and every effort was made to have them not work Canadian games.

"It was a no-win situation for everyone involved," Donohue explained. "You would have one referee from the other country whose career may be hinging on the result of the game and he is screwing us big time. It is impossible to complain because they either don't speak English or they pretend that they don't speak it. As a result, the Canadian referee, who is going out of his way to be fair, takes the heat for his partner's cheating. Our team is getting frustrated and the Canadian referee is getting yelled at for something he didn't do."

To make matters worse, the Canadian official traveled, roomed and ate meals with the team. If the coaches and players were upset about some calls, it could make for some very uncomfortable situations. Ron Foxcroft found that out first hand early in an illustrious refereeing career. His officiating career included refereeing in the Olympics, World Championships, and Canadian National Championships and was one of the few Canadian officials to work regularly on NCAA Division I games. He was elected to the Canadian Naismith Hall of Fame and invented and patented the FOX-40, an innovative, pea-less whistle. In 1973, Foxcroft was one of the top young officials in Canada, a rising star who was excited about accompanying Donohue and the national team on a European tour.

"We were in a tournament in Italy and there was an agreement that I wouldn't do any of the Canadian games," Foxcroft said. "But an official scheduled for one of the Canadian games got hurt and I was asked to take his place at the last minute. Sure enough, my partner is calling against

Canada and Jack is yelling at me that they are getting cheated. I tell him I know, but what does he want me to do about it."

"Cheat for us," was Donohue's reply.

"Jack, you know I can't do that," Foxcroft said.

"Sure you can!"

Despite the one-sided officiating, the game was close until the final seconds when Foxcroft, fed up with the Canadian complaining, handed team captain Phil Tollestrup a technical foul. Incensed, Donohue jumped on the court to argue the call.

"You are a chicken, Ron," Donohue screamed. "You give Tollestrup a 'T' but you won't dare give one to me."

Donohue continued his emotional tirade until Foxcroft could take no more. He raised his hands together to signal a technical on the coach, provoking another verbal outburst from the enraged Donohue. The game ended with a Canadian loss and now Foxcroft faced another dilemma. His roommate for the trip was Donohue and he was worried that it would take time for the coach to get over the night's incidents.

Foxcroft slowly made his way back to the hotel and when he tried to enter his room he found that it was locked from the inside. Meekly, he knocked on the door and heard Donohue's voice from within.

"Jack, its Ron. The door is locked."

"I know."

"Aren't you going to let me in?"

"No!'

Foxcroft pleaded a few more minutes but eventually realized that the door wasn't being opened that night and found alternative sleeping arrangements for the evening.

* * * * *

Donohue entered the 1974 season with optimism but he would have to make some changes to his staff though before heading to Puerto Rico for the World Championships.

As the club began training camp, Donohue received a phone call from Gib Chapman telling him that he had just received new responsibilities at Acadia and could no longer commit to the national team program.

Donohue was at a loss to find a replacement at the last minute so he told Konchalski that he would get his opportunity to coach with the team.

"I was only an assistant coach at Loyola College and there were 37 head coaches in Canada that would have been upset that I was named Jack's assistant," Konchalski said. "Jack never announced my appointment publicly and by the time people found out that I was his new assistant, I had a summer of experience under my belt."

The highlight of that summer was the World Championships, an event in which Canada had never advanced to the medal round and their chance of breaking that sacred ground was diminished when McKenzie elected to forego the trip to spend time with his girlfriend in Alaska.

Donohue instructed Konchalski to make a weekly call to the big man to see how things were going without pressuring him to join the team. Donohue, the psychologist, believed that such contact with the team would eventually bring him back to the squad.

Konchalski continued the calls when the team arrived in Puerto Rico but McKenzie gave no indication that he was interested in joining the squad. One day, at a team breakfast in San Juan, a few days before the competition was scheduled to begin, the subject of the wayward post player came up.

"Do you want McKenzie here?" Robinson asked bluntly.

"Of course we do." Konchalski replied.

"I will get him but you have to pay for the phone call and let me stay on the phone for as long it takes."

Konchalski agreed and the next morning he passed Robinson in the hotel lobby.

"Anything happened with Ken?" he asked.

"Yeah, he will be at practice this afternoon," Robinson said matter-of-factly.

With Robinson scoring and McKenzie rebounding, the team got off to a fast start.

They advanced to the medal round and suddenly, all the newspapers back home were talking about the Canadian basketball team, a team that would eventually finish eighth in the tournament. Robinson was selected to the all-tournament team and McKenzie was the tournament's leading rebounder. Things were shaping up for Montreal just fine.

* * * * *

Ken Shields was appointed head coach of the Laurentian Voyageurs prior to the 1970-71 season at the tender age of 22. He tried out unsuccessfully for the national team the following year but was cut. With his playing days over Shields decided to focus entirely on coaching. He compensated for his lack of experience and for his age by gathering every bit of basketball knowledge he could. He observed the national team tryouts, read books and attended clinics.

"Jack would bring in guest coaches like Tates Locke, Red Sarachek, Lou Carnesecca and Vince Cazzetta and I would pick their brains at night," Shields said.

(In 1989, when Shields succeeded Donohue as the national team coach he initiated a similar program that brought Canadian and guest coaches into training camps so they could share ideas.)

"No one went to more clinics than I did," Shields said. "I wanted to soak up as much information about basketball and coaching as I could."

So when Puerto Rico was awarded the World Championships, Shields arranged to fly down with John Restivo and stay with the executive director at the tournament hotel.

A day before departure, Restivo had to back out, leaving Shields to go it alone.

"I didn't have a hotel room or tickets to the tournament but I was going anyway," Shields recalled. "On the plane ride down, I was talking to a pilot who lived in Puerto Rico and he told me to forget about staying in a hotel and suggested a guest house that was half the cost. Then, I ran into Jack at their hotel and he asked me if I had tickets. When I said no, in typical Jack fashion, he gave me his ID so I could see all the games free. I was going to all the games wearing Jack Donohue's ID and sitting in the VIP seats. It was great."

Shields did some scouting for the team, stayed an extra week and worked with Herb Brown who was coaching a club team in Puerto Rico.

Donohue was impressed with Shields' dedication and commitment.

"We can't get coaches in Canada to come to our national tryout camps and here is a guy who goes all the way to Puerto Rico to watch us."

It would not be long before Shields became much more involved with Donohue and his program.

Donohue was getting more comfortable with his surroundings and developing a small base of coaches whose advice he sought and respected.

But Donohue was disappointed that there weren't more Canadian coaches participating at practices.

He admired Shields' enthusiasm and would encourage other coaches to attend training sessions.

"Jack had an open door policy for practices and tryout camps and if you walked into the gym you were likely to be put to work quickly," Konchalski recalled.

Coaches who did drop by to take a peek at a national team practice soon found themselves on the court conducting drills minutes after walking into the gym. Donohue would ask anyone's advice who cared to venture an opinion about a player's ability or the merits of a particular drill or offensive set. During tryout camps, Jack would assemble all the coaches present in a room off the gym while Konchalski would place the names of the players on a blackboard. One by one, the coaches would decide, based on the last practice, whether or not a player deserved to be on the team. They could be placed in three categories; on the team, on the fence, or off the team.

Most tryouts lasted three days and that gave Donohue and his staff nine practices to evaluate and pick 12-15 players. There were always players who started hot but quickly faded as fatigue or familiarity set in. During evaluation meetings, Donohue would sit in the back of the room and play a passive role for the first few meetings. But as the time for cuts approached, he would be more active and often had to make a point that other coaches often overlooked: "We are looking for the 12 players that will make us the best team, not the 12 best players!"

* * * * *

Off the court, Jack also continued to increase the number of people he could count for advice and friendship. One day, in 1974, he made a phone call to a young lawyer named George House who had a strong background as an amateur athlete. House was a competitive swimmer and basketball player who played varsity basketball for the Carleton University Ravens, remarkable feats considering that he had overcome a battle with polio at the age of eight. The two arranged to meet for a coffee in Ottawa and that meeting led to what House referred to as "the beginning of a great friendship."

Donohue respected not only House's views on sport and business but admired his passion and soon had the barrister involved with the Canadian Amateur Basketball Association.

"I had tickets for several games for the 1976 Olympics when Jack called me up and asked me if I wanted to go to the Olympics," House recalled. "I told him I had tickets and was planning on going but Jack had other plans."

Donohue arranged for House to go on the team bus to Plattsburgh for an exhibition game with the United States prior to the opening of the Games and then got him floor accreditation for the Canadian games.

"I wasn't allowed in the Olympic Village but I was on the bench for every game, it was a tremendous experience," House said.

A few years later when the CABA was having budget problems Gerry Regan, the sports minister, named House as the minister trustee. House straightened out the organization's bookkeeping and became a member of the CABA Board of Directors, giving Donohue support on a board that didn't always agree with the way the coach did things.

Donohue found another strong ally in Ray Jones although their relationship started off on a bad note. In Donohue's second year in Canada, an Ontario coach was involved in a heated argument with a referee at a National Championship and there was talk of suspending the coach for a year. Donohue was asked to make a decision in the matter and in an effort to gather more information on the incident, Donohue called Jones who was then president of the Ontario Basketball Association.

"Mr. Jones, this is Jack Donohue, the commissioner of Canadian Basketball and I would like to discuss an incident in Winnipeg last year," Donohue said as a matter of introduction.

Jones cut Donohue off in mid-sentence and delivered an unexpected response.

"I don't need an American coming up here to tell us how to run basketball,' Jones yelled and then promptly hung up the phone.

Donohue was beside himself and his first reaction was to confront Jones. Discretion being the better part of valor, Donohue took another avenue and befriended Jones. Within a year, Jones was the team's trainer, a position he held for over six years before accepting a similar job with the Hamilton Tiger-Cats of the Canadian Football League. Their working relationship developed into a strong friendship and Donohue knew that he could always count on Jones to deliver when needed.

"Jack Donohue was one of the best two coaches that I worked with because he gave you a job to do and then he let you do it," Jones was to say years later.

Donohue gave Jones the freedom to do his job properly and in turn Jones provided a sense of security, particularly on the road. If something needed to be done, he would find a way overcoming language problems, differences in native customs and would not be above breaking a few rules or local ordinances to get the job done.

*   *   *   *   *

In 1975, Canada participated in the Intercontinental Cup, playing four games against National Teams in Europe and then hosting the same four countries in Canada.

The format was great for Canada since it gave them an opportunity to play against potential Olympic opponents without any pressure to win. Donohue and Konchalski could experiment with different strategies and at the same time develop scouting reports for the Montreal Games.

"In Europe, we played in front of capacity crowds every game," Robinson said. "But that wasn't the case when we came back home."

The final game of the series was against the Soviet Union at Toronto's Maple Leaf Gardens where the Canadians recorded an exciting victory over the defending Olympic Champions. In a post-game interview Donohue talked about playing the number-one team in the world in front of a home crowd.

"We have 21,000 fans watching us but unfortunately 18,000 were disguised as empty seats."

Regardless of the lack of fan support, the team delivered one of the finest performances in the history of Canadian basketball and the main reason for the win was the play of Robinson.

"When I think back to the game, I remember Billy Robinson coming down and putting an amazing move on his defender and then scoring on a jump shot," Konchalski said. "He may or may not have been our top scorer that game, but he was the reason we won."

Despite the absence of home crowds or media attention, it was obvious that Canadian basketball was on the rise. All of a sudden, people were talking about a possible medal for the men's team at the Montreal Olympics and the person doing the most talking was Jack Donohue. The team was starting to believe in itself and just at the right time.

CHAPTER 16

Double Duty

In the early days of women's basketball, the most successful program in the world played out of Edmonton, Alberta. The Edmonton Grads, a senior women's team, amassed an incredible 502–20 record during a 25-year period that spanned two World Wars and the Great Depression. Canada's dominance in women's basketball began to wane in the 1950s and 1960s as the rest of the world began to take the sport more seriously.

The United States, the dominant power on the men's side, did not take to the women's game until the 1960s when many high schools changed from a more specialized form of the game that featured six players on the court with players restricted to either a defensive or offensive zone, to the more conventional five-on-five game invented by James Naismith. Women's rights groups changed the landscape further by demanding scholarships and equal funding for female players. The women's game, therefore, experienced an explosion in numbers and talent with the passage of Title IX in the United States in 1978 whereby American universities were required to offer equal opportunities for male and female athletes to qualify for federal funding.

Elsewhere, the sport underwent similar growth in Europe, particularly in the Eastern Bloc countries of the Soviet Union, Poland and Czechoslovakia. Women's basketball did not have the same prestige as their male counterparts on the international stage but the sport received a boost when it was announced that women's basketball would be included in the 1976 Montreal Olympics. Canada was going to be the site of the first Olympics to host a women's basketball tournament and Sport Canada wanted to field a representative team.

While the men's national team was showing steady improvement as it prepared for the 1976 Games, the same could not be said for the women's team. Unlike the men they did not have the benefit of a full-time coach and were losing ground to other countries.

The women's team was scheduled to go on a trip to Omaha, Nebraska, when they discovered that they no longer had a coach. Darlene Curry, who had handled the job for several years and had helped raise the status of the program, unexpectedly resigned in the fall of 1973. Curry was considered a good coach but her practical evaluation of the team riled some players.

"Darlene cared about us but she was blunt in her observations and that bothered some players," point guard Joyce Slipp said. "There were some complaints: players were tired of her negative attitude. We would go into the games and her pep talk would be 'try not to lose by 40 points.'"

Donohue stepped in to lend a helping hand and added the women's team to his long list of duties with the CABA. He had never coached women before but he rationalized that basketball was the same game for men and women. He agreed to take the team to the Omaha tournament in December. He soon realized that certain aspects of coaching women's basketball were indeed different while his new players learned that there was more to a basketball team than just Xs and 0s.

"We were all excited when we heard he was going to coach us and we wanted to make a good impression in our first game," Slipp related. "We were playing against an American team in Omaha and we are going 100% in warm-ups trying to show Jack how serious we were and there he is off signing autographs, not paying any attention to us at all."

The players didn't realize that Jack didn't like watching warm-ups and used that time to talk to opposing coaches or people in the stands. "We came to the bench sweat pouring down our uniforms, completely exhausted," Slipp said. "By halftime we had nothing left and got beat in the second half."

Donohue blasted the team in the locker room and then decided to make a quick exit and allow the team to think about his comments as they changed and showered. But his plan hit a snag as he exited from a side door of the locker room and found himself in the main women's locker room facing several women who were casually undressing.

It was a problem he had never faced at Holy Cross or in his high school coaching days! Sensing that this was not a good place for a man to be strolling through, he quickly retreated to the team locker. The only logical solution was to re-enter the Canadian locker room and leave by a different door, but by now the team had started to get undressed. "Close your eyes I'm coming through," Donohue cried as he barged through one door and made a bee-line for the other door that led to the outside and safety while players scrambled to make themselves appear halfway decent.

Donohue agreed to continue coaching the club for one more season giving Basketball Canada a full year to find a suitable full-time replacement for the Montreal Olympics. He would take the team to a tournament in Brazil and then hold a tryout camp in Ottawa in conjunction with the men's training camp.

By the time they reached the South American country, the players were discovering that Donohue's coaching methods were different from any other coach they ever had. He talked to them about things other than basketball and when they replied, he listened and seemed genuinely concerned with their lives.

"For the first time, I felt like someone was coaching the national team that really cared for me as a person and a player," Kathy Shields said in an interview prior to her induction into the Naismith Hall of Fame.

"Jack was always taking us for long walks and we would go arm-in-arm and he was a touchy-feely type of guy," Slipp recalls. "He cared about us as people as well as players and it showed."

Even when he lost his temper or was angered about a player's performance or conduct, he would reprimand them in a caring manner. "He had a habit of making you understand that while he was unhappy with you at a particular moment he still valued you as a person and a friend," Shields said.

Patti Tatum was one of the veterans on the team that had experienced some lean years and she found Donohue a refreshing change. "In seven years with the national team, I had six different coaches," Tatum said. "This was wonderful, we had a coach that spent a lot of one-on-one time with the players and would ask you what you thought about things."

One night prior to the start of the Brazilian tournament, Shields and a teammate were walking down one of the local streets when Donohue appeared and asked where they were going. They replied they were going for a walk to get an ice cream cone and he asked if they minded if he joined them. As they strolled towards the ice cream stand Donohue entertained them with stories about New York and stayed with them until they returned to the hotel. A few days later, the two players realized that they had been in a red light district and Donohue, concerned about their safety, had accompanied them until they were safely back in the hotel. "He never said anything about where we were headed because he didn't want to upset us but he was concerned about us and that meant a lot," Shields said.

Donohue continued his practice of holding countless meetings while on the road and in one such conference he laid out strict rules about sun tanning. "He told us no more than twenty minutes in the sun the day of a game and we all said 'Come on Coach; give us a little more time'," Shields said. "We squeezed a few extra minutes out of him and some of the girls took their time walking back to the hotel, soaking up some extra rays."

Neither Donohue nor the players realized how hot the sun was that close to the Equator. "We were right on the Equator and even twenty minutes was too long in that sun," Slipp said. "We all showed up for out first game against the Soviet Union wearing white uniforms, our skin red as a beet and we could hardly move," Shields recalled. "Everyone was laughing at us as we tried to warm-up. It was embarrassing!"

Canada won the game although with great difficulty and when they arrived back to the hotel Donohue decided it was time for a team walk.

The women dispersed to their rooms to change and shower but most of them found those two chores extremely difficult. Shields's embarrassment at the game turned into fright back at the hotel as her temperature rose to unhealthy limits.

As she descended the stairs to the hotel lobby, she asked Donohue if she could skip the walk. As the words left her mouth, she closed her eyes and collapsed in front of her startled coach and teammates. Her temperature had risen to over 102° and she was quickly rushed upstairs. Team trainer, Al Millier, stripped her down, put her in a bathtub and packed it with ice.

Shields woke up in a tub of ice and wondered what was happening. But she was out of danger. The next day, the collective sunburns adorning the bodies of the Canadian squad had begun to blister and once again the team had trouble warming up. Playing in the championship game became a near impossibility and the team had to settle for silver medals.

"I still have a scar on my arm where the skin cracked and fell off after being hit by an opposing player when I was shooting," Slipp recalled 30 years later.

* * * * *

Chris Critelli stuck out at the regional tryout in Toronto for the women's national team like a sore thumb. Not only because, at age 17, she was by far the youngest player at the camp, but also while the rest of the players wore proper shorts, jerseys and shoes and gave the appearances of being basketball players, Critelli looked like she was dragged off the street. She wore cut-off jean shorts, a ragged T-Shirt and a pair of $2.99 sneakers that her mother had brought the day before.

She had no expectations of making the team or being invited to the main camp later that month in Ottawa. A local coach from her hometown in St. Catharines encouraged her to show up at the open tryout and she figured she had nothing to lose.

But as she looked around the gym and saw the older more polished players perform drills effortlessly, she felt out of place. That all changed when Donohue called her over for a talk. "I am going to give you some very important advice," he said to the attentive Critelli. "You are a terrible player but you are a great athlete and you have the potential to be a great player. I am going to bring you into Ottawa for the main camp to get some experience. I'm not expecting you to make the team but it will be a good experience."

Critelli was in a state of shock. She had never traveled anywhere before and now she was going to Ottawa, miss a few days of school and do nothing but play basketball. For the high school girl who loved the game it didn't get any better. The competition in Ottawa was a notch higher and Critelli was pitted against players used to the rigors of three-a-day tryouts and who were more focused on securing one of the 12 spots on the team.

Shields, who was at the Toronto tryout, couldn't believe the teenager was invited to the main camp in Ottawa. "I remember saying to myself 'What is Coach Donohue doing inviting that kid?' In my mind there was no way she should have made it to the final camp." Yet Critelli's athleticism and enthusiasm kept making an impression on Donohue. He believed that basketball should be played with passion and few players he had ever coached demonstrated as much desire as Critelli did at the Carleton University camp. As the final practice came to an end, she went up to Donohue to say good-bye and thank him before departing for home. Donohue seemed surprise by her comment and asked her to follow him to an office adjacent to the gym. The office was a small cubbyhole with a desk and two chairs filling the room's entire space. The coach asked Critelli to stand-up facing him and to listen carefully. "Chris, you are not going home, you made the team," Donohue said. "We are practicing at Carleton for the next two weeks and then we are going on a Canadian tour. You are on the National team."

"I had no idea what that meant," Critelli would say later, "I was expecting to go back and finish the last two months of Grade 12 and now Jack is talking to me about staying in Ottawa, going on a cross-country tour and then embarking on a month trek to Europe with the team."

To provide her with some guidance and direction, Donohue roomed Critelli with Shields, the veteran who questioned her presence at the tryout and was still in disbelief when the teenager made the final cut.

Shields was paired with Critelli in Ottawa ostensibly to keep an eye on the rookie but that task proved to be a larger chore than anyone expected. "I was awoken late one night by Chris who was climbing through the window so she wouldn't be caught breaking curfew by Coach Donohue," Shields said. "Years later, when we were coaching together, we would kid about how good we were for each other because I kept Chris under control and she helped me have a life. In those days, I was focused completely on basketball. Everything I did revolve around basketball."

As an unpolished rookie, Critelli saw little playing minutes, a situation she understood and accepted. But she thought her national team days may have been numbered when she showed up late for a game in Halifax. "We were staying at the dorms at St. Mary's University and we always napped in the afternoon when we had a night game," Critelli said. "Normally our manager came by and woke us up but either she forgot me or I slept through her knock on the door. I woke up late and the team had already left for the gym. In a panic, I took a cab to the game, putting my uniform on in the cab as we drove to the gym. I arrived at the gym just as the game was about to begin."

Donohue was adamant about being on time and that meant showing up at least ten minutes before the appointed time. Critelli walked gingerly to the team's bench as the National Anthem was playing; the rookie was expecting the worst. But instead, Donohue demonstrated the patience of a saint as he inquired about her tardiness.

"I explained what happened and he told me not to worry about being late," Critelli recalled. "He told me that I would play in the game, for a minute or two and he wanted me not to be nervous and to stay focused." At the end of the conversation, he reminded her not to let it happen again and Critelli was on time for the rest of her playing days.

In Europe, Critelli was not only introduced to different cultures and some of the best women basketball teams in the world, she also learned that the life of a rookie had its perils. "We won a tournament in Piazza Armarina in Italy and Coach received this big ugly vase that he was going to bring home to his wife," Critelli said. "Since I was the rookie, he gave it to me for safe-keeping. He told me that if anything happened to the vase he was going to send me back home to St. Catharines." By now, the rookie knew Donohue well enough to know that she wouldn't be sent home but realized that the threat was Donohue's way of telling her to take care of their newly acquired trophy.

As the team made its way through Europe, young Critelli dragged the three-foot vase with her, enduring constant kidding from her teammates along the way. Keeping track of the bulky ornament was not always easy, but she and the vase made it to a Germany train station when disaster struck.

"We were at the end of a long trip and everyone else was at the Duty Free shops doing some last minute shopping," Critelli recalled. "Not me, I was left to watch over the luggage and the vase." She had placed the vase on top of several bags aboard a trolley and watched in horror as the vase became dislodged and slowly slid from bag to bag and finally hit the cement floor before she could reach it. "It was like watching something in slow motion and when the vase hit the floor, it shattered into a million pieces," Critelli said. "I was devastated although my teammates were laughing their heads off. I was supposed to protect this vase and now it was cracked beyond repair. How was I going to tell Coach?"

The rest of the team showed little sympathy and sensing her concerns, they teased her about what Donohue was going to say. She cleaned up the mess and when the team checked into a hotel, she wondered how she would break the bad news to Donohue.

"We were having a big dinner that night at the hotel so I composed a poem that would explain the accident." She went to the dining room early and left a poem at his place at the dinner table.

Donohue had no idea to what the poem was referring, so Critelli had to muster enough courage to deliver another anonymous message that the vase broke while under her care a little more bluntly.

Addressed to Clueless
If that poem left you clueless
This may help you decipher that mess
There once was a girl unnamed
Who is feeling totally shamed
It was just her luck
She knows she's a schmuck
For that is her claim to fame
There was once a lovely gift
Which she always had to lift
Under her arm it always stayed
Until that one regrettable day
When among the Piazza's (hint) the luggage did shift
If you still don't understand
Here (you stupid) is a helping hand
Don't drop your jaws, I broke the vase

When Donohue discovered the meaning of the poems he turned to Critelli and said "It's about time you broke that ugly vase Critelli, you should have done it a month ago and then you wouldn't have had to carry it all over Europe."

During some of the more trying times in Europe, Donohue would tell the team that they had nothing to worry about because secretly he was Superman. "If something bad happens I will just pop into a phone book and change into my Superman costume," he told them on numerous occasions. Finally, towards the end of the trip the women had heard enough. As they checked into a hotel, several members of the team pushed him into a pay phone booth in the hotel lobby. It was just what Jack wanted. As the players looked in disbelief, their coach undid his tie, stripped off his dress shirt to reveal a red and blue Superman T-shirt, complete with the superhero's trademark S across the chest. He emerged from the phone booth flexing his muscles as the team shook their heads in disbelief and passers-by stared in amazement.

Kathy Shields was a competent power forward and a mainstay on the Canadian team when Jack took over the team in 1974, but her playing career was cut short by a debilitating back injury. Basketball was her life and she believed that she could play through the pain with the help of medication but the pressure of daily workouts deteriorated her condition.

In the winter of 1974, Donohue was taking the team to Cuba with several other Canadian national teams as part of an exchange program. While the rest of the team was packing for the trip, Shields checked into a Toronto hospital to have surgery on her spine.

"Coach came by to see how I was doing and before he left he asked me if I needed anything," Shields said. "I said I was fine but he slipped me $50. He was always looking out for us."

Donohue only coached the women's team for a year, his reign ending when Brian Heaney was appointed full-time head coach in the fall of 1975, but he had a positive impact on the growth of the women's basketball in Canada. Six of his players later became head university coaches and at least four of them credited him as a major influence in their coaching lives. Shields would spend the rest of her life battling back problems but, with the support of her husband Ken, became the country's most successful women's university coach. She captured an unprecedented eight National University Championships at the University of Victoria and coached in the Canadian national team program for 14 years. She won a battle with breast cancer in 2002 before recurring back pain, stemming from her playing days, eventually forced her to retire. Yet, even as she watches from the sidelines, Shields remains one of the most influential coaches in the country. She has advised two of her predecessors with the national team, Bev Smith and Alison McNeill, whenever they asked for advice, and the University of Victoria program is the standard by which other women's basketball programs measure themselves.

Shields's greatest gift to the Canadian sporting scene was the manner by which she both achieved success and handled adversity. She won National Titles and developed Olympic and pro athletes without cheating or taking short cuts and her drive for success was always tempered with a genuine concern for her athletes, a trait she learned from

Donohue. She was exposed to some outstanding coaches including her university mentor Norm Vickery and, of course, her husband Ken, but she also credited greatly her year's association with Donohue. "There are two things that I remember the most about playing for Jack, two things I tried to incorporate into my coaching," Shields said. "I admired the time he spent with each player for I saw how important it made me and my teammates feel. He could sense when you were down and would try to pick you up. When someone behaved improperly he would tell them that while their behavior wasn't great, he still cared for them as a person." Shields said. "The second thing I tried to emulate was the positive feedback he provided in games. When I started coaching, I wanted to treat my players the same way Jack treated us."

Critelli, Joyce Slipp, Coleen Dufresne and Shields applied the lessons taught by Donohue to their own players. The first lesson Donohue imparted to the women's team in 1974 was the importance of team play. "I will never forget the time that Jack told us that he didn't want to see long faces in the locker room after a win because someone didn't get enough playing time," Critelli recalled years later. "At the same time, he also didn't want a player who had a great game celebrating afterwards, if the team lost. The most important thing was the team and that is a message that I delivered every year to my teams."

Joyce Slipp knew that she was destined to join the coaching fraternity even before her playing days were over. "I always knew I wanted to coach," Slipp said and a few months after the 1976 Olympics, she was named the head coach at her *alma mater*, the University of New Brunswick. There, she utilized many of Donohue's coaching techniques and UNB maintained its position as one of the top programs in the country.

"I tried to copy everything that he did, his relationship with players and how good he was with people. I honestly don't remember a lot of the technical stuff in practice; his assistants did a lot of that. He was the quintessential game coach. I have never seen anyone better. He could work the officials and us and always made the right decision at the right time."

Several weeks after the 1976 Olympics, Slipp invited her former coach to her wedding to Dick Slipp. "He flew in for the wedding, which was very nice," Slipp recalled. "He was the MC and had everyone rolling in the aisles with his stories."

Critelli's coaching was postponed for a few years as she became one of the country's most successful players. She is the only player to be a member of both a Canadian University championship team (Laurentian University) and an Association of Intercollegiate Athletics for Women (AIAW) National Championship team (Old Dominion University). She also spent one year playing in the Women's Professional League (WBL) in the United States. She was named head coach of the Brock University women's team in 1984 and spent six years as member of the Canadian national team coaching staff. In retrospect, she looks back at her rookie year with Donohue with fond memories. "He did the little things for me and the other players that were so important," she said. "We were both Catholic so he took me to church a lot. It was so important for me to have Jack as my first national team coach. He had a much greater impact on my coaching career then all the Xs and Os I learned from other coaches."

CHAPTER 17

Montreal Olympics

When Mayor Jean Drapeau successfully bid for the 1976 Olympics, he envisioned Games that would showcase Montreal as one of the most beautiful, vibrant cities in the world. Everything had to be on a grand scale and even though Drapeau was a frugal man personally, when it came to his city, no expense was spared in his attempt to turn Montreal into a North American version of Paris. Unfortunately, his vision nearly bankrupted the city.

In 1967, the city hosted the World's Fair, called Man and His World, and that event was a financial and artistic success. Two years later, Drapeau played a major part in bringing Les Expos, an expansion National League baseball team, to the city. With Les Expos and the famed hockey team, the Montreal Canadiens, calling Montreal home, the city could boast of being a major sporting town. The Olympics would be the crowning jewel in Drapeau's dream: an international sporting event that would bring the world to Montreal. For Canadians, the Games would be the first Olympics at home. For the Canadian athletes, whose feats on the international sporting scene were often overlooked, the Games were a chance to compete before their families and fans.

But the Games were in trouble from the start. Even though Drapeau received financial aid from both the provincial and federal governments and a televised national lottery raised millions of dollars, there never was enough money or time to build the needed venues.

One of the selling points that the organizing committee used in their fundraising attempts was the fact that new facilities would be a lasting legacy of the Games, sites that could be used by elite athletes and the general public long after the Olympic athletes had departed from Montreal. Unfortunately, Drapeau was more interested in the buildings' aesthetics than their practicality. The Olympic Stadium, which would later house the Expos and a variety of professional teams, was the first stadium with a retractable roof. But, a few years after its completion, the roof was inoperable and the stadium had to close its doors on several occasions because of structural damage.

Costs spiraled out of control as corruption and Drapeau's grandiose plans threatened to bankrupt the Games a year before they were scheduled to be held. A labour stoppage by construction workers nearly scuttled several playing venues, but the Games opened on time amid rumors of scandal and drastic cost overruns.

Politics also caused problems as 16 African countries boycotted the Montreal Games in protest of New Zealand's participation. The African bloc was protesting New Zealand's acceptance of a touring South African team. The Canadian government refused to allow Taiwanese competitors to enter the country unless they competed under the Olympic banner and not their own country's name. The Olympic Games prided itself on being non-political, but in this case, Canada was reacting to pressure from mainland China, the largest market for Canadian wheat.

As the opening of the Games neared, the controversial Drapeau angered many when he built a concrete wall to conceal some of the poorer sections of town, keeping visitors from seeing Montreal's least glamorous areas. However, there was no hiding for the Canadian athletes who were going to be in the spotlight after years of toiling in anonymity. The Canadian government, under the auspices of Sport Canada, had poured millions of dollars into amateur sport in an attempt to upgrade international performances and improve the country's medal count in the 1976 Games.

After poor performances in the two previous summer games the heat was on the coaches and athletes to perform well. The public, media and government officials expected medal performances from many of its athletes and teams and nothing less was acceptable.

One of those teams projected for a possible medal was the men's basketball team. The team, whose core had been together for three years, had played well in the 1974 World Championships in Puerto Rico and in 1975 had beaten the defending Olympic champion, the Soviet Union, in Maple Leafs Garden.

The most optimistic was Donohue himself who kept the team in the headlines in the months leading into the Games. While most national team coaches were following the time-honoured policy of keeping quiet about their team's chances, Donohue was telling anyone that would listen that the men's team was going to win a medal in Montreal. He wasn't being cocky when he said it but rather following the advice he had often given to others.

You will never exceed your own expectations. If you don't plan to win, if you don't think you are going to win, then you won't.

In the four years he had lived in Canada, he had observed a national mentality that accepted mediocrity in everything but hockey, where conversely nothing but the best was good enough. Donohue wasn't satisfied with just being competitive and he emphasized the importance of wanting to win, trying everything to win, and feeling hurt if you failed to meet your goals.

If winning isn't important, then why are we keeping score?

He was fulfilling a dream by coaching in the Olympics but he wasn't satisfied just being there. He wanted to win and wasn't afraid to say it.

* * * * *

When James Naismith, a Canadian, invented the game of basketball while teaching at Springfield College, Massachusetts, in 1891, he did so to give football players an activity to keep them in shape during the off-season. Springfield College was affiliated with the YMCA and it was through the efforts of that organization that the game was soon being played on six continents.

Men's basketball was introduced as a demonstration sport in the 1904 Olympics where the United States finished with the best record although no medals were awarded. It officially became an Olympic sport in the Berlin Games in 1936 and, that year, the Canadian team advanced to the finals against the Americans. The game was played outdoors in a tennis stadium on courts of clay and sand. On the day of the gold-medal game, a heavy downpour turned the courts into mud and the game into a defensive struggle. The U.S. prevailed 19-8 after holding a 14-4 halftime lead. During that initial tournament, the International Basketball Federation passed a rule that banned all players taller than 6'3", an edict that would have sidelined three of the top players on the American squad. The U.S. objected, and the rule was withdrawn. In the championship game, one of the players in question, 6'8" center Joe Fortenbury, scored eight points, equaling the score of the entire Canadian squad.

The 1936 Berlin Olympics was the last time a Canadian team would finish in the top eight in an Olympic competition. In spite of those earlier, less successful Olympics, Canada was a medal hopeful leading up to Montreal, even though these Games would see the strongest field in Olympic basketball history.

The Americans, upset by their controversial second place finish in the 1972 Games, were going to leave no stone unturned in their efforts to regain the gold. The U.S.S.R. was equally intent on proving that their 1972 gold medal was not a fluke while the Yugoslavian, Italian, Czech and Cuban teams were all capable of pulling off upsets. Even the Australian and Puerto Rican teams each featured star power in Ed Palubinskas and Butch Lee respectively, a pair of guards who earned All-American status playing NCAA ball. Still, Donohue knew that his team was ready and hoped that with some hometown support anything was possible.

* * * * *

The Canadian team set up their headquarters in Hamilton, Ontario, 45 minutes west of Toronto and the site of the pre-Olympic qualifying tournament, in the days leading up to the Olympics. Physically and mentally, Donohue had the team where he wanted them, now it was simply a question of execution on the court.

"Coach had a replica of a medal made out of cardboard and used to wear it to practice all the time," Jamie Russell. "He would point to the piece of cardboard and tell us that is why we were in Montreal, to win an Olympic medal."

They arrived in Montreal a week before the competition began and scheduled an exhibition game against the U.S. in Plattsburgh, sixty miles south of the Olympic site. The game was played before a capacity crowd in the diminutive State University of New York-Plattsburgh gym and the

Canadians played very well against the stronger American team. Robinson and Riley were hitting from the outside while Hansen and McKenzie were making their presence felt inside as Canada proved up to the challenge of facing the pre-Olympic favourites.

The U.S. held a slim two-point lead at halftime and the game was nip and tuck until the final minutes of the contest when Canada not only lost the game but their most valuable post player in the process. Battling for a rebound, McKenzie landed awkwardly and hurt his knee. As he was carried off the floor, Canada's chances for an Olympic medal suffered a serious setback. With McKenzie on the bench, the Americans dominated the final minutes of the game and came away with a 10-point victory, but Donohue was more concerned about the condition of his big man as the team boarded a bus back to the Olympic Village. X-rays confirmed his worst fears: McKenzie had torn the ligaments in his knee and would be sidelined for the Games.

The Canadian Olympic delegation requested and was given permission to make a last minute replacement and John Cassidy was added as the team's 12th man while McKenzie returned home to B.C.. Before boarding the plane, McKenzie took verbal shots at Donohue and the national team program, comments that soon appeared in every major Canadian newspaper.

McKenzie was upset that Donohue did not keep him on the 12-man roster but the Coach decided that he needed 12 healthy bodies and McKenzie was sent home.

*   *   *   *   *

The men's basketball draw consisted of two pools of six countries each with the top two teams from each pool advancing to the semi-final medal round. A master of goal planning, Donohue refused to allow his players to think about medals during the preliminary round robin. The message was clear: *Let's concentrate on one game at a time and advance to the next round!*

They started the Games with a relatively easy 102-76 win over Japan. Phil Tollestrup wowed the crowd with his outside shooting and finished the contest with a game-high 26 points, one of five Canadians to hit for double figures. Canada faced its first formidable opponent two days later when they squared off against Cuba. The Cubans entered the game on the heels of an impressive 111-89 win over a good Australian team and were basically the same team that had hammered Canada three years earlier. It was after that humiliating loss to Cuba in 1973 that Donohue had challenged his team and insisted that he didn't want players on his roster who didn't believe they could eventually beat the Cubans or were unwilling to spend the effort to improve both individually and as a team.

Canada had spent the next three years preparing for the rematch and when the time came, everyone on the squad knew not only that they could beat Cuba, but also that they were the better team. The game plan was simple: control the tempo, deny the Cubans easy scores and keep the game close in the early going. The longer the game remained close, the better Canada's chances were of winning. Donohue knew that if the offensive-minded Cubans jumped to an early lead and took the partisan crowd out of the game, Canada would have a hard time coming back.

The strategy worked to perfection. Cuba held a 42-40 halftime lead due to the scoring of guard Roberto Herrera, but the Canadian team had neutralized Pedro Chappe, a power forward who played well against Canada in the past. The Canadian scoring balance was the difference in the second half as Bob Sharpe came off the bench to spark a second half rally that resulted in an 84-79 win for Canada. Tollestrup led Canada with 25 points while Robinson and Jamie Russell had 16 points a piece and Sharpe contributed 15. Herrera was the game's top scorer with 31 points while Chappe was limited to a mere six points.

The Soviets, the defending Olympic champions, were Canada's next opponent and Donohue's crew was able to match the bigger, more experienced Soviets for 20 minutes. The Canadians trailed 57-51 at the intermission but the Soviet Union started the second half with a 17-4 run that prompted Donohue to clear his bench to give his starters a much needed rest.

Derek Sankey did an excellent job pouring in 18 points as Canada's record dropped to 2-1. The team got back on the winning track two days later as Canada rode a strong first half en route to an 81-69 win over Australia. The game featured two of the Games' more flamboyant players: Australian guard Eddie Palubinskas and Canadian guard Billy Robinson. Palubinskas won the individual scoring battle with 28 points but Robinson, who had a tournament high of 23, was the better player as he set up teammates Tollestrup (19), Hansen (19), and Russell (15).

One more win and Canada would be in the medal round, but they would have to do it without their emotional leader as Robinson was sidelined with an ankle injury for their next opponent, Mexico. Tollestrup picked up the slack with 28 points to lead the Canadians to a 92-84 win over Mexico, good for second place in Pool A and a berth in the semi-finals. After a day off, they would play the powerful United States in the semi-finals.

For the semis and finals, the action moved to the Montreal Forum, and despite the fact that Canada was the host country, the States had plenty of fan support inside the historic building.

Canada needed one win in their next two games to win their first medal in basketball since their 1936 loss to the United States. The Americans had more than just talent in their favour as they prepared for their match against Canada. Their national pride was at stake as they sought to re-establish themselves as the dominant basketball power in the world.

The United States had dominated the basketball courts at the Olympics since the game's introduction, winning gold medals in seven consecutive Games and entering the 1972 Games in Munich as the gold-medal favourites. Over the years, their rosters included such basketball greats as Bill Russell, Oscar Robertson, Jerry West, Bill Bradley, Alex Groza, and Charley Scott and the team that played in Munich consisted of some very talented college players in the U.S., although the NCAA Player of the Year, Bill Walton, was one notable absentee.

That team was coached by a living legend, Hank Iba, who insisted his team walk the ball up the court, thus depriving his players of doing what they did best: run and shoot. That strategy, and an unusual decision by FIBA boss R. William Jones, sent the Americans down to defeat in the most controversial ending in Olympic history. The Americans' slowdown tactics played right into the hands of their taller Soviets opponents who held an eight-point lead with six minutes to play in the gold-medal game. Forced to play an up-tempo style, the Americans stormed back and finally took their first lead of the game when Doug Collins sank two foul shots to give the U.S. a 51-50 lead with just three seconds left in the game.

A last second shot by the Soviets failed, but as the Americans celebrated, Jones ordered the two teams back on the court. Three seconds were put on the clock and the Soviets awarded the ball under their own basket. Jones had ruled that the Soviets should been given a time-out after Collins' foul shots although skeptical Americans felt that Jones had secretly believed an American loss would be good for international basketball. Given a second chance, the Soviets in-bounded the ball the length of the court to Aleksandr Belov who overpowered two American defenders to score the winning basket that handed the Americans their first-ever Olympic defeat.

The U.S. protested Jones' decision but lost the appeal 3-2 and back in America hoop fans cried foul about the supposed injustice and vowed to get revenge in the 1976 Games. Basketball USA changed coaches, replacing the conservative Iba with Dean Smith whose North Carolina teams were well known for their fast breaking and defensive pressure tactics.

Smith's 1976 squad consisted of some of the country's best collegiate players including three members of the NCAA championship Indiana Hoosiers, and eight players from the Atlantic Coast Conference.

From the opening day of tryouts the American team's goal was simple – to avenge the 1972 defeat by beating the Soviet Union in the gold medal game. The Americans went undefeated (though they nearly lost their second game in Olympic history when they squeaked by Puerto Rico and Butch Lee, 96-95) in the preliminary round and everyone was anticipating a final with the tournament's two undefeated teams.

For Smith and the Americans, the semi-final game against Canada was just a formality, a tune-up to be used to prepare for the Soviets. In the morning papers the day of the contest, Smith was quoted as saying that Canada played in a weaker pool, implying that the Canadians weren't one of the best four teams in the Games. Smith denied making the comments and threatened to sue the *Montreal Gazette* while Donohue also appeared upset over the comments.

But the story gave him a chance to further motivate his club, imploring them to go all-out against a superior team. He had spent the last four years convincing his players not to be afraid of the Americans and now he had a little ammunition to help pump up his players.

The pep talk didn't help as the Americans jumped to an early lead and never looked back. Billy Robinson tried to rally his teammates in the first half but it wasn't enough. Canada trailed by 13 at the half and the Americans cruised to a 95-77 win.

"We were outmanned particularly after we lost McKenzie," Robinson said. "He was a natural athlete who at 6'9" and 240 lbs. was the only player we had who could hold his own against the Russians and

Americans. He wasn't a great scorer but he played great defence and could rebound with anyone."

Before the game even started, both the Americans and Canadians were dealt a blow when Yugoslavia defeated the Soviets 89-84 in the other semi-final game. The Soviet loss deprived the U.S. of a chance to avenge their 1972 loss while the Canadians now had to beat the U.S.S.R. to garner a bronze medal. Over the years, the Canadian team had a fair amount of success playing against the Yugoslavians but now they had to face a Soviet team they did not match up well against, particularly with McKenzie back in British Columbia. Tickets for the finals were among the hottest at the Games, but many fans lost interest after the Soviets lost to Yugoslavia and ticket scalpers who were expecting a big demand for a Soviet-USA final took a financial bath.

The atmosphere in the Forum was low key as Canada took to the court and any vocal support from American and Canadian fans was stymied by the Soviet domination on the court.

"We beat them in Toronto but that was an exceptional game," Robinson said. "They were a team we could beat on a particular night, but not on a regular basis. They had too much talent."

The Soviets finally figured that Robinson was the key to the Canadian attack and put the taller Sergi Belov on the 5'10" guard.

"It was almost like a box and one," Robinson remembered. "Everywhere I went on the court, there was Belov right next to me."

The Canadians stayed with Russia for the first ten minutes behind Robinson's outside shooting, but the Soviets slowly pulled away. They held a 51-34 halftime lead and won by 28 as both coaches emptied their benches in the second half.

"Losing McKenzie cost us a medal," Steve Konchalski would reminisce years later. "He was the one guy that could bang and hold his own against the Yugoslavian, American and Soviet post players. Lars Hansen was an excellent offensive player but he didn't have the strength that Ken did. But even without McKenzie we still could have beaten Yugoslavia – we matched up better against them and had success in previous games with them. When the Soviets lost in the semis our medal hopes were in trouble."

* * * * *

Throughout the Olympics, the Canadian media, which always maintained a good relationship with Donohue, kept raising the issue of Donohue's contract. It expired with the team's final Olympic appearance and everyone wanted to know if he was returning or was going to accept a more lucrative contract in Europe where several Italian club teams were said to be offering incentive-laden contracts.

In a newspaper interview a few weeks before the Games began, Donohue expressed his displeasure with the slow nature of negotiations with the CABA.

"I've been trying to renegotiate my contract for the past 14 months," Donohue told the *Ottawa Citizen*. "So far, no satisfactory solution has been reached. Unfortunately, the pressures which go with such negotiations are mounting at a time when my mind should be devoted exclusively to the Olympics."

What most of the media did not realize was that Donohue had already turned down a European offer in 1975. Two different clubs offered a contract that included housing, transportation and private schooling for the children. The contract would even end in the spring allowing him to return to coach the national team in the Olympics.

When he stalled on giving an answer, one of the clubs sweetened the deal further, offering riding lessons for his oldest daughter, Carol. As Donohue discussed the latest offer with Mary Jane, her response surprised him.

"There is no point talking about this; we are not going," she said calmly.

Jack was surprised by Mary Jane's strong stand.

"What do you mean we are not going? This is an opportunity of a lifetime!"

"What about the players? Who are they going to call when they have a problem? Can you help Billy Robinson when he has problems if you are in Italy?"

She was right and he knew it. He wasn't about to desert the players who had battled with him the last three years. But now, with the Olympics over and with most of the players headed for retirement, the scenario had changed. While he had enjoyed his four years with the national team and had become a national sports celebrity, he was tired of fighting with the CABA and the resignation of its executive director, John Restivo, a year earlier added to his frustration. In the months leading up to the Montreal Games, the most important in the team's history, the organization was without a full-time executive director and the constant bickering between board members was starting to take its toll.

As he walked off the Forum floor after the Soviet game, Canadian reporters surrounded him, wanting to know his future plans.

"Just give me a chance to talk to the players and then I will talk to you in the media room," Donohue said.

But on the way to the locker room, he was stopped by a CBC television reporter who queried him about his future plans. In the media room the waiting reporters watched the live telecast as Donohue told the nation that he was unsure of his future plans but that his contract with the CABA had just expired.

He sounded very much like a man who was headed for a new job.

CHAPTER 18

Post Montreal

The 1976 Montreal Games had offered such promise to Canada, to the city of Montreal and to the Canadian athletes who participated in the XXI Olympiad!

When the curtain finally came down on Jean Drapeau's spectacle, there was disappointment on all sides. Canada's infusion of cash and personnel did not bring about the anticipated results. The total medal count of 11 surpassed the 1972 total, but had fallen short of the predictions made by the media and Sport Canada. Canada became the first host country in the history of the Olympic Games to not win a gold medal.

For the athletes, whose personal sacrifices meant putting careers on hold and borrowing money to help training costs, the final results and negative reaction from the public were hard to accept. As for the citizens of Montreal, the memory of hosting the world's greatest athletes for three weeks was soon forgotten as the city was forced to deal with cost overruns that resulted in special municipal taxes. The original budget called for expenditures of $310 million but the final bill was closer to $1.5 billion!

The men's basketball team's performance at the Montreal Games represented one of the great turnarounds in the history of Olympic basketball. A team that failed to qualify four years earlier had finished a strong fourth and should have been the talk of the country. In reality, the club's finish, the best showing by any Canadian team at the Montreal Games, was overlooked by the media, which preferred to dwell on the lack of overall production by the host country. Men's basketball was one of the sports projected for a medal and to the casual observer, who knew little of the history of the team or the sport, the fourth place finish was a disappointment. Sport Canada and the basketball community, however, knew the progress the team had made in four years and were anxious to keep Donohue on board. His contract expired the day the team lost to Russia in the bronze medal game and there were legitimate concerns that Donohue would pack up his family and move back to the States or accept one of several offers from club teams in Europe. It would have been the perfect time for him to head for greener pastures. But uprooting the family would not be as easy this time. All six children were now in school and Mary Jane had developed roots in the community, its schools and the local church. For his part, Donohue had also become attached to his adopted country. There were several issues with the CABA, that had to be ironed out before Donohue would agree to a new contract. The biggest problems were to whom he would report within the organization and what to do about the payment for his speaking engagements. For years, Donohue had supplemented his coaching salary with motivational talks and speaking engagements and the CABA wanted a piece of the action.

"Somebody on the board said that since I was under contract to the CABA the money should go to them and not me," Jack told me. "They were willing to pay my expenses and a small honorarium. I told them that would be a good way to end my career as a speaker."

The impasse between the two sides was broken when Carling O'Keefe Breweries entered the picture with an interesting proposition. The brewery would hire Donohue and loan him out to CABA. Carling O'Keefe wanted Jack available a few days a year for meetings and to give talks to company employees. The rest of the time he would be free to coach the national team. The brewery would allow him to speak to outside groups and keep the fees, and they would help him procure more speaking engagements. It was a match made in heaven. The brewery enjoyed the publicity Donohue gave them as he roamed around the country with his blue Carling O'Keefe blazer and the coach appreciated the professional manner in which they treated him.

"Carling O'Keefe would call up and ask if it was possible for Jack to be at a meeting or give a talk somewhere," Mary Jane remembers. "I would tell them 'Of course it's OK, he works for you.'"

Once Donohue inked a new deal, he quickly began to focus on what needed to be done to get to the next Olympics in Moscow. Canadian teams were given free entry in the 1976 Games because they were the host country but in 1980 they would have to qualify for the Olympics, and that put added pressure on the team and their coach.

* * * * *

The first order of business was putting together a staff. Konchalski, who had taken over as head coach of the St. Francis Xavier X-Men in Antigonish, Nova Scotia, was more than willing to commit to another four years, and Ray Jones, who had developed a strong relationship with Donohue, was happy to continue as the team trainer. Ed Brown, who hailed from Newfoundland where he was instrumental in the development of basketball, came on board as the team manager. Brown, like his boss, had strong religious beliefs and was an engaging conversationalist, who could spend hours talking about the evils of Liberal politicians, the virtues of living on an isolated island or the importance of enjoying life. Most importantly, he was very good at his job: keeping Donohue on schedule and keeping problems with the CABA to a minimum. With the staff in place, the most important task still remained: finding players who would commit for the next four years.

Unlike European countries, Canadian national team players did not get paid for participating with the national team program. The federal government had set up a "carding" system in which national team athletes received a monthly stipend based on their international performances. In 1977, the highest level of carding provided approximately $800 a month, hardly enough to support an athlete. Donohue talked about centralizing the team 12 months a year but the money for travel and salaries simply wasn't available. As a result, most of the country's top athletes were forced to train part-time or go overseas or to Latin America where they could play for a club team and receive generous expense money while maintaining their amateur status. Donohue looked at the rest of the world and realized that every other country had a national basketball league, supplemented by two or three imported players, that paid players to play and developed local talent.

"What we need is a Canadian league, like they have in every country in Europe and Australia, so our players don't have to spend every winter in a foreign country," Donohue appealed to anyone who would listen.

Everyone agreed that a semi-pro league would be beneficial for national team development providing Donohue with a built-in feeder system, but the plan never materialized. The federal government didn't have the money or inclination to jump-start the league and not enough financial backers could be found to support franchises.

The Montreal Games saw the retirement of a majority of the team and now the rebuilding process had to start with new players. Billy Robinson, Lars Hansen, Jamie Russell, Romel Raffin and Martin Riley were the only returning players at the 1977 tryout camp and Donohue had serious doubts about Robinson and Hansen's ability to stick with the team until the 1980 Olympics. Robinson had come to realize that his dreams of playing in the NBA were rapidly fading and spent the winter trying to decide whether to continue with the national team program or retire from the sport that had been the focal point of his life. He had played exceptionally well at the Olympics despite being ill and had developed into Canada's best player by transforming himself from a temperamental scorer to an all-round player and team leader. But, at age 26, he now had a family to think about and Donohue had doubts whether Robinson could stay motivated over the next four years. Robinson gave Jack a call shortly after Christmas to discuss his future and the pair talked frankly about the star player's future. Donohue had formed a strong bond with his point guard and had concerns that he would continue playing past his prime.

"I told him that I could play for four more years and wanted to play in the Moscow Olympics," said Robinson. "He told me that he would never cut me, I didn't have to worry about that, but asked me not to embarrass him."

Hansen, on the other hand, was actively pursuing a career in the NBA, a move that would make him ineligible for international competition.

* * * * *

As he did in 1973, Donohue conducted tryout camps throughout the country and it was in Toronto that he first got a glimpse of the future of the national team in a 17-year-old named Leo Rautins, a promising high school basketball player at St. Michael's College. He had good size, could shoot the ball, possessed great basketball instincts and had good lineage. His older brother George had played at Niagara University and spent a few years with the national team.

In the spring of 1977, the younger Rautins was crushed when he got cut from the Ontario team and decided to spend the summer away from basketball. Two weeks after being rejected by Ontario, Rautins' father urged him to attend an open tryout for the national team and the teenager made an instant impression. Rautins' skills were evident, but as the day-long training camp progressed, Donohue was even more impressed with Rautins' attitude. He took the youngster aside and told him that he was inviting him to Ottawa to see how he stacked up against the rest of the country.

"They were going to pick two teams that year, one that would play in Cuba for two weeks and the A team that would go to Europe for the Intercontinental Cup and then host the European teams back in Canada," Rautins said. "I was still in high school and I thought it would be easier to schedule my schooling around the Cuban trip."

So a few days before leaving for Ottawa and the main tryout camp, Rautins called Jack and asked if he should pack for two weeks or two months.

"If you are just interested in making the Cuban squad, don't bother coming to camp at all, stay in Toronto," was Donohue's blunt reply.

"That was exactly what I wanted to hear," Rautins recalled. "All of a sudden I became excited about the tryouts and the possibility of making the A team."

When Rautins arrived at camp, he caught the attention of everyone in the gym when he came down the court on a fast break and dunked over 7' Jim Zoet.

"I remember the play well because it gave me a lot of confidence," Rautins said. "I knew then that I could play with these guys, I wasn't out of place."

However, he soon found himself watching more than playing and quickly feared that he was going to being cut without a good look.

"Billy Robinson called me little Georgie because he played with my brother George and he would tell me 'don't worry little Georgie you made the team'," Rautins said. "But I thought for sure that I was going to be sent home."

Donohue had become sold on the kid back in the Toronto tryouts and was giving other players who were on the bubble an opportunity to play themselves on or off the team. One night, right before the final cuts, Robinson grabbed the teenager and told him that they were going out for a beer.

"I said, 'What are you nuts? I'm only 17 and I am trying to make this team'," Rautins said.

Robinson reassured the teenager once again that Donohue wasn't going to cut him, but Rautins had prepared himself for the worse. When decision day finally came, Donohue called Rautins over to the corner of the gym and suggested that they go outside for a walk.

"All I could think of was, 'Here we go again, I am going to get cut just like I did with the Ontario team'," Rautins remembers. "But we started to talk about goals and what Coach expected of me and I knew then that I had made the team."

Rautins wasn't the only high school player to wear the Canadian uniform for Donohue. A year before, Donohue attended the British Columbia high school boys' basketball championship when the tournament Most Valuable Player, a 6'3" guard who played with flair and passion, caught his eye.

"Coach D dropped into the Vancouver Coliseum to watch the 1975 B.C. Boys' High School Championships although I doubt he was there to see me." Howard Kelsey said.

After the tournament was over Donohue requested a meeting with the high school star and Kelsey got the first glimpse of what his life would be like for the next eight years.

"My father and I basically spent half that day driving him around Vancouver, listening to Coach simply talking and telling his now-legendary stories," Kelsey recalled.

In between tales about New York City and traveling with the National Team Donohue posed three questions for the future national team player.

"He said he had three principal questions for me: did I want to play and win in the Olympics, did I think I could make it to the pros and, if affirmative, was I prepared to commit everything to achieve those goals?"

Kelsey didn't waste anytime saying "yes" to all three questions and Donohue made a commitment to him.

"Coach D said that although my talent wasn't overwhelming, that he'd take me straight out of Point Grey High School to the national team program because he said that he could quickly see that I'd likely work hard enough to get there."

*   *   *   *   *

Forty players were invited to Ottawa where Donohue and an expanded group of coaches put the prospects through three grueling practices a day. Each of the players was a star player on their university, club or high school team and as the three-day tryout period drew to a close, Donohue was faced with some difficult decisions, particularly at the guard position and he sought the advice of the participating coaches.

"During one practice Jack came up to me and asked whom I liked better, Tom Skerlak or Paul Armstrong," Eddie Pomykala said. Pomykala was a young, enthusiastic assistant coach at McGill University and would later enjoy a successful coaching career at both McGill and Bishop's Universities.

"That is an easy one Coach," Pomykala replied. "Armstrong is a great athlete who can do a lot of things for you while all Skerlak can do is shoot the ball."

Donohue nodded his head and slowly walked away. He knew that he had to take the 12 players who would make the team better, not necessarily the 12 best players. He also knew he needed a shooter against zones and sagging defenses and no one in camp shot the ball better than Skerlak.

"Jack knew what he needed for his team and that was a shooter," Pomykala said. "But it made me feel good that he would ask a young coach his opinion and listen intently to what I said, even though he didn't take my advice."

So Skerlak joined the A team while Armstrong was placed on the B squad. Before making the final selection Donohue had a chat with Armstrong. The player sat in the bleachers of the Algonquin College gym facing Donohue who was telling the young forward how well he had played.

"A lot of coaches have been telling me good things about you and you certainly have played well in the tryouts," Donohue said.

Armstrong face lit up when he heard the remarks. "Yes!" he said to himself. "I made the team."

Donohue sensed that he was giving Armstrong the wrong impression and quickly put everything back into perspective.

"Hang on; there weren't that many coaches who said it."

They both laughed and then talked about Armstrong joining the B team and traveling to Cuba.

"It was typical Jack," Armstrong would say years later. "First he built up my self-esteem and then when it was time to let me down he did it with that smile of his and a joke. I just got cut from the national team but I left feeling good about myself."

After the final scrimmage, the remaining players were ushered into two classrooms off the gym, one for the players on the A team and one for the players headed for Cuba. As Rautins walked into the A room there was Robinson right behind him saying, "I told you that you were going to make this team."

It was the start of a great international career for Rautins but the end of a storied career for one of Canada's greatest players. Robinson had a good camp and deserved to be on the team but came to a painful realization that his days on the national team were over. It was Rautins' dunk over Zoet that gave a rookie confidence and a veteran a clear understanding that it was time to move on with his life.

"We were scrimmaging and Leo Rautins took off from the point position and dunked the ball over big Jim Zoet," Robinson related. "I had always said that I would pack it in when there was a better guard and he was better than me. I went to Steve Konchalski and asked for a ticket home."

The spirit of the Canadian team during Donohue's first quadrennial had officially retired and the coaching staff had a big hole to fill.

* * * * *

Donohue was flying back from Halifax and the 1977 Canadian University Championships when he noticed Peter "Doc" Ryan waiting to board the same plane to Montreal. Ryan had just completed a season with the University of Quebec at Trois-Rivieres where he was the nation's leading scorer and an All-Canadian selection.

Although born and raised in Montreal, Ryan attended high school in Brooklyn and later played two years of college ball in the States before returning to Montreal in 1976. The Quebec Basketball Federation tried to arrange a tryout for Ryan with the national team prior to the Olympics, but Donohue's roster was set and he didn't want to take a chance with someone he didn't know. When Ken McKenzie was hurt a week before the Games began, Donohue bypassed Ryan and brought back John Cassidy who had plenty of international experience and knew the team's systems.

Meanwhile, Ryan joined a pick-up team of local players that scrimmaged against some of the Olympic squads and showed that he could definitely play at that level. That fall he returned to UQTR and was basically a one-man team, a jumping center, bringing the ball up against pressure and finishing the season as one of the top rebounders and scorers in the country. Donohue received positive reports about him from other coaches and arranged to sit next to him on the plane.

"Doc I would like to invite you to a tryout camp in Ottawa in May," Donohue said as the plane lifted off the tarmac.

"Coach, it would be a pleasure to play for you," Ryan said.

"Doc, I don't think you understand, I want to invite you to our tryout camp," Donohue repeated, this time with emphasis on the word tryout.

"Coach it will be a pleasure to play for you this summer," Ryan replied with more confidence.

Donohue began to get agitated over Ryan's inability to understand that this was an invitation to a tryout and not a guarantee of a spot on the national team roster.

"I think you are having trouble understanding the concept of a tryout camp," Donohue said as he started to lose patience. "We would like to invite you to our tryout camp in May and give you an opportunity to make the team."

Never one to be suffering from a lack of self-confidence Ryan said once again that it would be his pleasure to play for the Coach and two months later, after a very good tryout camp, Ryan was indeed playing for Donohue. He would continue with the national team as a player and then as a coach until Donohue's retirement in 1988.

* * * * *

Even with the departure of Robinson, the coach had a difficult task trimming down to a workable number of guards and he opened himself to criticism with some of his selections. Some of the criticism came from Don Punch. Punch was a legend in Northern Ontario, a legend he helped create himself. He had a habit of making outlandish remarks, often just to see how people would react to his opinions. In 1977, Punch was coaching a Lakehead University team that included Jim Zoet and a shooting guard named David Zanatta. He became upset with Donohue when the coach kept Zoet but cut Zanatta. He wrote a series of letters critiquing Donohue's coaching ability, his team selection, his American pedigree and just about anything else he could think of. The epistles were spiced with expletives deleted and actually threatened to harm Donohue if he continued coaching in Canada.

The problem was that the letters were sent to Donohue's home and Mary Jane would open the letters and get upset with their contents. When she showed the letters to her husband and asked what he was going to do about them he had a simple solution – don't open any letters from Don Punch.

"But what about the threats in the letters?" Mary Jane asked.

"I'll take care of it, it is not something for you to worry about," Donohue replied.

True to his word, Jack took care of it and gained a friend and ally in the process. He called his rancorous critic and offered a simple solution to the problem by inviting Punch to the next training camp and asking him to take part in the selection process. He knew that getting into a war of words or a shouting argument with the fiery Punch wouldn't solve anything and he appreciated the passion that Punch displayed for Canadian basketball. In Donohue's mind, if people weren't happy with his decisions, then they should become part of the decision-making process. Punch became a staple of the national team tryouts and a strong Donohue supporter long after he retired from university coaching.

Punch wasn't Donohue's only critic. Five years after his arrival in Canada, there was a group of Canadian coaches who didn't like the idea of an American invading their soil and coaching the national team. Another coach would fire off letters to Iona Campagnolo, the national sports minister at the time, complaining about Donohue's coaching tactics.

Campagnolo, who was a strong supporter of the Nation Team coach, simply passed the letters on to Donohue asking him to take care of the problem. He assured her that he would and promptly filed the letters in the garbage when he got home. Eventually the letters stopped.

* * * * *

After breaking camp, the A team competed in the Intercontinental Cup that began with a five-game European swing that included a game oddly enough in Israel. While the country is actually located in the Middle East, it was considered a European country by the International Olympic Committee (IOC) for political and security reasons. Team Canada did not fare well overseas, losing all five games with Rautins seeing little or no action. In one game in which the Canadian defense was non-existent, Donohue jumped out on the middle of the court as a Soviet player brought the ball up the court and immediately got into a defensive stance. As play stopped, a stunned referee gave Donohue a technical foul, the coach slowly walked back to the bench and said in a loud voice

"Well, someone on this team has to play defense!"

While the rest of the team got the message, Rautins was more concerned about getting an opportunity to get on the court.

"Coach could see that I was upset about not playing, so we went for one of those walks in Israel," Rautins said. "He basically told me that I had to be patient and keep working hard in practice. Then he asked me what my goals in life were. I told him I wanted to play in the NBA."

Donohue told Rautins that he was going to make it to the NBA, but to do so he had to keep working hard and believe in himself.

"That meant so much to me, the fact that he believed in me."

That belief did not, however, translate into playing time. Rautins wondered if he would get any court time when the series moved to Canada. He felt his time had come when starter Ross Quackenbush, an experienced two-way player from St. Mary's University, hurt himself prior to a game against Italy. But that morning, in a pre-game walk-through, Rautins did not practice with the starting five and figured he would spend most of the game on the bench.

"Coach came up to me after the practice and told me to be ready to play and I started the second half and played well as we beat Israel."

Rautins was in the starting line-up the following night against Italy and played a pivotal role as Canada edged Italy 69-65 in overtime despite the fact that two starters, Martin Riley and Quackenbush, missed the game due to injuries. Rautins' foul shot in the final minute of regulation sent the game into overtime and he finished the game with 19 points. Skerlak, the shooter that Donohue kept over Paul Armstrong, led Canada with 21 points.

Rautins' coming-out party came three days later when he was the leading scorer in Canada's stunning victory over the powerful Yugoslavian team in Winnipeg. It was an awesome performance against one of the best teams in the world and established Rautins as a prime time international player. He no longer had to worry about playing time; he would be a starter and the team's go-to player for the duration of his tenure with the national team

* * * * *

Jack continued to give clinics and speeches in every part of the country, preaching the importance of the pick and roll and the honour of playing for Canada. He had a hard time saying no to anyone and as a result found himself taking a trip to the city of Prince Rupert in north western British Columbia to provide workshops to the All-Native Basketball Tournament at the behest of Sports Minister Iona Campagnolo.

Following Canada's poor performance at the Montreal Games, Prime Minister Pierre Trudeau formulated the Sports Ministry to over-see the National Sports Organization and surprised everyone by picking Campagnolo to be its first minister.

"I was rumored to be appointed to the Post Office but when the Prime Minister called me in and asked me to be the new Sports Minister I asked 'Why me?'" Campagnolo recalled.

Trudeau wanted someone new and fresh in the position and believed that Campagnolo could also help promote the development of women in the sport.

While many outside of government questioned the appointment, Donohue embraced it. In Campagnolo he found an intelligent minister who was working hard to improve the status of sport and fitness in

Canada. The two supported each other and developed a strong working relationship built on mutual respect and friendship.

"Iona asked him to give a clinic up North to the Inuit First Nations and Northerners who were often off the beaten track for Canadian services and Jack gladly went," Dan Pugliese recalled. "A lot of people would turn down such a request but Jack was glad to go and made similar trips up North on several different occasions. To him it didn't matter where he was – as long as he could talk basketball, he was happy."

The minister not only appreciated Donohue's visit to the North but the way he handled himself.

"When he went up North he acted is if he was dealing with the national team and made everyone feel so important," Campagnolo said. "Jack Donohue also showed Canada that you didn't have to be a tyrant to be a successful coach. We had this model of a dictatorial coach and here was this very successful coach who had a different approach, a more humanistic approach."

Donohue was also making numerous trips to Manitoba at the request of Maureen Orchard, the president of Manitoba basketball.

"Maureen was probably Jack's biggest supporter on the CABA board so whenever she asked him to go to Manitoba, he gladly went," Scott Taylor said.

Taylor, now a columnist with the *Winnipeg Free Press*, was executive director of Basketball Manitoba in the late 70s when Donohue conducted a series of clinics in the province's northern region.

"We were way up north giving clinics in these remote mining towns," Taylor said. "People from the outside who visited would complain about the conditions and isolation but Jack was having a great time. As long as he could interact with people he was enjoying himself. The clinics were sponsored by Converse and at each stop we had raffles for Converse shoes and gear. In one town there was this kid who was dressed very shabbily and had holes in his running shoes."

"What is your name, son?" Donohue asked.

"Kelly, sir," the youngster replied.

"I can see the name tag on your shirt says Kelly but what is your first name?

"Kelly," the boy repeated.

"Your name is Kelly Kelly. Why did your parents call you that?" Donohue asked in an incredulous voice.

"Well, sir, I was the 13ᵗʰ child in the family and my father couldn't think of any more names."

With that comment Donohue began to laugh out loud and walked over to Taylor to tell him that day's drawing for shoes was going to be rigged in Mr. Kelly Kelly's favour.

"I think Kelly Kelly ended up with just about every spare piece of Converse gear that we had," Taylor said.

CHAPTER 19

Olympic Boycott

The 1978 World Championships in Manila presented the national team with its first major challenge following the Montreal Olympics and the team solidified its place among the world's basketball elite with a sixth-place finish. They also came within seconds of recording their first-ever win over the United States in international competition. With only two players from the Montreal Games on the roster, it also validated Donohue's stature as one of the premier coaches on the international scene.

The team picked up more than just wins and respect in the Philippines: they also enlisted the services of a young idealistic doctor who would serve both Basketball Canada and Donohue well over the next 25 years.

Andy Pipe was in Papua, New Guinea, working in a mission hospital, when a picture on the front page of a Manila newspaper caught his attention as he was on a plane headed to the Philippines.

"There was a picture of Jim Zoet getting off a plane at the Philippines airport with the caption 'Canadian team arrives for World Championships'," Pipe said.

Pipe was en route to another remote hospital in the interior of the Philippines but he did not have a set schedule. A former university soccer player at Queen's University, he had served as a team doctor for the Canadian national ski team and was part of the Canadian Olympic medical team in Montreal. He decided to check out the tournament and see if he could possibly pick up some free tickets from anyone connected with the team. Upon his arrival in Manila, he booked himself into a cheap hotel and then proceeded to the Philippines Plaza, a five-star hotel overlooking the Manila Bay where the teams were staying.

"I entered the lobby of this beautiful hotel and looked for some familiar faces and perhaps a few free tickets to the games," Pipe said.

He got a lot more than he bargained for when he ran into Ray Jones in the hotel lobby. He recognized Jones's name from the Montreal Olympics and explained his situation.

"You ought to go see the old man," Jones advised him.

Pipe was taken aback by how Jones referred to Donohue but, before he realized what was happening, the young doctor was in an elevator heading to the coach's hotel room, despite a fear that he would not be well received. That fear became reality when his knock on the hotel room door was answered with a grunt from inside. Pipe waited a few nervous seconds before Donohue opened the door. The coach was dressed in his underwear and holding a can of Pepsi in his hand. Pipe once again explained his situation while Donohue listened intently.

"We are leaving for practice at 4 o'clock, why don't you meet us in the lobby and come with us," Donohue suggested to the nervous doctor.

"Fantastic, going to practice is a lot more than I expected," Pipe thought as he headed back to the lobby.

He returned a little later and waited anxiously for 4 o'clock and the bus ride to the practice gym. The first seat on the bus was always reserved for Donohue and the coach asked Pipe to sit next to him.

"We had a police escort to the gym and coach Donohue started asking questions about my background and what was I doing in the Philippines," Pipe said.

When they arrived at the gym, Pipe, sat in a chair watching the practice and soaking up everything he could as the players ran up and down the court. Towards the end of the practice, Donohue called the team in and then motioned for Pipe to join them.

"Unbelievable," Pipe said to himself, "not only am I watching practice but Coach Donohue is going to let me listen to his instructions."

But when he arrived at the huddle, Pipe was surprised to hear Donohue introduce him as an expert on acclimatization.

"Guys, this is Dr. Pipe. He is going to spend a few minutes talking to you about playing in this climate and things you need to do to prepare yourself."

Pipe tried not to act surprised, but he was definitely caught off guard. Here he thought he was just going to watch a practice but he quickly realized that there was no such thing as a free ride with Donohue's national team. As he cleared his throat he reassured himself. *I know some of this stuff, I can do this.*

He went on to give the team five things to do in the tropics and five things not to do and everyone, including the staff, seemed to appreciate his comments. On the way back to the hotel, Donohue and Pipe continued their earlier conversation.

"We don't have a team doctor but the tournament organizing committee has given us accreditation for one," Donohue said. "Would you be able to help us out?"

Pipe quickly said yes and Donohue told him to check out of his hotel and move in with the team.

"There I was checking out of a flea-infested hotel and moving into the nicest hotel in the country," Pipe said. "Less than 48 hours earlier I was working in a part of the world that was literally one step above the Stone Age and suddenly, I am the Canadian basketball team doctor living in a five-star hotel."

*   *   *   *   *

The Philippines are an archipelago of 7,100 islands including the larger more populated isle of Luzon that contains the capital city of Manila. The islands possess a mountainous terrain, creating a beautiful landscape of narrow coastal plains, interior valleys and numerous dormant and active volcanoes, beauty that is often overlooked because of the poverty and political instability that has characterized the island nation for several centuries.

The political structure of the islands changed forever in 1521 when Ferdinand Magellan staked a claim to the island country for Spain, the first of several foreign countries to lay sovereignty over the Philippines.

The Spaniards held control of the islands until 1896 when the United States made it a protectorate following the Spanish American War. Japan occupied the islands during World War II and the Americans regained control following the fall of the Axis powers and promised independence and free elections. Instead, the Americans helped Ferdinand Marcos establish a dictatorship under the guise of democracy.

The country opened its doors to the competing teams in the 1978 FIBA World Championships but its own citizens suffered under the harsh conditions of martial law that Marcos had imposed in 1972. The country the Canadians visited was a paradox with a high level of literacy and a strong commitment to education; yet the population was saddled with a high rate of unemployment as Marcos drained the nation's economy for his personal advantage, forcing many to seek employment abroad. Under Marcos' regime, the difference between the have and have-nots grew and calls for reform were often met with strong government resistance. The government, sensitive to negative world opinion, tried to shield the competing teams at the World Championships from the reality of the country's poverty and dissatisfaction with Marcos.

Team Canada and the rest of the competing teams were treated like VIPs and every time they stepped out of the hotel, armed guards and motorcycle escorts accompanied them. The Canadians got a different view of the country when they went inland to play some exhibition games prior to the opening of the championship games.

"We went to play in a village and as we traveled the countryside the Canadian players got a glimpse of the poverty that was rampant in most of the country," Pipe said. "I remembered as our bus climbed up a hill overlooking shanties, Coach Donohue made a point of reminding the players that not everyone was as fortunate as they were."

The sight of poverty-stricken villagers was hard for some of the players to deal with, but the weather presented a more tangible threat to their sense of security. Their stay inland was extended when a monsoon hit the main island and made travel impossible. When the team finally returned to Manila, they turned their full attention to basketball. They easily defeated Korea and Senegal before losing a 10-point decision to Yugoslavia to finish 2-1 in the preliminary round. They didn't fare as well in the semi-finals as they lost consecutive games to Brazil, Yugoslavia and the United States before they rebounded with wins over Australia and the Philippines.

While Yugoslavia battled the Soviet Union in the gold medal game Canada drew the United States for fifth place. The Americans were represented by Athletes in Action, a group of former college stars who toured the world playing basketball and preaching the Gospel. Prior to the game Donohue reminded the players that they were capable of great things if they played together and the team responded with an outstanding effort. The score was tied 94-94 and Canada had the ball with just a few seconds left on the clock.

"We ran a play following the time-out and we executed it to perfection," Doc Ryan said. "Leo came off a screen and was open for a shot when he slipped on a wet spot on the floor and fell down."

One of the American players picked up the loose ball, took a dribble and then launched a half court desperation shot. Rautins was lying on the court floor and looked up in disbelief as the desperation shot sailed through the basket as the final buzzer sounded to give the Americans an improbable win. Canada's chance at beating the United States and recording their highest finish at a World Championships were erased by a wet spot on the floor. Rautins still remembered the play as if it were yesterday.

"There was a monsoon and on the bus ride to the gym we passed people in boats on the streets," Rautins said. "When we got to the gym we rode the bus up the stairs of the coliseum so we wouldn't get wet. The roof leaked onto the floor – thus my slip!!"

In the time-out prior to the final play several players tried to warn Rautins about the wet floor and remind him to wipe his sneakers before heading onto the court. But as the players huddled for final instructions, Donohue insisted that everyone be quiet and listen to his instructions.

"A couple of guys tried to talk to me about the wet floor but all I heard was Coach," Rautins said. "They were trying to tell me to wipe my shoes but I didn't hear them."

* * * * *

The 1980 season represented the biggest challenge since Donohue first arrived in Canada – qualifying for the 1980 Moscow Olympics. The team was performing well when they arrived in San Juan, Puerto Rico, for the qualifying tournament. In fact, Donohue's only real concern was an off-the-court skirmish that was occurring in Asia.

In December 1979, the Soviet Union invaded neighboring Afghanistan, an action criticized by Western-bloc countries. Unwilling to physically challenge the invaders, the United States threatened to boycott the upcoming Moscow Olympics and enlisted the aid of its allies in applying political pressure on the Soviets. The Canadian government of Prime Minister Joe Clark stayed true to its conservative label and announced in January that they would join the U.S. in boycotting the Moscow Games if the Soviets did not pull their troops out of Afghanistan by February 20, 1980.

"There was nothing that we could do about it, it was in the hands of the politicians," Donohue said afterwards. "What we didn't want to do was to worry about the boycott and then not play well and fail to qualify. If we qualified but the boycott stopped us from going, then at least we did our job. But if we didn't qualify because we weren't focused, then the threat of a boycott became a non-issue."

Donohue and the rest of the Canadian Olympic hopefuls received a reprieve when the Clark government lost a snap election in February that returned Pierre Trudeau and the Liberal Party to power. One of Trudeau's first acts was to reconsider the government's stance on the Olympic boycott, giving Donohue and his players a glimmer of hope.

Canada opened the qualifying tourney in Puerto Rico on April 18 with a hard-fought three-point victory over the Cubans and then recorded wins over Mexico, Argentina, Uruguay and Brazil to secure one of the three berths to the Moscow Olympics. But while the team was winning on the court they suffered a loss in Parliament on April 22 when the Interior Minister announced that Canada would join the Americans and their allies in the boycott of the XXII Olympiad. The Canadians had one game left against the host Puerto Rican squad. Both teams had already clinched an Olympic berth but the Canadians were playing for pride as they took to the court for the final game.

"Jim Zoet was having a great tournament and it was easy to see that the Puerto Rican strategy was to try and get him out of the game," teammate Romel Raffin said.

When the home team was unable to get the big man into foul trouble, they took the matter into their own hands. They started throwing elbows in the directions of Zoet's face and sent the big man to the bench for good with a carefully placed knee to his groin.

As Zoet lay on the court in pain and Donohue shouted at the refs and opposing team, the Canadian players knew there was no way they were going to win the game. With Zoet sitting out the rest of the game, Puerto Rico took the gold medal game by a score of 82-62.

"The atmosphere was unbelievable," George House said who was accompanying the team as its *chef de mission*. "The fans were throwing things at us and we needed a police escort to our buses and once we got in the bus fans started to rock the bus."

After the Canadians received their silver medals Donohue walked up to George House who was standing behind the team's bench and gave him his silver medal.

"Take this," Donohue said as he placed the medallion in House's hand. "I will get another one for myself later."

"That was Jack, always thinking about someone else," House said. "He wasn't getting another medal but he wanted to make sure that I received one."

The team returned home hoping that somehow the government would reverse its decision but the Canadian government stayed its course and boycotted the 1980 Summer Olympics. Donohue was disappointed but understood the government's position and publicly supported it. But to a man, the Canadian players felt that they had the team that could have brought home a medal if presented with the opportunity to go to Moscow.

"It was the strongest team Canada ever had and it was a shame that we weren't allowed to go to Moscow," Steve Konchalski said.

* * * * *

Bill Wennington and Danny Meagher looked out of place among the 40-plus players who had assembled in Ottawa's Algonquin College gym in the spring of 1981. The rest of the invitees were either university players or European pros while Wennington and Meagher were still high school students who had to return to school after the camp to finish their schooling.

"I had just turned 18 and felt so out of place," Wennington remembers vividly. "I looked around at the other players and thought they were more skilled and confident."

212

Wennington grew up in Montreal and was a competitive swimmer before Bernie Buckley, a high school teacher at Beaconsfield High School, convinced him to try out for the basketball team. A good all-round athlete, Wennington had grown to 6'10" by the time his parents moved to New York and began investigating high schools that would satisfy their son's academic and athletic needs. They decided to send him to Long Island Lutheran, a private high school that had a strong basketball history. There, Wennington ended up playing for head coach Bob McKillop, the first of three coaches who would develop Wennington into an outstanding player.

"I was very fortunate to have three coaches, Bob McKillop, Lou Carnesecca and Jack Donohue, who worked on my fundamentals and help make me a player," Wennington said at the conclusion of a career that included three NBA Championships.

Wennington earned a scholarship to St. John's University to play under Hall of Fame coach Lou Carnesecca. It was Carnesecca who mentioned to Donohue that he should give the untested player a look.

"Jack sensed that I was a little nervous and would talk to me about just doing my best and not worry about things I could not control," Wennington said about his first national team camp. "After a few days, my confidence level rose and I knew I could play with these guys."

Donohue took a mixture of young veterans and younger rookies to the team's first competition, a tournament in Uruguay and he made an effort to make the two teenagers comfortable.

"We were on our first trip, to South America, when Jack came back to my seat in the plane to show me a card trick," Wennington said.

"Pick a card, any card," Donohue said as he started telling his rookie center one of his stories.

Wennington selected the eight of spades as Donohue talked about growing up in New York. He interrupted the story to take the card, placed it back in the deck and put the cards away.

"I don't want to know what card you took," Donohue insisted.

After a few minutes Donohue asked Bill if he liked reading and when he said yes the coach asked him if he read *Sports Illustrated*.

"You should go up to the front of the plane and ask the stewardess for a copy of *Sports Illustrated*," Donohue suggested. "I am sure she has a copy, and if she does, open it to page 19."

Wennington obediently trooped up to the front of the plane and asked for the magazine. The stewardess obliged him and when he turned to page 19 he saw the following written across the page:

Your card was the eight of spades!

"Years later I learned how he did the trick, but what impressed me then and still impresses me, is the fact that Coach would go to all that trouble just to relax me on my first trip."

Wennington would spend four years with the Canadian national team and under Donohue's guidance developed into a premier post player.

"In my final year with the team we would talk about being the best players in Canada," Wennington said years later, "yet every day in practice we would be doing the same basic drills; dribbling drills using both hands, drop steps to the basket, all fundamental drills. We joked about it, but those drills helped us become good players."

After his senior year in college, when St. John's advanced to the Final Four, Wennington was drafted in the first round by the NBA's Dallas Mavericks and played four years with the Mavericks and Sacramento Kings before heading to Italy in search of more playing time. After two productive and profitable seasons abroad he returned stateside looking to give the NBA one more shot.

"I came into the Chicago Bulls camp in 1994 as the team's fifth center but Coach Phil Jackson said that they would keep me around for a while because they didn't want to play Bill Cartwright a lot in the beginning because they didn't want him to wear down in the second half of the season."

It wasn't too long before the veteran was getting a few minutes of playing time and making the most of his opportunities. He slowly but surely moved up on the coaches' estimation and when the season began Wennington was wearing a Chicago Bull uniform.

He spent six seasons with Chicago and earned three championship rings, an unlikely scenario for a kid who didn't take basketball seriously until the age of 15. When he was inducted into the Canadian Basketball Hall of Fame, Wennington said that playing for Donohue prepared him for his days in Chicago.

"Phil Jackson taught many of the same philosophies and tactics as Jack did," Wennington said. "But I always thought I was ahead of everyone else in those days because I had been coached by Jack."

"You have to give Bill a lot of credit," Carnesecca said. "He always did whatever it took to become a better player. The four summers he spent with the Canadian team really helped him improve as a player. When things weren't going well in the NBA he went to Italy for two years and came back a better player."

* * * * *

Unlike Wennington, Danny Meagher came off as a bit cocky in his rookie camp despite his age and lack of experience. His tough guy persona, however, covered up the true feelings of a young man who had self-doubts and a self-professed bad attitude.

"When I first came on this team, I really didn't fit in," Meagher told a newspaper reporter prior to the 1984 Olympics.

He had just landed a scholarship to Duke University and the St. Catharine's native figured he had the lay of the land.

"I was getting ready for my first year at college away from home. My language was bad, my manners were bad. I was like an untamed horse. I lacked a sense of maturity."

To many observers Meagher was a bad apple that would ruin the rest of the team, but Donohue looked past the rough exterior and saw a lot of good. Meagher wasn't a problem child, he was a challenge, a young man in need of direction, and Donohue provided that direction.

"Coach D was the one who went to work on me. He taught me how to channel my energies, how to set goals. He made me think about what I wanted to do and what kind of person I wanted to become. Things just came together."

The 1981 camp was heavily loaded with players from the University of Victoria and the NCAA's powerful Big East Conference. Ken Shields left Laurentian University in 1978 to become program director and head basketball coach at Victoria and immediately turned the school into the most dominant basketball powerhouse in Canadian university history. He had five members of his Victoria team invited to the '81 training camp and all five players earned a spot on the team.

Point guard Eli Pasquali, who migrated from his native Sudbury to Victoria for the opportunity to play for Shields, remembered a certain comfort level at the '81 camp despite his rookie status and the strong competition at the point guard position. Gerard Kazanowski was undersized at the post position, a deficit that he compensated for with his intelligence and skill. The other Vikings included Greg Wiltjer, Kelly Dukeshire and Ken Larson.

Wennington was joined by two other members of the Big East, players who had already established their basketball reputations. Rautins had just recently transferred to Syracuse University while Stu Granger, a gifted 6' point guard, started at Villanova University. Granger's family moved from Montreal shortly after his birth and he grew up in Brooklyn where he played for Nazareth High School and was selected to the all-city team. He was a pure point guard who could set up his teammates with pin-point passes or score when needed. He quickly established himself as the starting point guard in front of the veteran Kelsey and fellow rookie Pasquali.

Rounding out the roster was Jay Triano, a player who first came to Donohue's attention back in 1977 when he tried out despite a painful leg injury. He was cut that year but Donohue kept abreast of his progress at Simon Frasier University and before long the Niagara Falls native was one of the team's top players and according to Donohue, one of the hardest working players he had ever coached.

The high and low of the 1981 season came in the preliminary round of the World Student Games in Bucharest, Romania. The name World Student Games is a bit misleading because many of the competitors are not students in the truest sense of the word. To be eligible, an athlete has to have taken at least one course in an accredited school within a year of the Games and can not be over 28 years of age. The lax rules usually provided for a very competitive men's basketball tournament. Because there are no qualifications for the Student Games, the calibre was weak in the preliminary round but much stronger in the second and championship rounds. In previous Universiades, Canada would breeze through the first round against much weaker opponents before meeting the world's elite teams in the later rounds. That was not the case in Bucharest. The Romanian organizing committee, in an attempt to help the host country's medal hopes, stacked the deck in the opening round.

"They put the United States, Soviet Union, Mexico and Canada all in the same pool with only two teams advancing, "Donohue said after his return home. "It was ridiculous."

After beating Mexico in the opening day of play Canada met the United States in an emotionally charged game that featured several lead changes and a bench-clearing brawl. Granger had a game-high 21 points but it was Jay Triano that provided the big plays down the stretch as Canada held on for a 78-76 win, their first ever victory over the USA in international competition.

"It's incredible," Donohue shouted in the noisy Canadian locker room. "This is a group that has only been together for four weeks. They just came through. They have so much talent, but I was worried because we haven't had a lot of experience."

The Canadians had no time to savor their victory; they still had to face the Soviets. A win would advance Canada to the medal round although they would also advance if they lost by less than three points. But a determined Soviet squad and very questionable officiating crushed Team Canada's hopes.

The Canadians appeared primed for a win as they jumped to an early lead behind some torrid shooting by Kelsey that provided Canada with an emotional lift. However, he was quickly assessed three fouls and spent most of the game on the bench. Canada trailed by two points in the dying seconds of the game and appeared headed for the medal round. But a foul on Triano with four seconds left to play gave the Soviets two foul shots and a 77-73 win. Canada's coach erupted, protesting the game because of the quality of officiating.

"By North American standards the whole operation here is corrupt," Donohue was quoted by a wire service. "The thing is cancerous, but they won't do anything about the protest because it is the same people who run the tournament who will be making the decision on the protest."

The Canadian appeal was turned down.

CHAPTER 20

Kids, Kids and More Kids

A coach's life takes him or her away from the family for long periods of time, but Donohue was absent a lot more than the vast majority of coaches.

"There is nothing more important in my life than my family," Jack once said to a journalist at the 1982 World Championships in Bucaramanga, Colombia. "It may not seem that way because I spend so much time away from them, but they are the reason for anything I do. A second thing is that if you are going to be a good provider for your family, then you have to take care of yourself first and the rest of the family second. I know that sounds strange and selfish, but unless you are healthy and taking care of yourself, how can you help anyone else?"

Anyone who visited Donohue at his Kanata home quickly saw how devoted he was to his family. The six children raised by Mary Jane and Jack were by no means perfect, but as a unit they were a family that could laugh and cry together and despite differences and conflicts were always ready to support each other. While many families drift apart as the children leave home, marry and have children of their own, the Donohue family grew even closer with each passing year. When the Donohue kids began to move out of the house, the Donohue parents didn't downsize their living accommodations, but actually built two additions onto their

Lismer Crescent home to accommodate the growing number of in-laws and grandchildren that still today convene for Sunday dinner.

It was hard not to be in a good mood in the Donohue household when Jack was home because he simply wouldn't allow it. An early riser, he would take great delight in waking the kids for school and pronouncing to them in a loud voice that it was a beautiful day, and it was not to be wasted by sleeping.

The Donohues' six kids were born within an eight-year span and Mary Jane often felt her life revolved entirely around diapers and elementary school, particularly with Jack on the road so much of that time. The family moved three times after the birth of their first child, Carol, yet the Donohues were able to provide their offspring with a semblance of order and continuity. Rules were established, challenged and reinforced. School work was monitored, outside activities supported and discipline delivered without malice or hate.

"When I would get mad at them, I would tell that I love them, but I didn't like what they had done at that particular moment," Mary Jane said. "Often I would only have to count 1, 2, 3 and things would settle down."

When Jack returned from long trips, it gave the children a perfect opportunity for one of the oldest tactics in the world, playing one parent against another.

"He would be gone and a certain routine would be established," Mary Jane said. "When he came home, I would say no to something and they would go to their father and get a different answer."

A parental meeting quickly called by Mary Jane usually put both parents on the same page and limited future problems.

"The key to raising our kids was communication," Mary Jane said. "Even when Jack was gone for long periods of time, he was kept abreast of what each of them was doing."

When the six Donohue children were growing up in Kanata, they had no idea how famous their father was or how many lives he had touched in a positive way. It was not unusual for his face to appear on TV or in the local papers, but it was no big deal for the kids, who knew their father in a more conventional manner. When he was home, he disciplined them, acted as chauffeur, pumped them up with feel-good stories, told dumb jokes and basically seemed like every other dad. Dad had a reputation for being funny, but over time Mom, perhaps out of desperation, developed a similar sense of humor, and would display it often when deal-ing with her husband. Jack liked to tell a story that demonstrated not only his wife's wit, but also the problem of being on the road so often.

"I was coming off a long trip and was just spending one day at home before hitting the road again," Jack explained. "I knew that the time away from home was bothering Mary Jane, but she understood that my work paid the bills, and she knew that the most effective way to deal with most issues was with a smile. So I walked into the house expecting to be mobbed by the children, but instead saw them lined up in a row, shortest to tallest."

"Children, this is your father," Mary Jane deadpanned. "I want you to go over and shake his hand and introduce yourself to him."

The introductions actually made sense, considering Jack's difficulty with calling people by their right name – even his own kids! On one occasion, he came home and before entering his own house, he spotted a pair of twins whose family had just moved in across the street. Jack crossed the street and spoke to the youngsters for a few minutes. Later that night the twins' mother was remarking to another neighbor that Mr. Donohue was such a nice man to go and speak to two children he didn't even know.

"It is no big deal," the second neighbor said. "He probably thought they were his own kids."

* * * * *

Carol and John Joe were the oldest and as the family increased over the years, they had to assume a certain amount of responsibility over their younger siblings. Carol seemed well groomed for the role of older sister – she was intelligent, serious, and fair-minded, and at times more mature than her age might indicate. Yet, despite an exterior that exuded confidence, she had problems like any other child growing up in the 70s. She was small for her age and in the eighth grade she had to wear braces, long before they became commonplace. Then suddenly, in high school the A student started to get only average marks. When an alarmed mother expressed concern, Carol's teachers said she was a good student and perhaps her parents were expecting too much from her.

"I knew that wasn't the case. We didn't push our kids, but some-thing was wrong," Mary Jane said.

So at Mary Jane's request the school's guidance counselor arranged a meeting with the teachers in question and the concerned parents. One by one the teachers reiterated their belief that Carol was not a discipline problem and was working to her potential. However, the teachers' outlook changed when the guidance counselor took out a nation-wide aptitude test that showed Carol in the top 5% of the country. Maybe she could work a little harder!

The problem, however, had been solved even before the evening began. Carol had stopped working hard because she thought her parents had taken her for granted and she was jealous of the younger children, particularly Maura. When she found out her parents were going to visit the teachers, she realized that she was indeed loved, and was soon working to potential in the classroom.

Carol did struggle at times in her role as the family's babysitter, possibly because she took the responsibilities of the job so seriously.

"We would come home and she would be in tears, because the other kids didn't do what they were supposed to do and Carol thought it was her fault when they misbehaved," Mary Jane explained.

In reality, the elder Donohues just wanted the house in one piece and everyone unharmed whenever they returned from a rare night out. Once, Mary Jane took Jack to the airport in the midst of a snowstorm and as she returned home on a local highway, the storm picked up in intensity. She noticed that even the city buses and tractor trailers were slowing down as they climbed the hill that led to Kanata. As she exited off the highway she saw that a car just up ahead had failed to stop at a red light, and watched in horror as the vehicle slid along the icy street and into a utility pole.

"Just a few minutes more on the side streets and I will be home," a nervous Mary Jane told herself.

By the time she reached home she was a bundle of nerves, but was surprised to see the six children waiting in the driveway, shivering in the snow.

"It is our fault, Mom," they all cried out at once as she got out of the car. "It is not Carol's fault; we were misbehaving and made her do it."

Made her do what, Mary Jane pondered.

"She broke the glass on the door but it wasn't her fault, we weren't listening to her."

Mary Jane's eyes moved to the storm door and the shattered glass that lay on the ground. The kids were expecting their mother to explode, but she calmly ushered everyone inside and made sure that Carol was okay and that the broken glass was all cleaned up. She then quietly, but firmly, told the frightened children that she wanted them to go to their rooms and think about what had happened. As they ascended the stairs Mary Jane left the house, walked across the snow covered lawn and let herself into the neighbor's house, calling out in a loud voice, "I need a drink." After a few sips, she relaxed and relayed the story of her last few hours. The next time Carol was in charge of the house, the rest of the brood was on their best behavior!

*   *   *   *   *

John Joe's high school experiences were a combination of successful ventures, coupled with unrealized dreams. He was a regular at national team practices whenever the team was in town and often accompanied his father on trips overseas. In fact, John Joe did too much traveling with the national team for Mary Jane's liking.

"You have other children, you know," she would remind her husband.

But Jack had difficulty with the logistics of taking young girls on a trip with a men's team. He later solved that problem by taking two daughters at a time.

John Joe was a decent high school basketball player, but always felt he was forced to live up to his family name. Coaches were often afraid to tell the son of the national team head coach how to do things, and believed that Jack had spent a lot of time teaching his own children. Eventually, Mary Jane had to tell the kids' high school and community team coaches that her kids needed instruction like the rest of the players.

Dan Pugliese was visiting Jack one afternoon when John Joe came home from basketball practice. Pugliese asked him how the team was doing and John Joe told him that they didn't really have anyone qualified to coach them. That got Jack and Dan thinking. Certainly, a national team coach and a former university coach could spend some time helping a high school team out a few afternoons a week. So they started showing up at Earl of March High School, John Joe's school, and were enjoying the experience of working with young, undeveloped, but appreciative high school players.

One day, a physical education teacher walked in during one of their impromptu practices and asked who they were and what they were doing. Jack explained the situation, but the information was not well received. The two volunteer coaches were asked to leave the school's premises. A week later, John Joe brought home a letter from the school stating that Jack was not allowed to coach the high school team because he lacked the proper qualifications!

After being cut from the Queen's University team in his freshman year, John Joe spent the summer with the national team and was often used in drills and the occasional scrimmage. When he returned to school that fall, he felt he had a good chance of making the team, but was among the first cuts. Although he felt he deserved to make the team, John Joe directed his energy to other endeavors. An above-average student, John Joe earned two bachelor's degrees and eventually a doctorate in education.

But his passion for basketball did not lessen, and he continued to play in intramural leagues and ended up coaching a senior boys' basketball team at a Kanata high school. Donohue once asked a friend who had seen John Joe play high school basketball on numerous occasions for an honest appraisal of his son's basketball ability.

"He's not a bad player and has decent skills," the friend remarked. "But he is too nice a kid to be a really good player."

"I guess if I had to choose between the two, I'd rather have my son be a really good kid," Donohue replied.

He got his wish.

*   *   *   *   *

If Carol and John Joe were at times too serious, Marybeth and Kathy provided an interesting contrast. They were dubbed the "Irish Twins" because they were born less than a year apart and, according to Jack, shared a brain. The pair was constantly providing laughs because of their unintended gaffes.

"Whenever one of them would do something dumb, we would say the other twin must be using the brain today," Carol said.

Kathy was the older of the two, and possessed the most maternal instincts of the family. Whenever Mary Jane needed help with one of the younger children, Kathy would volunteer. She loved babies and the younger, the better.

"I remember once after a long day, she came downstairs and said that Marybeth had gotten sick," Mary Jane said. "As I pulled myself out of the chair to go upstairs, Kathy said 'It was okay, Mommy, I cleaned it up and took care of her.' She was always like that."

She also possessed a rebellious streak and would often lock horns with her mother over the smallest of things. Like her father in his childhood days, her answer to perceived injustices was to hurt the rest of the family by running away from home.

As Kathy left the house in a huff, her mother would call out to her to not be late for supper.

The other "twin," Marybeth, was a very good athlete, possessed a winning personality and intelligence that more often than not were overlooked by her siblings. Sunday dinner was not complete unless there was at least one Marybeth story.

One winter morning, Marybeth was alone in the Donohue house when she went out in the backyard to feed the dogs. As she stepped out onto the porch, the door closed behind her, locking her out of the house. She thought the front door might be open, but she had nothing on but slippers and pajamas and the path to the front was covered with a foot of snow. She noticed an empty bag of dog food and quickly used it as a boot for her left foot. She then emptied a full bag of dog food onto the ground and placed this bag on her other foot and proceeded to the front of the house. As luck would have it, the front door was also locked but Marybeth was saved by a neighbor who was walking by and figured the young woman wearing pajamas and dog food bags on her feet in the middle of winter was in need of some help.

"The neighbor asked me if I needed to call anyone and I was able to get my brother-in-law Denis to come with a spare key," Marybeth said.

Another time, when her car was stuck in a snowdrift in her apartment parking lot, she figured that she could pull it out by herself using a little Donohue ingenuity. She started the engine and put the car in reverse. She kept the engine going by placing her briefcase on the gas pedal and she moved to the front of the car and started pushing.

Her plan worked as the car moved out of the drift, but with the briefcase still on the gas pedal, the car continued to move until it hit a parked car. The impact of the hit, though minor, pushed the gear back into drive, and the car moved forward and returned to the original snow-drift. Marybeth finally gave in and called the CAA.

* * * * *

"Bryan was just a sweet kid," Mary Jane would say when the name of her second son came up. That simple statement spoke volumes because Bryan Donohue was the nicest, most unassuming member of a family that bred nice kids. In his early years, he was considered the quiet one in the family, though it turned out that there was a good reason for his quietness and not just because he was somewhat intimidated by his older siblings. In the second grade, it was discovered that he was partially deaf in both ears – a condition that caused him problems in the class-room. In sports, Bryan's athletic ability was often stifled by his easy-going personality and lack of aggression.

On a trip to Ireland with his father and Maura, Bryan visited Blarney Castle but refused to kiss the legendary stone. In a phone call back to Ottawa, his mother chided him for not kissing the landmark that purport-edly gave the gift of gab to anyone who kissed the ancient piece of slab.

"If anyone needed to talk more it is you, Bryan," Mary Jane insisted.

"I wasn't going to kiss that stone and get everyone else's germs," Bryan said matter-of-factly. "Besides when I have something to say, I say it. Otherwise I keep quiet."

His comments caught Mary Jane off guard, but after a little thought she had to agree with her son.

"Bryan would take a lot but once he got his back against the wall, watch out," Mary Jane said afterwards. "When he had something to say, it was worthwhile."

His older brother John Joe found out the hard way that Bryan could be pushed only so far. The two fought a lot, and John Joe had a tendency to pick on his younger brother, knowing that he would win the ensuing fight. But when Bryan reached his mid-teens, he was suddenly as big as John Joe and could hold his own, putting an end to the physical confrontations.

Bryan would refer to his late teens as his rebellious years, a term that few would equate with the mild-mannered, fun-loving kid.

"Everyone else in the family was very talkative and I was quiet. They all took physical education in college and I took computers," Bryan said.

Bryan also struggled in his first year at university, where he found the co-op program at the University of Waterloo overwhelming.

"I was lost; it was so big with more than 300 students in some classes," Bryan recalled.

He investigated the possibility of changing schools and was considering joining Maura at St. Francis Xavier, when his father sat him down for a serious talk.

"Bryan this is your life and you can do what you want with it," Jack told him in no uncertain terms. "But it is time to start pulling your weight."

The talk was just what Bryan needed.

"It woke me up and I decided to go to St. Francis and get my life straightened out. I knew Maura was there and so was Coach K [Steve Konchalski] and Doc Ryan and the classes were small."

Maybe too small!

"If I was late for class the teacher would know it," Bryan said. "They would come up and say, 'Bryan, this is the third time this semester you have been late. Is everything OK?' There was a strong support system there and I needed that."

* * * * *

Maura was the youngest child and with five older siblings there was a strong possibility of her being spoiled, a possibility that Jack ended quickly. She was only five years old when Jack wrote in a weekly column in a local newspaper that his youngest daughter was Chinese.

"I read recently that every sixth child born in the world is Chinese and since Maura is our sixth child, she must be Chinese," Jack wrote.

The comment would have passed as just another family joke, like Jack's comments about Mary Jane's cooking, but the other kids wouldn't let it die. They told Maura that not only was she Chinese, but adopted as well. Whenever the family ate out at a Chinese restaurant, they would ask their "Chinese" sister what was the best thing to eat. Each time Maura would emphatically deny that she was Chinese.

Maura may have been the youngest, but she quickly developed a strong will and was adamant about challenging established norms that she perceived to be wrong.

"We would all argue with Dad about the environment, women's issues or even about taking the girls on trips with the national team, but eventually we would give up," Kathy said. "But not Maura, she wouldn't take no for an answer and Dad knew that when the two disagreed he was in for a fight."

Maura attended St. Francis Xavier and originally wanted to follow Marybeth's footsteps and become a teacher but later changed her mind and became a physical therapist. Regardless of her occupation, Maura's remained vigilant when out in public and was not one to look the other way or mind her own business when something appeared to be amiss.

"She had 911 on her speed dial and the OPP (provincial police) would answer her calls with 'What now, Maura?'", her brother-in-law Denis would joke.

* * * * *

Sundays were family days at the Donohue household. The day began with Mass at St. Isidore Church and was followed by some form of sporting activity: football in the autumn, softball or basketball in the spring. The day would end with a big meal, where everyone was fair game for kidding and practical jokes.

The Donohues literally had an open-door policy and very often Jack would invite the parish priest and any visitors in town over for the Sunday feast. After grace, Jack would tell why he had a great day, and then everyone would have to share one great thing that happened to them that day.

"No matter how bad a day you thought you had, he made us come up with something positive," Kathy said.

Even worse than putting up with their father's perpetual sunny disposition was trying to stay mad at him. Jack would draw the ire of his children for a number of reasons. He would volunteer the kids for stuff and neglect to tell them until they would already be committed. He established a house rule that boys did outside work while girls did chores inside the house which included cleaning up after the boys. That rule did not last long. Finally, he would organize everybody to do a big family project, get them started and then disappear to "make a phone call" or something – only to be found later lying on the couch, watching TV, drinking a Pepsi or fast asleep.

"But he did make the best Submarine sandwiches!" Mary Jane said about his one redeeming grace.

As the kids got older, married and moved out, it was decided that they should keep Sunday dinner as a get-together for the family, and the weekend gathering included spouses, boyfriends, grandchildren and anyone that Jack might invite on the spur of the moment. In more recent years, the number for dinner ranged from 22 to 30 and forced the Donohues to renovate the house for a second time. This time, they added a new dining room to accommodate everyone for Sunday dinners, holidays and birthdays.

As the number of participants increased, it was decided to rotate cooking responsibilities, whereby the food was not the only thing roasted. The cooks were fair game for criticism whenever the culinary delights weren't up to anyone's particular liking. Each meal usually included a chicken or vegetarian dish for those who didn't like red meat, and an attempt was made to satisfy the particular epicurean delights of each person. Jack, never one to be picky about food, ate whatever was put in front of him.

The one standing rule was that chips could not be included in the meal. That rule was put to the supreme test whenever it was Maura's and Marybeth's turn to cook. On one occasion, they forgot to get to the grocery store on time and ended up serving potato and cheese salads – dishes that looked, smelled and tasted like potato chips and cheetos. "Everyone would spend a lot of time planning and preparing menus, when it was their turn –except Marybeth and Maura," Kathy said. "It would be mid-afternoon when one of them would say 'Oh, is it our turn to cook?' and then, they would be scrambling for the rest of the day and more than once we had pizzas."

Playing football or softball was part of the Sunday family day ritual, and whenever Jack would bring the national team out to Kanata for a home cooked meal, the players and the Donohue kids would head across the street to the park for a sandlot baseball game. The children used sports to stay together after their school days, playing on basketball, volleyball, ultimate Frisbee, touch football and softball teams.

The extended Donohue clan, including in-laws and friends, has been a mainstay in the Kanata mixed softball league, fielding a team dubbed Donohue Legends for years.

League championships have eluded the squad despite a fair amount of expertise. They win some and they lose some, but mainly it gives the siblings an opportunity to spend time together. Of course, any major guffaws or mental miscues are replayed in the evening, when everyone sits down to dinner. "The family that plays together, stays together", was an adage that Jack passed on to his children.

CHAPTER 21

The year we fell in love with talent

Jack Donohue and Basketball Canada were very optimistic as they approached the summer of 1982, and with good reason. The team roster was the most athletic in the history of Canadian basketball and funding was arranged to field both an A and a B team and conduct an extended training camp. The highlight of the summer program was to be the World Championships to be held in Cali, Columbia. Donohue felt so good about the team's chances for a medal that he had talked CBC Sports into coming to the Championships to televise the finals.

The list of players invited to the training camp included several who had distinguished themselves in NCAA competition over the previous winter and would later play in the NBA. Leading the list was Leo Rautins who was coming off an outstanding year at Syracuse University and was expected to be a high draft pick in the 1983 NBA draft. Bill Wennington was now the starting centre for a very good St. John's team and Danny Meagher saw plenty of minutes with the Duke University Blue Devils. The big news was point guard Stu Granger from Villanova University who was expected to be the team's number-one ball handler. Granger who was born in Canada but grew up in Brooklyn played well for Donohue in Bucharest the previous summer. The line-up also included four players (Gerard Kazanowski, Greg Wiltjer, Eli Pasquali and Kenny

Larson) from the University of Victoria's defending Canadian National Championship team.

Donohue brought in ten coaches and 40 players for the tryouts in Ottawa. Donohue would coach the A team while Ken Shields and the recently retired Doc Ryan would coach the B team that was going to a tournament in Cuba in July. The training camp was competitive and while the senior team was fairly set, the battle for positions on the B team was fierce. There were lively debates in the evaluation sessions after each practice as the guest coaches lobbied for different players.

In the end, Donohue took a veteran team to a Taiwan tournament and made sure that the B team consisted of 12 players who had a chance to play some day for Canada. That meant cutting a number of excellent university players and when it came time to let players go, the process was quick. Donohue had a standing rule that players cut had to be on their way home the same day, and as soon as a decision was made, team manager Ed Brown had their plane tickets ready and transportation to the airport arranged.

Shields took a younger group to Cuba with the idea of developing players for the next quadrennial, but in the back of the minds of the coaching staff was the possibility that someone from the B team might be able to help the senior team in a complementary role in Columbia. Included in that group was Mike Smrek, an unknown 7-footer from Ontario who was about to start his first year at Cansius College in upstate New York. Smrek was just learning to play the game but he would eventually play in the NBA and earn two championship rings as Kareem Abdul-Jabbar's back-up with the Los Angeles Lakers.

The senior team played well in Taiwan but their performance was overshadowed by a stomach flu that sent Donohue to a Taiwanese hospital. Dr. Andy Pipe suddenly became the most important person on staff. He personally monitored Donohue's recovery and when the team returned to Canada, he gave the Coach strict orders to rest up. Meanwhile, the B team played well in Cuba, battling uncomfortable temperatures and teams that were older and more experienced. The team finished with a 2-3 record and had a few days on the beach for a little rest before returning to Canada.

* * * * *

The senior team reconvened in Ottawa a week before a preliminary tournament in Knoxville, Tennessee, the site of the 1982 World's Fair. The only question facing the squad was the availability of the head coach who hadn't responded to treatment as well as Dr. Pike had hoped. Donohue attended the three-a-day practices but tired easily and his usual unbridled enthusiasm waned at times.

The team was scheduled to arrive at the competition site a few days before the first game and the flight from Ottawa, with two connections, would take over four hours.

Pipe decided to have Donohue stay behind and take a direct flight to Knoxville the day of the first game against Yugoslavia, the defending World Champions.

When he arrived at the airport, Konchalski met him and the two grabbed a cab.

"What time is practice?" Jack asked.

"11 o'clock, but you are not going to practice." Konchalski replied. "We have a problem."

"Is this a five-cent problem, a 10-cent problem or a 25-cent problem?"

"I would say 25-cent. You have to go to the local courthouse while I handle practice."

The previous night, one of the players was having supper with a few local fans and on the way home the police stopped the car they were driving in. As the policeman checked out the car and its passengers, the Canadian player was uncharacteristically lippy and landed in jail.

The last thing Donohue needed was a discipline problem but he headed directly to the local courthouse. After talking to the policeman involved, he was able to convince the judge to release the player into his custody and was told that the charges would be dropped if there were no further incidents. Donohue assured the judge that there would definitely be no more incidents.

Jack returned to the hotel with the player and read him the riot act. He was here to play basketball, not to get into trouble at night. He was here to represent his country, not embarrass it. Donohue was upset, but he handled the situation one-on-one. He didn't humiliate the player in front of the rest of the team, and after the talk, everyone focused on basketball.

It was now time to see what this Canadian team was like. The 10,000-seat Knoxville Arena was virtually empty as the team warmed up for the opening game against the defending World Champions, the Yugoslavia team. There were a slew of NBA scouts in attendance, though they were there mainly to check out the American team that was playing China in the second game.

The Canadians started off well, particularly Leo Rautins. Rautins took the Yugoslavians to school with a variety of moves and long range shooting. When he was double-teamed, he dished off to open team-mates. The Canadians ended up winning the game.

The following night the U.S. team, who had witnessed Rautins's show against Yugoslavia, was intent on limiting his effectiveness. But Rautins and his teammates continued to shine as they led from start to finish and posted a comfortable double-digit win. Canada finished the tournament with a perfect 3-0 record after an uninspiring win over China and prepared for a trip to Columbia to take on the rest of the world.

* * * * *

International travel for sports teams can be adventurous but more often it is a tedious experience, particularly when planes are booked based on economical rather than logistical reasons. The team flew to Atlanta the day after beating China and, after a five-hour wait, headed for Bucaramanga, the site of the first round games. Because of the long lay-over it was decided that Donohue would stay in Knoxville, rest up and then join the team later in the week.

A few days later, Donohue arrived looking fit and ready to go and soon began to prepare the team for the battles that lay ahead. The Canadian traveling party on that trip included Matthew Fisher, a free-lance reporter who had covered the team before and was going to send game stories back to the Canadian media. He was considered *persona non grata* by Basketball Canada executives who didn't appreciate the fact that Jack had supplied him with free meals and rooms in the past. Fisher made a meager living following Canadian teams and athletes abroad. In the winter, he could make decent money covering the Canadian ski team, but demand for stories dried up during the summer months.

Fisher and Donohue had a solid relationship – Donohue loved the press that Fisher provided for the team and conversely Fisher found Donohue accommodating, approachable and entertaining. Whenever possible, Jack would find a room for the aspiring writer or invite him to team meals much to the chagrin of the bureaucrats in Ottawa. Since Fisher was getting paid for filing stories, Basketball Canada felt he should pay for his own meals and lodging.

"Here is a guy willing to write stories about us, has to live in strange countries from pay check to pay check to do so and we can't help him out?" Donohue would say to the rest of the staff. "It doesn't make sense."

And when things didn't make sense, Donohue tended to do what he considered logical. He instructed Ed Brown to help Matthew in any way he could and his presence in Columbia proved to be invaluable to the team.

*　*　*　*　*

In Bucaramanga, the team won its first two games in the opening round against Uruguay and Czechoslovakia. The wins assured a berth in the championship bracket but the team ran into serious trouble in the final preliminary game against Yugoslavia and that is when the wheels started to fall off the Canadian express.

"Yugoslavia knew that they had no one that could stop Stu (Granger)," Rautins said. "It was obvious their strategy was to get him out of the game."

Granger had poured in 31 points to lead Canada to a win over Czechoslovakia and his quickness caused match-up problems for the Yugoslavian defense. With Canada trailing 35-31 late in the first half, Jay Triano drove to the basket but was knocked to the floor. In an ensuing pileup of bodies Granger was accused by one of the referees of deliberating elbowing a Yugoslavian player and was ejected from the game. The pro-Canada crowd pelted the floor with debris and only stopped after riot police were called in.

"It was a unique experience," Donohue told Fisher after the game. "The weakest part of international basketball is officiating and it showed tonight."

The fight carried an automatic one-game suspension and Granger was forced to sit out the first game in the championship round against the Soviet Union.

The team flew to Cali, the setting for the next round of games. When they arrived at the Cali Airport, they expected to be driven to a downtown hotel close to the playing venue but instead, found themselves billeted in a UN experimental farm outside of the city with the other six visiting teams. The rooms were open-air and simple, with the smell of manure a constant reminder of where they were. Instead of chocolate mints on the pillows, each room had two fly swatters, necessary tools to battle the larger-than-life mosquitoes that were a constant threat once the sun went down. There were no TVs, radios or game rooms where the players could hang out during down time.

No one knew for sure where the host Columbia team was staying, but the other seven teams in the championship round were unhappy with the living arrangements. On the second day, Donohue was cooling off in the outdoor pool, the one amenity, when Alexandr Gomelsky, the Hall-of-Fame Russian coach came over for a brief chat.

"We cannot stay here," he said. "We are playing for a World Championship and they put us up in a terrible place. The players can't sleep at night and there is nothing to do. Coach Donohue must go to the organizers and get it changed."

Jack laughed and said he was powerless to do anything.

"No, you are a famous coach and they will listen to you. Tomorrow morning there is a meeting and you must be there. We get to the championship round and stay at a manure farm. The losers are at a resort by the seas. It is not right. There is a meeting tomorrow and you must be our leader. FIBA looks up to Jack Donohue."

Donohue knew that the teams were on the farm to save money. Columbia had bid for the World Championships in part to show the world that they were capable of hosting an event of this magnitude. The master plan was to do a good job with the basketball and then bid for the next available World Cup of Soccer. While hosting the basketball championships were a break-even proposition at best, the Soccer World Cup was a moneymaker.

But the organizing committee did a poor job of securing sponsorships and attendance in the preliminary rounds did not meet expectations. The tournament was losing money and moving seven teams to the UN farm would save a bundle. Before going to the FIBA meeting, Donohue had Ed Brown inquire about the availability of hotel rooms in the downtown area. At the meeting, Donohue sat back and remained quiet as country after country complained about the living arrangements. Finally, the head of the organizing committee apologized profusely and said that it wasn't possible to move because all the downtown hotels had been booked for weeks.

That was Donohue's cue.

"Maybe we can help the committee out. We made reservations this morning at the Hotel David and are moving in this afternoon."

The Columbians were surprised at the comment but rebounded quickly.

"That's good but it wouldn't be right to move just one team and leave the other six on the farm."

"That's not a problem," Donohue replied. "We also have reservations at five other hotels and would be glad to give them to the other teams. That will take care of six teams and perhaps the committee could somehow find rooms for the seventh team."

All seven teams moved in to five-star hotels that afternoon.

* * * * *

The move to luxurious quarters did not help the Canadians' play on the court. The cohesion that was always a trademark of Donohue-coached teams was painfully lacking. Without Granger, the team was easy pickings for the Russians and losses to Australia, the Americans and Spain followed.

In international basketball, the ability to deal with crazy travel itineraries, unfamiliar food and customs, and homesickness are just as important as basketball skills.

Under Donohue, the national team usually managed to cope with such problems by joining together to form a collective group and together raising the Canadian flag.

"There is no better feeling than playing for your country." Donohue would say. "Canada is counting on us." It may have sounded hokey but the immigrant coach believed it and so did his players.

When things started to unravel in Cali, the response was different. Granger became withdrawn and moody after his ejection in the Yugoslavian game while Rautins never duplicated his performances in Knoxville. Many of the younger players lacked the maturity to deal with the adversity and the high expectations placed on the team.

The team play that characterized the Canadians in Knoxville and the opening round of the World Champions was non-existent. As the losses began to mount up, the individual play increased, leaving Donohue searching for answers. He tried everything – team meetings, individual talks, even long walks with Rautins through the streets of Cali – but he couldn't right a sinking ship.

"I was playing scared because my knee (which was operated on the year before) was bothering me and I feared that it would affect my chances of playing in the pros," Rautins said. "Jack and I would go for these walks and he was concerned that things were falling apart. He thought the guys were more interested in having fun off the court than playing basketball. I told him the teams before always had fun but were also always ready to play ball. We just had a lot of guys who hadn't matured yet."

The team won their final game against a weak Columbian team that had fired their coach prior to the game. Brown arranged for the team to leave prior to the gold medal game while Donohue stayed with the TV crew from CBC. He felt bad that CBC had come to Columbia to televise a championship game that Canada would not be in, so he agreed to do the color commentary for the broadcast.

Besides, he needed time away from his players.

* * * * *

The team's departure from Cali was a fitting end to a disastrous trip. When they first moved into downtown Cali from the UN farm, Donohue held a meeting to warn the players about their new environment. Looking at his 7-foot twin towers, Wennington and Wiltjer, and tough guy Danny Meagher, Donohue stressed that size was not a deterrent to crime in the poverty-stricken city.

"I know that you are big, strong guys but some of these people either steal or starve. They will kill you if they have to. I don't want anyone going out by themselves and be careful where you go."

His fears were backed up by the team guides who told graphic stories of thieves who cut off fingers to steal jewelry. The team was leaving at 5 a.m. on a Sunday morning and met in the hotel lobby where a bus was arranged to take them to the airport. A wedding in an adjacent ballroom was winding down when the festivities ended literally with a bang. One of the guests became jealous, pulled out a gun and shot a man dancing with his girlfriend. As the Canadians turned to see what the noise was, the shooter ran through the lobby clutching the gun, chased by several friends of the wounded man. One of the pursuers hopped into an empty cab and began to pursue the man, driving up sidewalks before he finally cornered him in a scene right out of a movie.

As the bus pulled up in front of the hotel to take the team to the airport one of the coaches said, "I think it is time to get out of this place." Everyone nodded in agreement.

On the flight home, Konchalski tried to figure out where it all went wrong.

"I have been with the national team program for nine years and this is the worst performance in those nine years," he said to the other coaches. "We have our work cut out for us."

Thankfully for Canadian basketball, Jack Donohue was never afraid of hard work.

CHAPTER 22

The Edmonton Gold Rush, the Los Angeles Bust

Donohue had the entire winter to contemplate the failures in the 1982 World Championships and he came up with one conclusion – never fall in love with talent! He had allowed talent to supersede team effort: individual potential took preference over team development. And he knew better!

He knew better when he first started coaching CYO basketball and baseball at St. Barnabas, he knew better at Tolentine and Power, and at Holy Cross College and certainly in his first ten years in Canada.

Donohue-coached teams had always exceeded their talent level, even in the Alcindor era at Power Memorial. But in the previous summer, just the opposite was true – Canada had not played up to its potential. Now, the team was to start preparing for another major competition, this time on their home soil, and he had to get things right.

Canada was the host country for the 1983 World University Games in Edmonton and the Sports Ministry was once again looking for positive results on home turf.

On paper, the Canadian team appeared to be a lot weaker than the squad that self-destructed in Cali the summer before. Donohue was losing two of the team's more talented players to the NBA draft – Rautins and Granger.

Donohue would miss Rautins because they had become close off the court and Leo was arguably the most talented player ever to wear a Canadian uniform. There was talk about Rautins postponing the pros for two years to maintain his amateur status and be eligible to play in the Edmonton Games and the Los Angeles Olympics the following year, but Donohue advised against it. Rautins had been with the team since 1977 and it was time to move on. Jack knew it and Leo knew it.

"Playing in the NBA was a life-long dream and that dream was realized when I was drafted in the first round by Philadelphia (the 17th overall pick and the fourth highest Canadian ever picked behind Hall of Famer Bob Houbergs, league MVP Steve Nash and Bill Wennington)," Rautins said. "At the time it didn't make sense to stay with the national team and risk injury. But in hindsight, I never should have gone to the NBA."

The 76ers drafted Rautins, and Charles Barkley the year after, because they were expecting their two all-star forwards, Julius Erving and Bobby Jones, to retire after the 1982-83 season.

"But Philadelphia won the NBA championship in '83 and everyone decided to come back," Rautins said. "Billy Cunningham (the 76ers' coach) was not the kind of coach who trusted rookies, he preferred playing veterans."

Rautins played in just 28 games in his rookie year before being traded to the Atlanta Hawks but an injury sidelined him for all but four games in his second season and his NBA career came to an abrupt end. He signed with an Italian club team and had six productive years playing in Europe before returning to North America to pursue a broadcasting career.

"What I should have done was go to Europe right away, keep my amateur status and continue playing for Canada."

Granger was a different story. Although he was born in Montreal, he was bred in Brooklyn and never had any real closeness to Canada. Often, in an international player's career, there comes a time when the travel and homesickness become obstacles to performance. When such incidents would occur, Donohue reminded the team that they were playing a sport that was supposed to be fun and that they had the privilege that few athletes experienced: representing their country in international competition.

"There are hundreds of players back home who would die to be in your shoes," he would tell his troops when their morale began to falter.

When players complained about the food, he would talk about the millions of people throughout the world who were going to bed hungry.

"You are playing a sport you love for your country against the best players in the world. If you can't enjoy that, then you shouldn't be playing."

Granger had problems identifying with Canada and after the suspension because of the Yugoslavian game in the '82 World Championships, he appeared to have lost some of his drive. He was playing to prepare himself for a pro career and the Canadian national team was merely a means towards that end. He spent two summers with the team but never felt a part of the program the way a Howard Kelsey or Gerald Kazanowski did.

The departure of Rautins and Granger left two vacancies on the team's starting line-up. In typical fashion, Donohue stressed to the team the positive aspects of losing the club's most talented players.

"There is an opportunity for people on this team to get more playing time, to step up and help Canada win a medal in Edmonton," Donohue said at the beginning of the team's training camp in Ottawa in May.

* * * * *

Eli Pasquale, the talented point guard from the University of Victoria Vikings who spent two years backing up Granger, was now the undisputed point guard and team leader.

"It was great because Coach told me, and then told the players, that I was the leader on the floor and the confidence he showed in me was a big help."

Pasquali was coming off an exceptional season with Victoria that saw him earn "Canadian Player of the Year" honours as the Vikings won their third straight national title under Ken Shields. The coaching staff thought that Jay Triano and Tony Simms could conceivably replace Rautins. Triano wasn't as good a passer or shooter as Rautins but he played with unmatched passion, hated to lose and had improved each summer he had been with the team. Simms, a star player for Rick Pitino's Boston University Terriers, provided strong play at both ends of the court and was one of the team's best athletes.

Bill Wennington, Greg Wiltjer, John Hatch and Danny Meagher had one more year of maturity under their belt and joined Kazanowski to provide the team with strong play at the forward spot. While none of them could individually match up with some of the more talented forwards on the Yugoslavian and American squads, collectively they could hold their own.

Meagher was another example of a player who blossomed under Donohue.

While the power forward was considered a disciplinary problem in his earlier years with the national team, he slowly developed a strong bond with Donohue, and as the team prepared for the Edmonton Games, Meagher was displaying a new found maturity on and off the court. The team also welcomed back Romel Raffin who phoned Donohue in the winter of 1982 and said he was thinking about making a comeback. Raffin was a teenager when he represented Canada in the 1976 Olympic and had retired from the National Team program after the 1980 season.

"I thought I had basketball out of my system in 1980 but the desire was still there," Raffin said.

There was only one problem, his wife was pregnant with their first child and was due during the team tryouts. Donohue told Raffin he was welcomed to tryout but that his first priority was to his family. The coach was surprised to see Raffin come walking into the gym one Monday morning three days after the birth of his daughter, Jessica.

"I was at the hospital when she was born Friday night and stayed until Sunday when my wife told me to get to camp. I think she wanted to get rid of me," Raffin recalled.

Donohue also brought in a new staff member – sport psychologist Cal Botterill. While many coaches in the early 80s were wary of using sport psychologists, Donohue embraced Botterill and the pair complemented each other.

"Jack Donohue was the most impressive applied sport psychologist and life psychologist I have ever known," Botterill said. "Despite this, he believed I could help his players, his staff and him. He was unbelievably supportive as a person and as a professional – a real privilege to work with. All he expected in return was a total commitment to what we were trying to do. He had incredible perspective as a coach, leader, and friend. I believe now that this, more than anything, was the basis for his greatness. When I was introduced to the national team for the first time at camp, he said he knew that I could help the players and even more importantly, could help him and his staff. He showed incredible humility; he was a student of life."

Another staff addition was Doc Ryan who had made the transition from player to coach. Donohue loved Ryan's passion for the game, his ability to communicate with players and an insatiable appetite for dealing with people. Ryan also displayed a strong work ethic, a trait of which Donohue took advantage when needed.

"My job was to get the game tapes and break them down for the players to see the following day," Ryan said. "One day during the '83 Student Games we got back late to our rooms and I told Coach I was going to bed."

"That's a good idea, but are the films ready for tomorrow?" Donohue queried.

"I'll do them in the morning," Ryan replied.

"No problem, just make sure they are ready for me when I wake up at 6 tomorrow morning," Donohue said as he went to bed.

The 1982 season had ended in disaster but out of the wreckage Donohue and friends would once again raise the level of Canadian basketball to new heights.

* * * * *

The World Student Games are held every two years and outside of the Olympics are the biggest sports venue in the world, although they get little media play in North America. The Canadian contingent was governed by the Canadian Interuniversity Athletic Union that has since been renamed the Canada Interuniversity Sport (CIS).

When Donohue first arrived on the Canadian scene, he discovered that the national team would be participating in the Student Games but not with him as coach.

In 1973, Donohue's second year with the national team, the same team participated in both the pre-Olympic qualifying tournaments and the Student Games, but with different coaches. Donohue directed the team in Italy and then Paul Thomas, appointed by the CIAU, took over the coaching reins at the Student Games held in Moscow. It was an awkward situation that Donohue quickly corrected. If his team was playing, he was going to be the coach and over the years he used the Student Games as an opportunity to evaluate players.

From the moment it was announced that Edmonton would be the host, Donohue urged friends to be a part of the Games. Three of his own children served as volunteers and were able to watch first hand as their father led Canada to one of its more memorable basketball triumphs.

Canada had little trouble in the opening round, posting wins over Angola and Argentina. In the second round, they defeated Israel and China before dropping a close contest to Yugoslavia. The loss to Yugoslavia meant Canada drew the United States in the semi-finals, and would be playing a U.S. squad that included some of the best collegiate players available and several future all-stars.

Canada had recorded its first-ever international win over an American team two years earlier in the Student Games in Bucharest, but it was a transitional period for both programs and the victory received little coverage in North America.

This game was going to be different. CBC was televising the contest in Canada as part of its complete Student Games package, while the American channel CBS decided to televise the four medal-round games live providing plenty of pre-game hype.

CBC was only broadcasting parts of the basketball game live, cutting away from the game to show other events, and that forced Canadian basketball fans to watch CBS which was showing the game in its entirety. They heard Billy Packer complain that the Americans had taken the Student Games too lightly and had not sent their best players. While several big name collegiate players did skip the Games (the most notable being Michael Jordan), the American roster included two players who would later be named among the NBAs top 50 players, Charles Barkley and Karl Malone, as well as future NBA stars Ed Pickney, Johnny Dawkins and Kevin Willis.

The Americans entered the game as prohibitive favourites, but Donohue, with some help from Botterill, had his team believing that they could beat anyone.

"Every day the players completed a little form reviewing our preparation, readiness, and focus. Each day, as we shared the highlights of every game, the confidence in our preparation and focus grew." Botterill recalled. "At one stage, I suggested maybe we didn't need to continue the forms, but Jay Triano insisted we continue right through to the final game!"

The Canadians jumped out to an early lead as the Americans seemed unable to match the home team's intensity. Canada held a nine-point lead at halftime and in the second half the Canadians continued to outwork their more talented opponents. The Americans, unused to being behind in games, started to show their frustration, while Team Canada stayed focused and recorded a shocking 85-77 victory.

The following evening, CBS, expecting the United States to be in the finals, televised the basketball final between Yugoslavia and Canada. Once again, the Canadians got off to a quick start. When the Yugoslavians, the defending World Champions, mounted a comeback in the closing minutes of the first half, Donohue turned to an unusual source to stem the opposition tide.

He inserted Karl Tillman, an outstanding shooter in Canadian college ranks, who had sat on the bench against the Americans. Tillman promptly missed his first shot which Yugoslavia rebounded and converted for an easy hoop at the other end of the court. Undaunted, Tillman scored eight consecutive points to give Canada a much-needed lift and a lead going into the locker room at halftime.

"Karl Tillman came off the bench late in the first half when the Yugoslavian machine started to roll," Botterill said. "He was used to playing 40 minutes in college but sat out the entire emotional USA game. Things weren't looking great after he missed his first shot but he drained his next four shots to dramatically demoralize Yugoslavia and help put the game on ice."

The second half was all Canada as the partisan crowd cheered every basket and the home team cruised to a victory.

As the game came to an end, TV cameras from CBS and CBC captured Donohue being hoisted off the ground by his players, his fist clinched high in the air.

For Botterill, the Edmonton Games would be a learning experience that would assist him in future international competitions.

"I learned so much from the players, especially Jay Triano, and the staff. This was the first real team I was able to be part of and together we experienced the power and potential of real team dynamics and focusing. After defeating the powerful U.S. team in the semi-final, the victory against the World Champion Yugoslavia team felt like destiny. I will never forget our shared joy and running into Jay Triano walking the streets at 5 a.m. after the final game. We were appreciating the privilege of being able to represent Canada and be able to celebrate a tremendous team accomplishment."

"The bench staying so ready and supportive in the Edmonton tourney was huge... Tillman, Howard Kelsey and Kelly Dukeshire were as instrumental in our success as the starters. Dukeshire was the last player chosen for the team, but he was the ultimate 'support' player. He kept everyone playing well and when it came time to cut down the net in celebration – there he was boosting everyone up for a turn!! He waited the whole tourney to get on the floor. It was only justice that he got to 'stick' the last 2 free throws of the tournament."

* * * * *

The team that captured the gold medal at the 1983 World Student Games was intact for the 1984 Olympic and expectations for a medal performance in Los Angeles were high. In the eyes of the public, Canada's hopes for medals were buoyed by the Soviet boycott, a political move that saw several Eastern Bloc countries joining the Soviet Union in abstaining from the L.A. Games, a retaliation move for the United States-led boycott of the Moscow Games in 1980.

In reality, the men's basketball field was missing just one medal contender, the Soviets, and Canada had plenty of competition for the top three spots.

The U.S., playing at home, had pulled out all stops after the loss to Canada in Edmonton. Their roster included the top American university players including Michael Jordan, Sam Perkins, Patrick Ewing and Chris Mullin.

The Yugoslavian squad was a veteran group that had advanced to the finals of the 1982 World Championships and Spain, Italy and Brazil were teams to be reckoned with.

Still, Canada entered the Games with confidence and had all the necessary tools needed for success in international basketball: size, leadership at the point position, shooting ability, experience, depth and a savvy, knowledgeable coaching staff.

Prior to the Games, Donohue enrolled the team in the NYC summer pro league, providing the players with not only excellent competition but also a taste of his former stomping grounds.

"We played 14 games in 16 days; it was crazy," Wennington said. "But it was nice being in New York and the guys got to see an awful lot."

Donohue took the team to Yankee Stadium one afternoon and for many it was their first time at a major league baseball game. On another excursion, Donohue presented his players with a glimpse of high society when they visited the penthouse of Jack Mulqueen. Mulqueen was the Tolentine junior varsity baseball player that learned a valuable lesson about responsibility from Donohue 25 years before and was now a leading fashion designer in New York.

"They were playing in a local league down here and one day Jack called me up and invited me to dinner with the team at Mama Leone's," Mulqueen said. "After the meal, I had two Rolls Royces pick up the team and chauffeur them back to my apartment for an impromptu party. It was quite a sight seeing these tall basketball players squeezing into the two cars."

Back in Mulqueen's penthouse apartment, the players listened to music late into the night as the host told stories about his days in Donohue's 10th grade business class back at Tolentine High School and the lessons he learned as a junior varsity baseball player.

* * * * *

The basketball format had changed since Canada's last Olympic appearance in '76. The number of teams remained the same but now eight of the 12 teams would advance to a single elimination championship round. The key for Canada was to avoid playing Yugoslavia or the United States in the quarterfinals.

But it wasn't the opposition that would be the cause of the team's failure to capture a medal in Los Angeles – rather it came from two unexpected sources: injuries and uncharacteristic mental breakdowns.

The first injury came in New York when Wennington suffered a concussion during a game in the Pro-Am league. With Wennington still recovering from his injury, Donohue looked to Raffin to help pick up the slack.

"I was in the best shape of my life and playing well," Raffin said. "Then it happened."

A separated shoulder put Raffin's Olympic participation in serious jeopardy. Raffin was in Pennsylvania to spend some time with his wife's family and was hurt playing pick-up ball at Penn State. The injured player immediately called Donohue who calmly directed him to Pipe.

"Give Andy a call, tell him what happened and do whatever he tells you," Donohue said.

The team was scheduled to reconvene in a week but the normal healing time for such an injury was six-to-eight weeks. Pipe contacted an expert in the field of shoulder injuries and then told Raffin that he was willing to work with him every day to try and get him ready for the Games, but there were no promises that he would be ready in time.

Meanwhile, Donohue contacted Ken Larson, the last cut from the Olympic team and told him to get ready, that it didn't look like Raffin would be healed in time for the Games. But Pipe and Raffin beat the odds and after consulting an expert Raffin was given the OK to play.

"He knew that there was a risk the shoulder could pop out again but it was a testament to his determination that he was able to recover so quickly," Pipe said.

Raffin's good fortune was bad news for Larson who once again was left behind. Larson first made an appearance with the national team when he was the last invitee among 40 hopefuls at the 1979 tryout camp that would make up the 1980 Olympic team. Under normal conditions, his chances of making that team would be slight but this was an Olympic year which made his prospects a near impossibility since Donohue preferred to go to battle with more experienced soldiers. Yet each day Larson moved up on the depth charts and showed enough after three days to make the first cut. He continued to impress the coaching staff and was the last cut before the team headed for Puerto Rico for the Olympic qualifications. He was a member of the team that participated in the World Championships in 1982 but an ankle sprain prevented him from playing in the Student Games in Edmonton.

"I was back in Duncan, B.C., with my ankle in ice water, screaming at the TV, while my parents were behind the bench in Edmonton," Larson said. "It was very strange; I cried for joy and was heart-broken at the same time."

"Then Coach D picked 16 guys to be on the team for the year leading up to L.A. I played well, but not well enough. It came down to our last game of our cross-Canada tour. I was again the 13th man on a 12-man team. And when the team finally got to L.A., Coach called me and said to get ready because Raffin hurt his shoulder. Then, I got a call a few days later and Coach said Raffin would be OK. So I was about as close as one can get without actually going to the Olympics."

The near misses were disappointing to Larson but it didn't affect his strong feelings towards Donohue.

"If anyone had a right to be upset with Coach, it was probably me," Larson said. "However, Coach and I had a special relationship that lasted until his passing. He would always call me when he came into town. We'd get together for lunch. And when I started my speaker's bureau, Coach was my first booking. I eventually followed in his footsteps and I now speak professionally. Coach taught me more lessons than I can list; he helped me shape my core beliefs. He will always be an inspiration to me. I do my very best to pass on his teachings to my clients, kids I coach, and anyone else who will listen."

* * * * *

Prior to the opening of the Games, Danny Meagher told Mike Farber of the *Montreal Gazette* that the hype of the Olympics and Los Angeles would not have an effect on the Canadian team.

"What gives us an advantage is that we'll be ready for L.A. and all those other teams will have to adjust to the freak activity," Meagher said. "L.A. is no big deal for us, but they may not be able to handle the L.A. trip. Coach D has been talking a long time about this. We won't have family or tickets to worry about. Just basketball! They'll be thinking what clothes they should take home to the wife, and we'll be thinking totally about a medal."

Unfortunately, nothing could have been further from the truth.

"We lost our focus, there was too much outside pressure from family and friends and we allowed it to distract us," point guard Eli Pasquali said after the completion of the Games.

Canada was used to playing in the obscurity of European and South American gyms but the proximity of Los Angeles proved to be a burden on the Canadian players as demands by family and friends took their toll.

"Los Angeles was crazy, there were things going 24 hours a day," Raffin said. "Cal Botterill tried to get us on track but the distractions just hit us."

Donohue and Botterill had expected the distractions and tried to nip them in the bud by constantly reminding the players that they were going to Los Angeles for one thing only: play basketball well enough to win a medal.

"The L.A. Olympics were a unique challenge," Botterill said. "I noticed how powerful emotions can be at the Olympics. Since the Games were in North America, more of the players' families were taking in the games. Being a major media and celebrity centre produced tremendous potential distractions. We had players prepare their families by writing them a letter in advance explaining how focused they wanted to be. We worked daily at optimizing our focus and maintaining a strong team orientation."

The Olympic Village is usually a haven for the athletes, a space off-limits to media, family and outsiders. That was not the case in Los Angeles. Botterill got a better understanding of just how distracting Los Angeles was going to be when the team first arrived at the Olympic Village on the University of Southern California campus where the athletes were quartered.

"When we arrived, Lionel Ritchie was singing in the village square, people were trading pins and uniforms. The beautiful people and celebrities were everywhere inside the Olympic Village."

*　*　*　*　*

The distractions took their toll not only in the Village but on the court as well.

Two standards of all Donohue coached teams were rebounding and foul shooting. "A team that outrebounds their opponents and makes more foul shots will win most games," Donohue constantly preached to his players and coaching staff.

In Los Angeles, it was foul shooting that proved to be Canada's downfall. Canada got off to a poor start and after dropping their first two games in the preliminary round, their medal hopes were in serious jeopardy.

They suffered a heartbreaking 83-82 loss to Spain as Spain's Fernando Martin exploded for 27 points. The Canadians' balanced scoring was reflected in the fact that four players scored in double figures but the team's Achilles heel was their free throw shooting. They missed 17 foul shots in the one-point loss!

Things got worse the next game as Michael Jordan and his team-mates downed the Canadians 88-69 to leave Canada with a 0-2 record. Donohue refused to panic but rallied the troops with motivational talks and a request for a more focused effort from his veteran squad. He stated the obvious when he told the club that there was no longer any room for error – the team had to win their next three games to guarantee at least third place and avoid Yugoslavia in quarter final play.

"We talked to the team this morning about a lack of communication on the floor," Donohue told the press after Canada recorded is first victory of the Games, a 121-80 romp over China. "Over the first two games, we missed something like 31 foul shots."

The Canadians reeled off two more wins over Finland and Uruguay to finish the preliminary round with a 3-2 record, good for third place in Pool B behind the United States and Spain.

Canada met Italy in the quarter-finals and the game plan was clear – control the tempo of the game and not allow the Italians to turn the contest into a track meet.

The strategy didn't work in the first half as Italy jumped out to an early lead and held a 43-37 advantage at the intermission. In the Canadian locker room, Donohue stressed the importance of getting back on defence, of taking the ball to the basket and of not relying solely on perimeter shots. The halftime talk did the job as Canada took control of the game in the final 20 minutes and won 78-72. Jay Triano led all scorers with 25 points while Gerald Kazanowski added 20. For the first time in the Olympics, the Canadians executed from the charity stripe where Canada outscored their opponents 20-8.

Donohue and his team didn't have time to enjoy the hard fought victory, in less than 48 hours they would be back on the court facing the undefeated Americans. The semi-final match was never in doubt as the U.S. jumped to an early double digit lead and walked away with a 78-59 as the teams' benches saw plenty of playing time in the second half of the game.

Canada had little chance of upsetting the Americans and was looking forward to a rematch against Spain in the bronze medal game. But once again, an upset in the other semi-final game would prove disastrous for Canada's medal hopes. The first half of the Spain-Yugoslavia game went according to form with the Yugoslavians holding a 40-35 halftime lead. But Spain limited the opposing team to just 21 points in the final 20 minutes and ran away with a relatively easy 74-61 victory. That meant Donohue and Team Canada needed to beat Yugoslavia to realize their goal of winning an Olympic medal.

It was certainly a do-able task; they registered a double-digit win the year before to win the gold medal at the Student Games and had repeated the trick with a win over the talent-laden Yugoslavian team earlier in the summer.

However Drazen Dalipagic, a one-time European Player of the Year, exploded for 37 points to lead the Yugoslavians to an 88-82 win. Donohue used a variety of defenses – zone, box-and-one and man-to-man – but nothing prevented Dalipagic from putting the ball in the basket.

"I can't remember anyone dominating a game against us like Dalipagic did tonight," Donohue said after the game.

Canada trailed by one with less than three minutes to play but couldn't stop Dalipagic and future NBA star Drazen Petrovic down the stretch.

"We have always played tough against Yugoslavia but it is so hard to beat a good team three times in a year," Konchalski said repeating an old sports adage.

The Canadian players, many of whom were playing their last game under Donohue, wept in the locker room.

"We cried," Wennington said, "because we knew that this would be our last game together and it didn't turn out the way we hoped it would."

Back home, there were some complaints about the team's failure to garner a coveted medal by detractors who overlooked the team's injuries or underestimated the talent level of the opposition. It would be awhile before Donohue heard any of the criticism. He packed his bags and headed for New Jersey's Long Island Beach and a much needed family vacation.

CHAPTER 23

Surf City

When the Donohues were first married, their summer vacations were spent at Friendship Farm where Jack ran one of the more successful basketball camps on the American East Coast. Those early summers were not much of a vacation for Mary Jane who was caring for her ever expanding family while her workaholic husband ran the camp, but it was a change of venue and the open air of the Catskills was a refreshing alternative to the humid summers of Yonkers. The only real vacations they had in the early years of their marriage were joint trips south with his old army buddy, Ted Burns. The Donohues would hook up with the Burns family in New York City and head down to Florida.

"We would leave New York in two cars at midnight and drive all night," Burns explained. "We would hit South of the Border in South Carolina around nine in the morning and rent two rooms. The rest of the families would go to the beach or shopping while Jack and I slept. Then that night, we would start again, driving all night until we reached our destination in Florida."

When the family moved to Canada, Jack stopped running the camp and the family vacation revolved around the national team schedule.

"We went to Disney World once, but some years we didn't have the time to take a real vacation," Mary Jane said. "And we could never make final plans until the national team schedule came out."

In the early 1980s, Jack came up with a great idea and started a family tradition that has continued to this day. For years, his sister, Mary Castelli, and their cousin Anne took their families to Surf City, a beach community on New Jersey's Long Beach Island, forty minutes north of Atlantic City.

"We don't spend a lot time with Mary and her family and I think we should all get together for a week in the summer down in the Jersey Shore," Jack mentioned to Mary Jane in the spring of 1981. "And what are you going to do there?" Mary Jane asked skeptically.

"There are lots of things to do down there. We will be right on the ocean, there are plenty of facilities for sports and we will be close to Atlantic City."

"I am sure that there will be plenty for the kids and me to do, but what about you? You can't sit still for more than 20 minutes and there will be no phones or TV."

"Look, we will be an hour from New York and Philadelphia and I know a lot of coaches and I have friends in both places. When I need to get away I will just head to New York or Philly for a day or two. I will be fine. Let's give it a try."

What was started as an experiment turned into an annual highlight of the year for both the Donohues and their cousins!

Mary Jane discovered that Jack could actually stay in one place for more than 20 minutes and have a good time. In fact, once he hit the beach he didn't want to go anywhere else.

"The first year that we went to the Shore, each family rented houses for a week. Jack, who always enjoyed being on the ocean, acted as activities coordinator," Mary Jane said.

It was perhaps the most relaxing time the family had ever spent together and, to Mary Jane's surprise, her husband was content to hang at the beach house. There were no trips to Philadelphia or New York and he managed to curb his addiction to the telephone for a week. He was relaxed and enjoying the company of his family, his sister and his cousin and their families. The time on the Jersey shore was so enjoyable that it wasn't long before their stay was extended to two weeks.

"Uncle Jack loved the water but hated the beach," Gene Castelli remembered. "On a typical day he might spend an hour just floating in the water talking to whomever was by his side, but he would spend less than two minutes on the beach. Of course, he was never short of company. His favorite floating partner was our cousin Georgie."

Georgie, the son of Jack's cousin Anne, spent most of his life on dialysis, yet never complained and managed to keep an upbeat attitude towards life, traits that Donohue admired greatly. The pair would stay neck deep in the ocean and talk about sports (mostly about their favourite team, the New York Yankees) as their bodies rolled with the oncoming waves.

With a trip to New Jersey engrained in the families' annual plans, Mary Jane would phone Mary to plan the vacation as soon as the national team schedule was finalized. And as the kids got older, the need for more space became apparent as boyfriends and girlfriends were now included in the summer getaway.

"There was never a question of someone staying home and missing the Shore," Mary Jane said. "If their friends wanted to come, fine, otherwise they will see them in two weeks when we got back. No one was missing the trip."

And this included Jack who never strayed too far from the ocean. Instead of making those trips to Philly or New York, he ended up inviting his buddies to visit him on the shore.

"We couldn't get him to leave Surf City, not even for a trip to Atlantic City for a show," Mary Jane said.

* * * * *

Walking through an airport in the United States, Donohue was once stopped by a man who insisted he was an old acquaintance and wanted to know how the Utah Jazz were doing.

"The Canadian team is doing well thank you, but you have to realize that I am not Frank Layden," Donohue replied to the man.

"No, really Frank, how are the Jazz going to be this year?" the man said believing he was talking to the head coach and president of the NBAs Utah Jazz.

Donohue told him politely who he was and then went on his way, leaving the confused man behind. Donohue and Layden were often mistaken for each other and such errors were understandable. They were both Irish Catholics from the Metropolitan area, had strong New York accents, similar physiques and loved telling stories with the same New York City accent and deprecating sense of humor.

"Jack was much better known than I was, particularly outside of the United States, so I would be mistaken for him all the time," Layden said. "Once, I was on a flight and the guy sitting next to me on the plane starts talking about the Bronx and New York City basketball and I can pick up enough that he thinks I'm Jack. I just went along for the ride.

"Finally I told him that I wasn't Jack Donohue."

"Well, who are you then?" the startled man said.

"Harry Carry."

The fact that both Donohue and Layden enjoyed successful basketball careers just added to the confusion.

"There were certainly a lot of similarities between Jack and I although I was much better looking," Layden would deadpan to people who mentioned the resemblance.

Layden grew up in Brooklyn, played at Niagara University in the early 50s and then returned to Long Island to pursue a high school coaching career.

"I coached at St. Agnes High School and Seton Hall High School on the Island and we had very good teams," Layden recalled about the start of a legendary coaching career. "But I would go into the city and watch Power play; but as good as we were, the city teams played at a much higher level."

Layden soon took an interest in Donohue's coaching methods and was impressed that, among other things, he never ran up the score against weaker opponents.

"Years later, I told him that one of the things I really admired about his coaching was the fact that he would sit down his big stars at Power once the game got out of hand," Layden said. "He took a risk of having the starters upset because he was cutting in on their playing time. He seemed embarrassed by the comment but thanked me for making the observation and then gave a great explanation."

"The game only lasts for a night and the players are temporary," Donohue replied. "But these are my colleagues I am coaching against and they are my friends for life."

256

"As a young coach I learned a lot from Jack, he was a great role model," Layden said.

The two squared off in the late 70s when Donohue took the Canadian national team on a tour against American universities including Layden's Niagara University.

"They beat us and Jack was the reason," Layden said. "He was an excellent game coach and I learned a lot when we played against each other. After every time-out they came out better prepared; they would run a play for basket or change defenses that forced a turnover."

The friendship between Frank Layden and Donohue grew tighter when the Laydens joined the Donohues for a week in Surf City. If Jack had any desire to leave the ocean during his vacation time, it was eliminated with the arrival of Layden. The two entertained each other daily with stories about characters that they knew in and out of basketball and thoroughly enjoyed each other's company.

"Long Beach Island was a great time," Layden said. "We used to go down there all the time and the memories aren't something you can just relive or bring back. It was a special time."

The Donohue's rented cottage became a refuge for friends and relatives who would accept Jack's invitation to come and spend a few days by the sea. One year, Jack's open door policy for passers-by became a reality.

"There were so many people coming in and out of his house that the front screen door fell off the hinges," Layden said. "It was a very Irish family setting. People came down because they loved each other and Jack's place was a clubhouse with people sleeping anywhere they could find a bed or sometimes on the floor."

Frank, Barbara and their son Scott were in Surf City in 1984 when Jack flew in from the Los Angeles Olympics with bags full of clothing.

"It was amazing: he had shirts, sweat suits and all sorts of clothing from the Olympics that people had given him and he was distributing it to everyone," Layden recalled.

Donohue also brought back a case full of M&Ms, one of his basic food groups.

* * * * *

The Donohues would always stop at Mary Jane's parents' house for a few days before heading back to Kanata. And it was during one of those trips that Jack had a chance to take his son-in-law Denis Sicard, an avid sports fan, to his first trip to historic Yankee Stadium. In the process, Denis realized that the Donohue name still carried some weight in New York City.

"He said to me 'You have never been to New York? I'll take you in one day and we will go to a ball game at Yankee Stadium'," Sicard recalled.

Denis was looking forward to visiting baseball's most revered shrine but he got more than he had bargained for. They drove to the Bronx, parked Denis's car by a subway station and took the EL to the game. When they reached the Stadium, a few cops who recognized Jack asked him where he had parked. When he informed them that they had parked in the north Bronx and took the subway in, one of the cops admonished him for not driving into the Stadium.

"That's a bad neighborhood you parked in and who knows if the car would be there when you get back," the cop said. "Besides it is not good taking the train at night. Next time, call up and we will get you parking down here."

The cop then looked over at Denis who seemed a little worried about the fate of his brand new car.

"I'll call and have someone check on your car and when the game is over we will drive you there."

Sure enough, after the game the cops arranged for a patrol car to take them back to the parked vehicle.

"We heard a report on the radio that a car with Canadian plates was seen leaving the city but we don't know if it was your car," the officer driving the car said as he glanced at Denis who was now expecting the worst.

"But don't worry; if someone stole the car, we will drive you back to Mamaroneck."

Jack thought that was great but Denis was more worried about his car than getting a ride back to Mum and Pops.

"I didn't know if they were putting me on about the car being stolen and now Jack was expressing very little concern about the car, but it was my car," Sicard remembers. "I was relieved when the patrol car shone its light on the car which was still parked in the spot where we left it."

The following year, they decided to attend another game and this time Jack called a few friends and landed some tickets and VIP parking for an afternoon game.

"We drove to the exit for Yankee Stadium and Jack told me to pull up on the curb outside of the Stadium near some policemen," Sicard said. "He gets out of the car and says something to one of the cops who tells him that he can leave the car right there outside the stadium."

The patrolman pointed to an area right next to an ominous tow-away sign.

"We heard that you were coming Jack," one of the policeman said. "Just leave the car there, it will be fine."

Once again, Denis didn't feel comfortable leaving his new car in a tow-away zone. "Don't worry," the cop assured him. "I will be here for the whole game; no one is going to touch your car."

They picked up tickets at the "will call" desk left by a friend (Roger McCann, a former basketball referee who worked for the Yankees in the summer and the Knicks in the winter) and settled in some seats between first base and home plate. After the first inning, McCann showed up and apologized for the seats. He escorted them to box seats behind the plate and then brought hot dogs and drinks for everyone. When the game ended, they emerged from the park and there was Denis's car surrounded by other vehicles, all parked with the blessing of New York's finest.

"It was good to see you again, Jack, don't be a stranger," one of the officers said as the Donohues got in the car and headed back to Jersey.

Denis was impressed with the treatment his father-in-law received in a city he left over 30 years ago.

"It was amazing, everywhere we went not only did people remember him after all the years but treated him with the utmost respect."

A similar scene was played out when Jack took Denis and John Joe to a college basketball game at Madison Square Garden.

"Jack introduced us to one of the ushers who was working in the Garden back in the Power days," Denis recalled. "The usher asked John Joe if he knew how important his father was. 'Your dad was one of the finest gentlemen ever to coach in this building. As long as I am working here your family will have tickets for this building'."

* * * * *

Jack and Mary Jane's first grandchild was born to Kathy and Denis in 1989 and was named Taylor. Coincidently, cousin Gene and his wife had become the proud parents of their first child a few weeks earlier and he was also named Taylor.

"When we heard that Gene and Ellen were naming their child Taylor we thought about changing to a different name" Kathy said. "But they had different last names, lived 1,500 miles apart and would only see each other a few times a year, so we decided to call our child Taylor as well."

The two new-born cousins would soon spark an intense rivalry between the American and Canadian relatives. That summer, it was decided to have a contest between the two babies, a 'Taylor-crawl,' in the sands at Surf City. The Canadian Taylor won the event despite being a few weeks younger and some unethical tactics by the Americans. "It was a close race until the Americans tried to cheat by throwing a baby bottle at the finish line," Kathy Sicard says.

The ploy backfired as the Canadian Taylor raced for the bottle while his American counterpart sat stationary in the sand, eyeing all the grown-ups who were yelling "Go, Taylor, go."

"It was definitely an early form of baby doping."

That race inspired the Can-Am Surf City Olympics, a series of events between the cousins that included athletic and non-athletic competitions, plenty of trash talking and new levels of cheating. Jack, banking on his years of experience competing in the "other Olympics," appointed himself in charge of Surf City events.

They included such varied activities as beach volleyball, half-court basketball, miniature golf, softball, bowling, bingo and relay races. When the Americans complained that the Canadians had an unfair advantage because they were more athletic, non-traditional events such as eating contests and battles of the half-wits were added.

As the years passed, it became obvious that the ability to cheat was a far more important skill than athleticism. While the Canadians often complained that their American cousins were too competitive and cheated too much, they had an ace in the hole: their patriarch, who accepted the role of judge, officiated to his personal whim. "Since my Uncle was on the Canadian side, the majority of the 'cheating' was without a doubt instigated by the Canadians," Gene Castelli said. "However, to be fair, the majority of the arguing over cheating was clearly carried by the American side.

"Whether it was baseball, cards or mini-putt, Jack would make a call based on how he felt rather than what actually happened," said Denis.

The elder Donohue got his comeuppance one afternoon on the miniature golf course when he got into a debate with his cousin Mark Chomich.

"Mark had brain surgery earlier in the year and he and Dad started arguing with each other," Kathy said. "They got louder and louder and people playing thought they were fighting for real. When it was over, we told Dad that he lost a battle of wits to a person with only half a brain. We never let him forget it."

As a result the battle of the half-wits was designated an official Surf City Olympic event.

Mark was also the reigning champion in the Jayson's Big Breakfast contest, an event that requires eating a hungry man's breakfast in the fastest time at a local restaurant. The menu included eggs, bacon, sausage, potatoes and pancakes, and it was fitting that a person who worked in a city that turned the Coney Island Hot Dog eating contest into an international event, would be its defending champion. Mark received little competition, year in, year out, and in 2003 was named Champion Emeritus and appointed judge of the contest he once dominated.

Stories about Jack's naps became legendary among the cousins and at one point the Canadians, hoping to profit from his ability to rest at a moment's notice, proposed napping as an Olympic event.

"We would joke that if we made napping an Olympic event my uncle would have to be disqualified because he was a professional," Gene said.

The Great Baby Race, the event that spawned the Surf City Olympics, continues to this day with new entries every year, with the original combatants, the two Taylors, now acting as judges.

CHAPTER 24

The Final Run

Following the 1984, Olympic Games, Donohue persuaded Frank Layden to give Kazanowski and Triano tryouts with the Utah Jazz. Triano was drafted by the Los Angeles Lakers in 1981 but he was placed in a nearly impossible situation of making the team as a point guard against competition that included Magic Johnson and Michael Cooper. He joined the Lakers Summer Pro Team and played well but left to join the national team when they headed for a tour that included the World Student Games and the Pan-American Games. Three years later, he joined Kazanowski at the Utah tryout camp. Kazanowski was among the first to be cut although he gave a good accounting of himself in scrimmages.

Donohue called up Layden to see how his post player had fared in the tryouts.

"He was an easy cut," Layden told a surprised Donohue.

"What? He didn't play well?" Donohue asked. "I thought the kid was ready to have a good tryout."

"He was fine, not good enough to make the team, but he had a really good camp," Layden explained. "He was an easy cut because I knew that he had other options. He has a college degree, is a bright kid and is going to be successful in life. He can play in Europe and with the

Canadian national team, and when basketball is over, he will move on other things.

"But there are other guys who aren't that fortunate. Basketball is all they have, if they don't make this team they have nothing to fall back on. Those are the tough guys to cut."

Triano found himself in a different situation. The Jazz were counting on a first round draft pick by the name of John Stockton to handle the point guard responsibilities but Stockton was a holdout, giving Triano ample opportunity to play point guard in training camp.

"I returned to my hotel room one day after a particularly good practice just in time to see Frank Layden being interviewed on TV," Triano recalled. "He said he didn't care if Stockton signed, there was a Canadian kid named Triano doing a good job at the point. That made me feel pretty good!"

Unfortunately, the feeling was short-lived.

The next morning, as he was stretching before practice, Triano eyed Stockton walking into the gym in his basketball gear, ready for practice. The man who would set NBA career records for assists and steals had just signed with the Jazz.

"An assistant coach came over to me and said Coach wanted to talk to me," Triano said. "I knew what he wanted; I was going home."

Stockton's signing made Triano expendable, but the Canadian made a big impression on Layden.

"Triano had a very good camp and we came close to keeping him," Layden said 20 years later. "I was impressed with him."

* * * * *

Donohue faced another rebuilding task in 1985 as he prepared for his final quadrennial. Romel Raffin retired for the second time while Bill Wennington and Mike Smrek were early NBA draft picks. Wennington was selected in the first round draft (16th overall) by the Dallas Mavericks and would enjoy a roller coaster professional career that included pro stops with Dallas and Sacramento and a two-year stint in Italy before he eventually joined the Chicago Bulls during the Michael Jordan era. Wennington found his niche with the Bulls where he picked up three NBA rings and played a prominent role in one of the league's most memorable moments.

"People don't remember that Michael Jordan and I combined for 57 points and I hit the game winning shot in Michael's return to the NBA at Madison Square Garden," Wennington said with pride.

"What people do remember is that Michael had 55 of the 57 points," Wennington added with a laugh. "Still I had the winning basket."

These departures left the national team with only one experienced post player returning, Kazanowski, and he was undersized at 6'9."

At Power Memorial and Holy Cross College and with earlier national teams, Donohue achieved success by getting the ball into the hands of his post players. Now his team was playing "small ball," reverting to the guard-orientated style he used when he was coaching Tolentine High School.

Guards Triano and Pasquale were the team's focal points on offense although Kazanowski, Meagher and Hatch continued to provide scoring as undersized forwards. The team finished sixth at the 1986 World Championships, tailing off after winning their first three games. Donohue still enjoyed coaching and his relationship with his players, but the on-going battle with administrators over control of his team was taking its toll on him and the demand for him as a speaker exceeded his availability. He announced that he would retire following the 1988 Seoul Games allowing Basketball Canada time to select a successor.

"Coach always kept his battles with Basketball Canada away from the players," Meagher said. "It was only after he stopped coaching and we were no longer playing that he would tell me about the problems he had with some of the administrators. He always had a positive attitude with the team."

Still, in a newspaper interview, Donohue was quick to point out how he prioritized amateur sport in Canada.

"The most important things in amateur sport are the athletes and the coaches," Donohue said. "You should want to keep both around for more than one Olympics. Coaches are self-motivated guys. They need to have a lot of control.

"Nobody seems to have control. It's a committee idea. You go into a meeting and ask who made a decision about something and no one knows who made it originally. It's bad business."

Still it was a profession that Donohue enjoyed and, deep down, he knew he was going to miss it.

"But no one screwed around with this team. Not that they didn't try, but no one did. If it was so terrible, I wouldn't have been here for 17 years."

The setting was in place for a Hollywood ending with the Coach leading his team to a medal in his final Olympics, but there were problems as the team headed for Donohue's stretch run.

The team was already thin in the post position when Greg Wiltjer and Danny Meagher discovered that they couldn't get released from their European teams to play in a pre-Olympic qualifying tournament and might not be available for Seoul if the team did qualify.

* * * * *

Donohue was never afraid to go against conventional ways, particularly when it came to his coaching staff. He selected a young Steve Konchalski as his assistant over dozen of other coaches who were older and more experienced and Doc Ryan joined the staff just two years after his playing days were over. Donohue would invite high school and women coaches to participate in training camps, anyone that approached coaching with the same passion he possessed.

In 1986, he made history when he appointed Olga Hrycak as the team's apprentice coach, the first woman to coach a men's basketball team at the international level. Hrycak started her career in Montreal where she coached women at the high school and university level before Richie Spears picked her as his assistant with the Quebec provincial women's team in 1975. However, the competitive Hrycak found the women's game too laid back and it wasn't long before she was coaching a boys' high school team. In 1979, she broke ground as the head coach of the Champlain College men's basketball team and within two years she directed the squad to a provincial title and soon caught the eye of Donohue who appreciated her work ethic and commitment to the game as well as her drive to improve herself as a coach.

Not everyone shared his view.

"There was a tournament in Taiwan and I was promoted from apprentice coach to assistant coach when one of the assistants couldn't make it," Hrycak recalled. "A woman coaching a men's team on the international scene just wasn't going to happen. I got a lot of strange looks from referees."

Not to mention some snubs from other coaches.

"We had just finished playing the Americans and were just shaking hands afterwards and one of the American coaches refused to shake my hand," Hrycak said. "Jack saw it and shouted 'Is there a problem here?' Coach Donohue made sure that everyone knew that I was part of the staff and he told me that if they didn't want to shake my hand then that was their problem, not mine."

Hrycak worked with the men's team up until the 1988 Olympics and then returned to collegiate coaching. In 2003, she made basketball history when she was appointed head coach of the University of Quebec at Montreal Citadins, the first female head coach of a university men's basketball team in Canada.

* * * * *

As he prepared for his final run at an Olympic medal, Donohue was Canada's longest serving and most successful full-time national team coach. His visibility as a motivational speaker, champion of Canadian pride and his comedic comments overshadowed the fact the men's basketball was the only team sport to qualify for the last three Summer Olympic Games. They finished fourth twice and were denied an opportunity to compete in 1980 when Donohue had arguably assembled his finest team.

While the Coach had grown tired of the constant battles with Basketball Canada's governing board, the belief that a coaching change was needed was growing among board members. There was a strong feeling that Donohue had stuck too long with veteran players rather than develop new talent.

His last administrative battle was over centralization, a program that would bring the national team together for an entire year before the qualifying tournament for the Seoul Olympics. Scheduling games for that preparation year was no problem; Jack quickly arranged tours against the Big East and several other NCAA conferences in the States. Financing the project was another story.

Jack came back from a meeting with a figure for a monthly stipend for each player. Mary Jane recalls: "He asked what I thought. I told him I didn't think the figure met the poverty line. I checked with some people at Kanata Food Cupboard and they told me that the figure, in fact, was below the poverty line."

Several players decided to stay in Europe, so the team played a reduced schedule with a revolving door of players.

"It was crazy," Doc Ryan said, referring to the team's ever-changing roster. "During the tours we would wake up in the morning and Jack would ask me what players were available for a game that night. Guys would fly in for a game or two and then leave, and sometimes we would pick guys who were living in the area just for a game."

On more than one occasion, coach Ryan was pressed into duty as a player.

Not only was Donohue preparing the team for the Olympics, he was also making his final coaching rounds in front of friends and family along the Eastern Seaboard.

"We were playing St. John's University with Lou Carnesecca and just before the game, this scruffy-looking guy with torn jeans and a big beard comes over to our bench and puts his arm around Coach," Ryan said. "I didn't know what to make of it."

The two talked for a minute and then the stranger hugged Donohue and departed as quickly as he had entered.

Donohue turned his attention to the game when Ryan leaned over and whispered, "Coach, who was that?"

Donohue smiled and said it was a former student.

Ryan thought a moment and then asked what the guy did for a living.

"He's a cop," Donohue replied. "He's an undercover narcotics agent and he heard we were in town and just wanted to say hi before he went on a stakeout."

*   *   *   *   *

Qualifying for the Seoul Olympics represented the biggest challenge in Donohue's coaching career. The qualifying tournament for the Americas was held in Montevideo, Uruguay, and the Canadians knew before the competition began that the host country was likely to stand in their way for one of the three Olympic berths awarded to the Americas.

Without Wiltjer and Meagher, the team lacked size and experience inside, but the unexpected return of Romel Raffin helped ease the problem. Raffin had first joined the team in 1974 and was back for one more kick at the can.

Donohue decided that he needed experience in the qualification matches so he raised the ire of many when he brought back the 13-year veteran, a player who had already retired from the national team on two previous occasions.

"Jack had called Tom Bishop and told him that the team needed help at the forward position," Raffin said. "When I heard that, I contacted Coach and asked him if I could tryout and he said sure, but I could tell he wasn't real enthusiastic about it."

After getting permission from the school board where he was employed as a teacher, and the blessing of his wife and family, Raffin showed up at the training camp and played as well, if not better, than any of the other post players. Donohue kept Raffin, who had to pay $90 a day for a substitute teacher to cover his classes back in Calgary.

Donohue's teams had fought some epic battles on Uruguayan soil and they knew that they would be facing hostile fans every time they took to the court. What they hadn't counted on was just how cold the playing venues would be. Montevideo, the site of the pre-Olympic tournament, was below the Equator so the tourney was held during Uruguayan winter, and, at times, it appeared the playing venues and practice sites were unheated.

"We prepared for the cold, but we also expected to be warm inside," Dr. Pipe said. "Guys would come off the floor and bundle up with winter coats. It was funny to see the Puerto Ricans. They would be on the bench with ski jackets, oversized mitts, and caps and it was obvious that they weren't used to wearing such clothing."

Canada got off to a quick start with wins over Venezuela, Mexico, and Argentina before losing the next three games to Uruguay, Brazil and Puerto Rico. Their 3-3 record was good enough to advance to the second round and now they needed one more win to qualify for Seoul. First up was a rematch with Puerto Rico and, this time, the Canadians dominated the game but let it slip through their hands in the dying minutes of the contest. "We had a 15-point lead in the second half but allowed the Puerto Ricans back in the game," Steve Konchalski recalled. "They hit an off-balanced jump shot at the buzzer to win. We were devastated."

As the dejected Canadian players left the court with bowed heads, Konchalski wondered if Donohue's coaching career was coming to a premature end. Canada now faced a must-win game with the host Uruguayan squad, a contest that would decide the third and final

Olympic berth. A loss and Donohue's international coaching career would end on a disappointing note.

"We had a day off before that final Uruguay game and had an early morning practice scheduled," Konchalski said. "As the players dragged themselves on the bus it was easy to see how down and dejected they were. The one question that ran through my mind was: how was Coach Donohue going to bring this team back up and make themselves believe they could win this one last game in a hostile environment?"

"When we got to the gym I found out. Instead of a typical pre-game preparation type of practice with scouting reports, walk-throughs and so forth, Jack put the team through a full hour of 'fun' drills, shooting competitions, dribble tag, with big men competing against the little men. All were designed to put the tough Puerto Rico loss behind us and remind the team of the times we had enjoyed together over the years. By the time we left the practice facility, everyone was laughing and smiling and very upbeat.

"Over the next 24 hours, amazing things began to happen. Players began posting messages to the team on the trainer's hotel room door. Letters and poems appeared expressing how much we cared about each other and how no one could prevent us from achieving our goal of qualifying for one last Olympic Games."

Canada knew they were definitely the away team when they arrived at the stadium and discovered there was no heat in their dressing room. Once the game started, Team Canada not only had to battle a tough Uruguay squad but also deal with a rowdy sold out crowd that literally wanted blood.

And that is exactly what they got!

Canada jumped out to an early lead behind the inspired play of Triano, Pasquale and Hatch. As the game progressed, the determined, disciplined Canadians added to their lead. With just over four minutes to play the crowd, sensing that their heroes were not going to win the game, got ugly. They began to pelt the Canadian bench and players with coins and cans.

Donohue had experienced such treatment before and he urged his players to ignore the chants and the projectiles and concentrate on finishing the Uruguayans in style.

"Remember we are the ones going to the Olympics, they're not," Donohue said during a time-out.

The players listened intently and returned to the court and continued to dominate the play.

"Jack was always able to shut everything out and focus on the task at hand," Hrycak said. "I've never seen anyone doing a better job of staying on track mentally. We were under siege, but he kept everyone focused."

The players and staff on the bench wrapped white towels over their heads to protect themselves from thrown objects, but the players on the court were easy targets.

"One of the coins hit John Hatch in the head and caused a laceration that eventually opened up and started to bleed," Pipe said. "John, with his best Rambo impersonation, spread the blood across his face and on his uniform, clenched his fists and yelled 'Bring it on!'"

Hatch's dramatics was the final push the emotional Canadians needed to secure a victory and one more trip to the Olympics.

Coach D was going out in style.

"Qualifying for the 1988 Olympics was the best coaching job Jack did in Canada," Konchalski stated.

In the hotel that night, the players held a party that included alcohol, the first time they had had a drink in a year.

"We made a pact the year before that we wouldn't drink until the team qualified for the Olympics," point guard Norman Clarke said.

Before the party began, one player admitted that he broke the pact on one occasion.

"He was out with his girlfriend and had a glass of wine with dinner." Clarke said. "We forgave him because he was up front and honest about it, but he had to buy the first round."

Despite the win, the critics back home were out in full force accusing Donohue of staying with older players too long and not giving younger athletes an opportunity. The core of the problem was Donohue's decision to bring back Raffin after the forward had already retired from international basketball twice. Donohue had strong words and advice for the dissenters: "We had just qualified in the toughest environment possible and we were criticized for our personnel. We had the best, more experienced players going to Seoul and someone suggested that we bring younger players to give them experience. I had to explain that Sport Canada didn't consider the Olympics a developmental tournament; that our funding depended on a) whether or not we qualified for the Olympics and b) on how we finished at the Olympics. It wasn't the venue to be giving guys experience."

As the team prepared for Donohue's last hurrah, Raffin supported his coach's personnel decisions in an interview with the *Edmonton Sun's* Cam Cole.

"There are young guys out there who could have been on this team," Raffin said prior to leaving for the Seoul Games. "But we wouldn't have qualified in Uruguay with a different group of guys. You have to be there; you have to have been through it, and played under less than ideal circumstances. We have."

*   *   *   *   *

Distraction was not a problem in Seoul, but a lack of size and depth were. Newspapers back in Canada talked about how the Canadian starting five had an average age of 28, suggesting the team was perhaps too old, but that was actually normal for an Olympic basketball team. Meanwhile, six of the seven players on the bench were playing in their first Olympic competition. Raffin was the biggest starter at 6'9" in a line-up that included Kazanowski (6'8"), Hatch (6'6") Triano (6'4") and Pasquale (6'). The starting five had plenty of experience and certainly were focused, but they didn't match up well inside against teams like the USA, Russia and Yugoslavia.

"It's funny," Donohue noted to Konchalski, "when we don't play well our players are too old; when we win, we are experienced."

Canada prided itself on its ability to shoot the ball but they were no match for their first opponent, Brazil, who prevailed in a shoot-out, 125-109. The Brazilians connected on 15 of 24 shots from beyond the three-point line led by the incomparable Oscar Schmidt. Schmidt, who once scored 46 points against the U.S., led the high-powered Brazilian attack with 36 points. Canadian rookie Wayne Yearwood, playing in his first Olympic game, came off the bench to score 16 points before fouling out late in the game.

Canada was preparing for the next game – against a United States squad that featured David Robinson, Mitch Richmond and Danny Manning – when an old friend walked in on practice.

"Is that a basketball coach or what!?" Al McGuire said as he laid eyes on an unkempt Donohue who was giving last minute instructions to his team.

McGuire was NBC's color commentator for basketball and stopped by to get the goods on the Canadian squad. As he surveyed the team, he noted the Canadians were indeed the smallest squad at the Games.

"Boy, are these guys hurting for size!" he said to no one in particular.

Donohue directed McGuire to Andy Pipe who provided the retired coach a player-by-player analysis of the team.

"Tell me, what do you think your chances are against the U.S. tomorrow?" McGuire asked after Pipe finished his thumb nail sketches of Canada's top players.

Pipe prefaced his comments with a dissertation on how well the Canadians played as a team and the fact that the coaching staff had always devised strong game plans against the Americans.

"I think we have a good chance of keeping the score low and making it a real close game," Pipe told a disbelieving McGuire.

"McGuire didn't say anything but I could tell from his look that he thought I was nuts," Pipe remembered.

Pipe's assessment was more accurate than the good doctor could possibly imagine. The Canadians' game plan of slowing the pace of the game and forcing the ball away from David Robinson worked to near perfection. Canada led 42-40 at halftime and only a late rally enabled the Americans to emerge with a 76-70 win.

"Eli Pasquale was a one-man press break and his ability to dribble through the American press for 40 minutes gave us a chance to win the game," Konchalski said afterwards.

It was a moral victory; but long ago, Donohue had taught his players that you play to win, not to keep the scores close. He remembered how upset he was back at Power Memorial when Xaverian High School was more intent on losing by less than 10 points than by trying to win the game. A loss was a loss and losing to the Americans always stung a little more.

"This game would have meant a lot to this country," Triano said in the locker room after the contest.

The Canadians defeated Egypt for their first win before a 10-point loss to Spain left them in a precarious position. Donohue's tenure as national team coach was coming to a close and, during that time, the club had always advanced to the medal round of a world championship or Olympics. That run was in serious jeopardy. The Canadian team gave their coach one final present when they hung on to defeat China 99-96 as Pasquale drained a game-winning three-pointer with seven seconds remaining in the game to send Canada into the medal round.

Canada drew a taller, more skilled Yugoslavian team, which featured future NBA stars Toni Kukoc, Vlade Divac, Drazen Petrovic and Dino Radja, in the quarterfinals and the height and talent discrepancy was evident as the Yugoslavian team recorded a 95-73 victory.

Canada rebounded to beat Spain 96-91, avenging their first round loss to them in the process, and then met Brazil in a rematch for fifth place. Once again, it was too much Schmidt as Oscar lived up to his reputation as one of the greatest scorers in the history of international basketball by pouring in 48 points to lead Brazil to a 106-90 win.

Just like that, it was over. Unlike Los Angeles, there were no tears or emotional outbursts in the locker room following the final game. The team had played well but simply weren't as talented as the majority of their opponents. Donohue, who had always preached seeing the big picture, was heading back to Canada to spend some time with his family and to begin a new career.

CHAPTER 25

Canada's Coach

The Kanata competitive bantam team was practicing at the Earl of March gymnasium, when an older gentleman entered the gym, and sat on a bench in the corner that provided him a full view as the young athletes moved up and down the court. He watched the practice intently, waved to his grandson, Taylor at the conclusion, and then left as inconspicuously as he entered. It is a scene that is repeated numerous times during the season and the bantam coach doesn't give the man's presence much thought.

It's nice to see a grandfather, who comes out to support his grandson, especially one who doesn't offer unsolicited coaching advice.

Then one day a parent asked Walter Pamic how it feels to have Jack Donohue at your practices.

Jack Donohue?

"Yeah, he is Taylor Sicard's grandfather and he comes to a lot of the practices and games."

The next practice the young coach nervously approached the coaching icon and introduced himself.

"Tell me Coach, you have been watching our practices, what can I do differently?" Pamic inquired.

"I wouldn't change a thing," Donohue said with a smile. "You're teaching the kids the basics. They are getting to run up and down the court and the most important thing is that they are having fun. If young players are having fun, they will keep playing."

Then in typical Donohue fashion the retired coach turned the table on the younger coach. "I want to thank you for coaching these kids. You are doing a great job."

When Jack Donohue decided in 1951 that he was going to make coaching his chosen profession, he began to look at sports from a different perspective. He always took a cerebral approach to the games he played, but now he concentrated on observing other coaches; how they ran practices, handled games and interacted with players. He knew that if he could land a teaching job, it would open up coaching opportunities and he wanted to be ready when a position became available. New York Catholic High School coaches were paid a small stipend, and usually had a reduced class load to compensate for the time they spent with their teams. Successful high school coaches also had the ability to advance to better paying and more prestigious jobs in the college ranks.

When Donohue arrived in Canada twenty years later, he found a completely different scenario. Coaching was a volunteer endeavor, or at best, a part-time occupation. Most university basketball coaches had other responsibilities, while high schools relied on teachers who directed teams out of a love for the sport with little thought of advancing past the high school level. If they did move on to a university position, it often meant a pay cut and loss of job security. The one exception was in junior hockey, a league that was often used as a stepping-stone to coaching in the National Hockey League.

Coaching was not considered a profession by the general populace and there was no formal process to educate young coaches in place. Coaches learned their craft through a process of trial and error or by observing other coaches. As a result, there was a disparity in coaching expertise throughout the country that affected the growth of amateur sport. This fact was recognized by the Task Force on Sport for Canada in 1969, which made several recommendations to improve the status of sport in the country. Among the strongest recommendations were the development of a National Coaches Association; government sponsored coaching clinics and an exchange of methods and techniques between Canadian and international coaches.

Canada, after a poor showing in the Mexico Olympics, was getting serious about sport and expected strong leadership from its small group of elite coaches. And leadership is exactly what they got when they hired Jack Donohue in 1972.

Long before "mentor" became a buzz word, Donohue put the practice into good use; first as a young aspiring coach in New York, then later as the Canadian National Basketball Coach and Technical Director. When he arrived in Canada, the first task at hand was trying to qualify for the Munich Games. Unsuccessful at his first foray into the competitive world of international basketball, Donohue returned to Kanata to look at ways of giving more credibility to the coaching profession.

He attended the CIAU National Championships and gave an open invitation to all coaches to come to the National Team training camps. At the same time, Sport Canada had asked each national sport organization to develop a coaching certification program. In 1974, Donohue toured the country giving certification clinics that would serve as a springboard for the provinces to certify their own coaches. The presentation was short and just covered some basic coaching principles, such as practice planning. It was obvious that a lot more work was needed in the preparation and course material, but the first step was taken. For his part, Donohue traveled from Newfoundland to British Columbia, preaching the gospel and getting people excited about coaching.

Donohue made his presence felt among the Canadian coaching fraternity in 1973, when he took a leadership role during a sport exchange program with Cuba. John Bales, now the executive director of Coaching Association of Canada, accompanied the contingent to the island country as a team manager and saw first-hand how Donohue made a lasting contribution to Canadian sport on that trip.

"Jack came with the women's basketball team and from the beginning his leadership in the Canadian camp was evident," Bales recalled. "He was very assertive and made sure that things, such as gym and game times, were handled in a professional way. He wanted to be treated fairly and spoke up when there was a problem."

Very quickly, the transplanted New Yorker was establishing himself as a patriotic Canadian.

"He really became a very committed Canadian and did a lot for the sport system," Bales said. "He understood coaching, how important it was; he shared and promoted that belief throughout the country."

276

When a more structured certification program was reintroduced after the Montreal Games, Donohue jumped on board. He lobbied to make certification mandatory for university and national team positions, and pushed the concept of coaching as a profession and not just a hobby.

"If your child is playing in a serious high school or university program, they will spend more time in a week with their coach than anyone else, including their teachers and parents," Donohue said. "It is important for that person to be qualified and properly trained. They often have the most influence on our youth, so we'd better make sure that they know what they are doing."

*   *   *   *   *

In 1983, Donohue's role among the coaching fraternity altered when he helped form the Canadian Association of National Coaches, which eventually became the Canadian Professional Coaches Association. He understood as well as anyone, that a coach's career is perilous at the best of times and the time-honored cliché, "coaches are hired to be fired" was true more often than not. He had his share of run-ins with the board of governors at CABA, and discovered that other National Team coaches experienced similar problems. He did not believe it was fair that the roles, and sometimes the fate, of full-time coaches was in the hands of volunteer board members; many of whom were on the board for just a year or two. Instead, he felt that coaches should be reporting to professionals and an incident prior to the 1983 World Student Games spurred him into action.

Two months before the Edmonton Student Games, Basketball Canada fired Don McCrae as the women's national coach and Donohue had seen enough.

"Jack was the coach who, concerned for his colleagues losing their jobs after the 1984 Olympics, began a conversation with a group of us about the need to change the situation," Andy Higgins said in an article in *Coaches Report* following Donohue's death in 2003.

"Jack was not concerned about his own situation. He was, however, deeply concerned that once again career coaches with great records were being summarily dismissed by volunteer boards, most of whom had not been there a couple of years prior and would not be there a year or two hence."

Donohue's idea was to form an association, like doctors or lawyers, which would become a voice for coaches providing them with an organization that would act on their behalf and protect their rights.

"Jack was our leader for the first few years and a key part of the CANC for many more," Higgins said. "I am certain that he was also the first coach to sit in the minister of sport's office to address issues of coaching and the life of a coach in Canada. He was our voice on radio and television and in the newspapers."

Higgins believed that Donohue gained credibility because he was able to take the national team to a new level in a short period of time.

"Like all terrific leaders Jack had a unique way of making people believe in what they can do and he did that in two ways. First, he showed us on the court and then he talked about it and spread the word across the country. In 1983, at the World Student Games, Canada beat a team of future NBA players in the semis and then beat Yugoslavia for the gold medal. I always said that if you took the 12 players from Canada and played 12 one-on-one games against the U.S. team, Canada wouldn't have won a single game. But Jack turned the 12 players into a winning team."

Much of the work that Donohue did in this area and the rights of the coaches for which he fought are now taken for granted.

"As with so many great ideas, they became self-evident and we forget that at one time one person had to care enough to think this and then have the energy and commitment to make the idea a reality," Bales said. "Jack did that for all of us who coach in this country, and all who will in years to come. He truly was the coach's coach."

Bales added that Donohue gave young Canadian coaches an alternative to the stereotype of the loud, overbearing coach who achieved success through fear and intimidation.

"We always had this type of dictatorial screamers; coaches who were control freaks and who achieved success using these methods. But Jack showed that you could be successful using other coaching strategies. He used a style that reflected values that were built on interpersonal relationships, helping the athlete develop as a person. He was so successful with the National Team, that people could see that his approach to coaching was effective."

"Jack was *the* role model for coaching in Canada. His success was based on a deep respect for his players, and incredibly strong interpersonal relationships with everyone associated with the team. He has had an enormous impact on my life, and on countless others in Canadian sport," Bales said.

* * * * *

From the moment Jack Donohue arrived in Canada, he encouraged fellow coaches to succeed and, in the process, he made people feel good about themselves and their chosen profession. He had an open door policy for all National Team tryouts and practices, and if a coach wandered through the gym doors, chances were he would find himself involved in drills, making passes to post players or charting foul shots and rebounds. Through his training camps, Donohue developed a growing number of coaches that would participate in the National Team program.

"I had a passion for coaching, and Jack allowed me to develop it, and without his support I would not have been able to accomplish all the things I did," said Ken Shields.

Shields' coaching accomplishments are legendary. He coached the University of Victoria Vikings to seven National Championships, succeeded Donohue as the National Team coach for five years and is presently a coaching consultant to the Australian Basketball program.

"When I first started coaching, I would drive down to Carleton University in Norm Vickery's Volkswagen and watch training camp, sleeping in the car," Shields recalled. "The camps were like clinics. Jack would bring in great coaches like Tates Locke, Red Sarachek and Lou Carnesecca and, at night, we would go out with them and pick their brains."

When he replaced Donohue as national coach in 1989, Shields was able to get funding for a similar concept.

"We got the CIAU to fund the High Performance Initiative (HPI), a program that paid university coaches to come into training camp and work with Canadian coaches," Shields said. "We'd have guest coaches that would work with our university coaches just like they did under Jack."

* * * * *

Until 1983, coaching certification was left to individual sports to implement and was sport specific. However, the Coaching Association added a theory component to the mix and it was an addition that didn't go over well with a lot of older coaches who were set in their ways.

To show his support for the initiative and to help encourage other coaches to get on board, Jack took the theory course offered on two consecutive weekends.

"Jack felt that he could help promote the certification program, even though he wasn't required to take it," Bales said. "Not only did he show up for the course, but he was an active participant, and contributed like a normal student."

Donohue knew the certification process was a key element in the development of basketball coaches in Canada. His personal involvement in the process sent a message to everyone involved in Canadian sport – certification is important!

Donohue continued to support the Coaching Association in other ways. He was a member of the CAC Board of Governors for ten years, and when the Canadian government declared 1989 the Year of the Coach, the recently retired Donohue agreed to be its spokesperson. While he may have retired from coaching, he remained the profession's most strident supporter. Donohue was in great demand as a speaker and he took advantage of every opportunity to talk about the importance of coaching in Canadian society and the need to improve its status.

Chris Critelli, who played for Donohue at the age of 17 before embarking on a successful playing and coaching career, believes that his greatest contribution to the coaching community was the example he set.

"I told him that I became a coach because of him, and that a day does not go by that I don't think about him and the lessons he taught us," Critelli said.

Critelli holds the rare distinction of being the only player to win a CIAU and a NCAA championship, and also play professional basketball in the States before returning to Canada to assume coaching positions with Brock University and the Canadian National team program.

"I have a picture of Jack on my desk and when I have a problem I ask myself: 'What would he do in this situation?'. He was such a good person and he was always thinking of others."

* * * * *

Jack changed the face of basketball in Canada, but his influence was felt just as strongly in New York, Massachusetts and throughout the world. When Ralph Willard was named the head coach of the Holy Cross Crusaders in 1999, he made a point of singling out Jack Donohue's influence on his own coaching career to the Worcester media.

In international circles, Donohue was not only ranked among the leaders in longevity, but in stature as well.

"People in Canada do not realize the esteem that the Latin and South American countries held for Jack," Rick Traer said.

Traer, a sports consultant who worked in a variety of positions for Basketball Canada for eight years, watched Donohue in action as a volunteer member of COPABA, the governing body for basketball in the Americas.

"When Jack talked, people listened and respected his opinions," Traer said. "He worked hard, very hard after he retired from coaching, to help the National Teams."

"Once, in Argentina, they were holding a clinic for local coaches, and one of the speakers couldn't make it and the organizers asked Jack to fill in. Despite the obvious language problems and the fact that he hadn't had time to prepare, the organizers said he gave the best lecture in the clinic."

Jay Triano, one of the greatest players to ever wear a Canadian uniform and presently an assistant coach with the Toronto Raptors and a former head coach of the Canadian National Team, said that Donohue was the person other National Team coaches looked to for leadership.

"Coach was so far ahead of everyone in the profession, and this was sensed at major tournaments. Whether in Olympic Villages or at international basketball events, no one knew the other coaches, but everyone knew Coach. We, as his players, were the envy of the other athletes."

Bruce Pirnie, now Director of Development Programs for Athletics Canada, remembers being inspired by Donohue as a young basketball and track and field coach in the 1970s.

"Jack stressed the importance of coaches behaving as professionals and he did it in a way that made you feel good about yourself and your sport," Pirnie recalled. "He was Canada's Coach."

CHAPTER 26

God is Good to Dumb Irishmen

Basketball Canada announced a retirement dinner for Donohue in the spring of 1989, eight months after Jack's final coaching appearance at the Seoul Olympics. The venue was the Westin Hotel in Ottawa and the evening turned into a fundraising venture benefiting the Big Brothers and Sisters of Canada and Basketball Canada. The list of guests included members of government, national sport organizations, media, former players, friends and coaches from the United States and Canada, including Red Sarachek, Ted Burns, Freddie "the Spook" Stegman and the president of the Toronto Blue Jays, Paul Beeston.

Converse, an official sponsor of Basketball Canada, arranged to have Julius Erving as the keynote speaker. The two had met years ago when Erving worked for Donohue as a counselor at Friendship Farm. Dr. J had also played college basketball for Donohue's friend Jack Leaman. Erving-led teams played against Holy Cross from 1969 to 1971 before Donohue headed to Canada and Erving to professional stardom.

Erving hadn't followed Donohue's career in Canada and certainly was not the best choice for giving a keynote address about a man he hadn't seen in 20 years. But the NBA superstar talked about the love that was obvious between Jack and his family and Jack and his players. A pronounced born-again Christian, Erving praised Donohue's faith and how it had sustained him through the good and bad times.

The best speech of the night was delivered by Jack's son, John Joe. He started out telling a few jokes but then delivered a heart-warming account of his father's relationship with his family. As he finished, his father rose to give him a kiss while the audience reached for handkerchiefs.

"When I saw the names of the other speakers I decided to go with humor rather than too serious an approach," John Joe remembered. "The other part I recall is that I acknowledged that this was the first time I had the microphone and he had to listen to me!"

Later that year, the Donohues celebrated the wedding of daughter Kathy to Denis Sicard, the first Donohue child to be married. It was truly a case of gaining a son rather than losing their daughter. Denis was an ambitious, outgoing person who was constantly doing odd-man jobs around the Donohue household and supervised several major renovations to the Lismer house.

"My mom always said that if we ever broke up, she was keeping Denis, not me,' Kathy would say.

Two years later, the family celebrated another wedding when Carol married Dan MacIntoish. The wedding was on a Friday night and Mary Jane planned a surprise 60th birthday party for Jack on Sunday. While she had no pretensions about keeping it a surprise Mary Jane figured it was a perfect time since so many friends and relatives were in town for the wedding. What she didn't count on was Jack accepting an out-of-town speaking engagement on the Saturday between the two events and tried to dissuade her husband from accepting the job.

"Think about it, you have all these friends and relatives coming from the States so you will be out late Friday night," Mary Jane reasoned. "On Saturday, you are going to be on the road for six hours, give a speech and come back here tired. It is not going to leave you in very good shape."

As usual, Mary Jane made lots of sense but Jack never liked to say no to a speaking gig and came up with the perfect solution – rent a plane.

"It will take less than an hour to fly there and I can take Teddy Burns and some of the kids with me," Jack said.

"And leave me here to cook and entertain your friends and relatives?" Mary Jane asked.

"If that is what makes you happy, dear."

On Saturday morning, Jack, Teddy, John Joe and his cousin Gene Castelli boarded an executive jet at nearby Carp airport for the 45-minute flight. Gene bought a video camera at Jack's request to film his talk. No sooner had the plane reached cruising altitude that both Jack and Teddy, exhausted from the night before, quickly slouched down in the seats and began to sleep.

Amid the snoring Gene had a brainstorm! He started filming the pair and produced a short film entitled *The Lives of the Fat and Irish*. That night after they returned to Kanata, Gene showed the video to the Donohue extended family of friends and relatives assembled back at the Donohue house. Everyone sat and down and had a laugh at Donohue's expense for a change, but no one enjoyed the film more than Jack.

* * * * *

Donohue was now officially retired from basketball although he continued to lend a helping hand to the basketball community whenever asked. The Donohues still had five children in high school or university and while they had a comfortable lifestyle, Jack needed to continue working as a speaker to make a living. He put the same energy into his second career as he did coaching, the same preparation, and attention to detail, the same dedication to doing a job well and demonstrated the same concern for people.

And he got the same results: Jack Donohue – motivational speaker – was in great demand. With Denis's help, the Donohues put an extension on the house and made an office for Jack Donohue Enterprises above the family garage. The renovations also included a downstairs suite where the Donohues hoped to move Mary Jane's parents.

Mary and Leon Choffin were approaching their 90s and still living in the same Westchester home where Mary Jane grew up. For years, Mary Jane had tried to get Mum and Pops to move to Canada but her mother wanted to stay in familiar surroundings.

However after the passing of his wife at the age of 96, Leon decided to head to Canada to the delight of everyone.

Jack Donohue Enterprises soon became a family business and its clients included government agencies, schools, Fortune 500 companies as well as various retail department chains. Mary Jane would work part-time booking appointments and working out travel logistics while John Joe, himself an aspiring speaker, also helped out. They hired several speakers' bureaus to help procure jobs while Jack and John Joe joined the local Toastmasters clubs. Donohue realized that the majority of work would come from word-of-mouth references and he approached every speech and conference with the knowledge that a good job would bring more work and a bad performance could cost future employment, knowledge he gained through experience.

In 1977, following the Montreal Olympics, he was among an impressive line-up of speakers including Bobby Knight, John Wooden and Al McGuire at a coaching clinic in Boston. Donohue's topic, "Preparing for the Olympics", sounded promising but when he took to the podium in front of over 600 coaches, he soon began to lose his audience. Instead of talking about the on-court preparations, he spent an hour detailing his problems dealing with the CABA. His attempts at humor uncharacteristically failed and the audience slowly filed out of the room.

He wasn't very good and he knew it. For a person who motivated so many people throughout his life, the speech was out of character and he resolved not to let it happen again. And it didn't.

He practiced his speeches, watched others perform their art and was always looking for new ways to improve his act, particularly when he was on the road. It was not unusual for him to go to a local comedy club to see if he could steal a joke or two from an up-and-coming comic. Whenever he and Frank Layden met, they would discuss the ins and outs of public speaking the same way they used to talk about basketball.

He was an exceptional motivational speaker, relating anecdotes about famous people who overcame unbelievable adversity to be successful. He would encourage and challenge his audiences not to allow limitations or barriers affect their productivity. He would stress the importance of teamwork to overcome obstacles and the need for a positive outlook towards every problem.

Mike Keenan brought Donohue to work with the Chicago Black Hawks on goal setting and he was an instant success. As a favor, the team brought Jack in as their special guest for the NHL's all-star which was being played in Chicago in 1992. Jack brought along his son-in-law Denis who had a much greater appreciation for the sport.

"As soon as we got to the game, Jack told me that we would probably be leaving after the first or second period," Denis said. "He had no idea what was going on during the game but he stayed the whole time because he could see I was enjoying it so much."

In between periods, the two men went for a walk when a well-dressed gentleman came up and shook Jack's hand. They talked for a few minutes, shook hands again and departed in different ways.

"He is a great guy and we were on the main table at a charity dinner a few weeks ago," Jack said to his awe-stricken son-in-law. "I know he was a great hockey player but tell me again, what's his name?"

"That was Jean Beliveau," Denis said in amazement.

* * * * *

Donohue always left the audience with two messages. The first was the need to develop, teach and nurture the young; the second was that failure is always present on the road to success. How we handle failure would determine our future success. The messages were always delivered with his patented self-deprecating sense of humor.

"No matter what kind of speech I give, I need to tell jokes," Jack said. "I have three types of speeches: one-liners that I use at banquets, motivational speeches and talks on organization. But even in the serious talks, I should be saying something funny every seven minutes to keep the audience engaged."

For those who coached with Jack the thought of him giving a speech on organization might have seemed to be a stretch. It was the perfect case of "do as I say and not as I do". Jack's everyday life was hardly organized and he was never a detail man in many areas. When he coached his attention to game details was one of his strengths. When Jack walked in front of an audience of businessman or sales people, he would emphasize the importance of organization within their company, and would give concrete ways to improve productivity and communication in the workplace. Certain aspects of his life may have lacked organization but he certainly could teach it.

He was best known as an after-dinner speaker where he would have an entire audience roaring with laughter as he poked fun at politicians, CEOs, and most of all himself. Don Cherry, the former hockey coach and CBC hockey analyst, said that he hated to speak after Donohue because he was just too hard an act to follow.

When he first moved to Canada, Jack liked to remind Canadians, in a thick New York City accent, that "there are two official languages in Canada …unfortunately I don't speak either one particularly well."

When he received a particularly good introduction he would comment that it was the second best introduction he had received that week.

"A few days ago I was speaking in Toronto and the MC didn't show up and I had to introduce myself," he deadpanned.

On another occasion, after a brief intro, Jack told the audience that he had supplied the MC "with a seven page introduction and that's the best he could do."

Everyone was fair game when Donohue was at the mike.

"A lot of you might not realize this but John Smith was quite an athlete in his younger days. In fact, a lot of professional baseball teams scouted him before he went into the textile business. Before the dinner tonight he was telling me that his nickname was 'Home Run Smith' and that is pretty impressive… although I must admit 'Home run' is sort of a strange nickname for a pitcher."

Donohue took pride in the fact that he could be funny without using off-color material and often included his friends and family as fodder for his jokes.

"I want to tell you people that this is a really nice hotel we are staying at and I am pretty sure that they have fixed those security problems they had last year. It was a year ago this week that my wife and I were staying here and someone broke into our room while I was speaking to a group just like this one and this crook stole my wife's American Express card. We haven't reported the stolen card because the guy who took it is spending less than my wife."

He would relate a conversation with a friend to get his point across about the need for commitment. "I was having breakfast with Jack Cooper, the president of Cooper Canada one time and I told him that I was having trouble distinguishing between involvement and commitment," Donohue said. "So Jack Cooper says 'you sports people ought to know the difference between commitment and involvement for goodness sakes.'"

"But I said they seemed to be the same to me, so he asked what I was having for breakfast. I told him that was easy: I was having the same as he was, bacon and eggs."

"Listen up," Cooper said, "the chicken was involved in your breakfast, but the pig was committed.

* * * * *

Donohue was constantly looking for new ways to break the ice with an audience.

"You know if you are connecting in the first minute…if you're not, you are in for a long night," he said.

Jack was the MC for the Vanier Cup awards dinner honoring Canada's top university football players when a well-known guest started to heckle from the audience.

"Excuse me, but I like to work alone," Donohue said to the heckler after a rude comment.

A few minutes, later the heckler struck again but this time Jack ignored it realizing that the man had too much to drink. But when the third interruption came a minute later Donohue put the man in his place.

"Ladies and gentlemen excuse my friend in the audience but you have to understand – that's what happens when first cousins marry."

The man kept quiet the rest of the evening.

Whenever possible, he would make his family part of his story. When he tried to emphasize the importance of keeping everything in its proper perspective he would take a folded piece of paper from his jacket pocket and show it to the audience.

"This is a letter from my daughter Carol who is away at college at Queens University."

He would then read a series of harrowing events that Carol was recounting to her parents.

'There was a fire in the dorms but my boyfriend broke my fall from the second floor window… the doctors think I should be able to walk within a few months and the skin grafts are going well…luckily I was able to move into my boyfriend's trailer…"

The list of mishaps continues until she mentions that she might not be able to get married before the baby is born. Donohue would then read the last line in the letter.

"Mom and Dad, there was no fire, no hospital, no boyfriend or baby but I got an F in my last Business test and I wanted to make sure that you kept everything in perspective."

As the audience laughed, Donohue held up the fictitious letter and bellowed "This is a young lady who understands perspective."

"It started out with Carol and then Marybeth and finally Maura," Mary Jane said. "People who knew the family and heard the story would call up the house and ask if me if the story was true and I would have to explain that no, it was simply Jack's way of getting his point across."

He often referred to Mary Jane as a religious cook because she served "burnt offerings." Shortly after retiring from Basketball Canada, he was speaking to company executives when he explained how great it was to be able to spend more time with his family and at the same time delivered another message about perspective.

"The best thing about being retired from coaching is that I now have time to help my family out when there are problems at home," he said in a speech in 1991. "It was hard before because when I was coaching I wasn't home that much. So, the other day, my son Bryan brought home a report card and it wasn't good but I can help the situation now because I'm home.

"Bryan shows me his report card and his marks are F, F, F, F and D-. I take one look at the report card and I said to Bryan, 'This is not good but I am an educator and can analyze this and see what the problem is. It is obvious that you are spending too much time on one subject.'"

But the best jokes were always directed at himself. When he received an award or was credited for the success of the National Team or a business project, he would divert the praise by stating that 'God is good to dumb Irishmen'. When friends or newspapermen visited the house for the first time, Jack would leave a copy of his book, "All I Know About Basketball" within sight. At some time during the visit, the unsuspecting guest would ask about the book, a handsome hard cover edition with Jack's picture on the cover and a description of his life's accomplishments on the back.

"It's not much, just a collection of everything I learned about basketball during the last 30 years," Donohue would say as he handed the book over for inspection. He would then quietly go into the kitchen as his guest thumbed through 350 blank pages!

* * * * *

The town of Almonte, located 45 minutes west of Ottawa, is a quaint town that features restored buildings and a charm not often seen in North America in the 21st century. It was originally settled by Scots, English and Irish, who worked in many of the city's textile mills.

Daniel Shipman ran the town's first successful mill in the 1850s and in the ensuing years, other businesses sprang up along the Mississippi River, located in eastern Ontario. Almonte, which was named for a Mexican general and diplomat, was soon dubbed "The Manchester of North America" because of the proliferation of textile mills within its boundaries. In the first half of the 20th century, the mills provided steady employment and job security, but by the 1950s stiff foreign competition began to force the closure of the mills. The last mill ceased operations in the 1980s and was converted into condominiums with a splendid view of the river.

The town's main street is a handsome boulevard housing two-story buildings, many of which go back to the prosperous days of the mills and there are still several farms on the outskirts. It has become a destination point for many young professionals looking to escape city life. It was also home to the Peterson's Ice Cream shop, a family-run business that attracted customers from the Ottawa Valley who would embark on a long car ride to sample the home-made ice cream. Peterson's shut down its operation and has since relocated but the town of Almonte still draws visitors to visit the birthplace of two famed Canadians educators – Tait McKenzie and James Naismith.

McKenzie has been called the father of Canadian physical education while Naismith earned world recognition as the inventor of basketball. Naismith's ancestors were among the multitudes of Scottish immigrants to settle near the junction of the Mississippi and Indian Rivers during the 19th century. Naismith was orphaned at the age of nine and was raised by an uncle. He was educated in a one-room schoolhouse where he was instructed in reading, writing, arithmetic, advanced mathematics, Latin and other subjects. After graduation from high school, Naismith moved to Montreal where he obtained a physical education degree from McGill University and a religion degree from Presbyterian College. In 1891, he accepted a position teaching Physical Education at Springfield College in Massachusetts. As part of his duties he was given the task of introducing a new indoor game in 1891. He was given two main guidelines – make it fair for all players and free of rough play.

Naismith analyzed the games of the day (rugby, lacrosse, football, soccer, hockey and baseball) and made several observations that helped him devise the game of basketball. First, he chose a soccer ball as his first basketball and then disallowed running with the ball. He noticed that there was too much jostling and rough play in the defense of the goal, net or goal line in the other games and decided to place the goal overhead where it couldn't be guarded. This posed a new problem, since this was the first game with the goal above the plane of the playing area. How would they shoot to score? Remembering back to a game he played back in Almonte called Ducks on a Rock; Naismith incorporated an arching lob form of shooting as a method of getting the ball into peach baskets hung from the walls of the gymnasium for his new game Basket Ball. It wasn't long before the new game was being played on six continents.

When the CABA decided to establish a Canadian Basketball Hall of Fame it did not have a physical site for the new shrine but that did not stop the organization from inducting its first members in 1978. The group included Percy Page, Noel MacDonald Robertson and Dr. Naismith himself. Page, a Rochester native, coached the legendary Edmonton Grads, a women's senior team that posted an incredible 502-20 record over a 25-year span. Robertson was the star of that team and was voted the outstanding female player of the first half century.

The Hall of Fame had its first members but no place to call home. The CABA had tentative plans to place the Hall of Fame in Etobicoke, an up-scale area in Toronto, but changed its mind when Charley Kitts requested that the Board consider Almonte. Kitts was a member of the Almonte-based Naismith Foundation and his proposal to set up the Hall of Fame in Naismith's hometown received strong backing from Ruby Richman, the CABA president. Almonte was designated as the future home of the Canadian Basketball Hall of Fame.

Donohue was selected to the Hall of Fame as a coach four years after his retirement, and his inscription credits him with the promotion of basketball in Canada during his tenure as the National Team Coach from 1972 until 1988. Strangely, there is no mention of his four consecutive Olympic qualifications or the gold medal performance in the 1983 Student Games in Edmonton. At the time of his retirement, he was Canada's longest serving National Team Coach, a feat not likely to ever be duplicated in any team sport.

Before and after his induction, Donohue took an active role in promoting the Hall of Fame and he was a strong supporter of establishing a permanent site in Almonte. In 1988, he was named the Hall's honorary president, a position he held for 12 years.

He pushed for induction of staff members Ed Brown and Steve Konchalski and saw 17 of his former players inducted into the Hall. At one point, a farmhouse was moved to the Naismith property with the hope of making the house and property the permanent home for the Hall of Fame. But while memberships in the Hall were increasing, disagreements within the organization paralyzed efforts and money woes forced the foundation to sell the farmhouse which is now classified as a historical site.

The Hall of Fame was moved to another historic building, the old Almonte Town Hall, where the inductees' plaques adorn a second story hallway. The building itself is charming but the space allotted to basketball is woefully insufficient. There is much debate over the future of the Hall of Fame but little doubt of the contributions its members have made to Canadian basketball.

* * * * *

As the centennial of the invention of basketball drew near, Charley Kitts and Donohue came up with a unique way to promote the anniversary. It began when Kitts ran into a former postal worker at the Ottawa Airport.

"I was changing planes when I ran into Richard McCorkell who told me that the Postal Office was looking for new ideas for stamps and if I had any ideas it would be a good time to pitch them."

Kitts did have an idea, a stamp commemorating the 100th anniversary of James Naismith's invention of basketball. He also had the perfect man to help sell the stamp – Jack Donohue. Donohue quickly embraced the idea and accompanied Kitts when they met with Canada Post officials.

"They said it was a good idea but didn't think it was feasible because we needed a sponsor that was willing to pay more than $250,000 to have the stamp printed," Kitts said. "When we replied that we felt that we could come up with a sponsor, Canada Post asked for a list of names of potential sponsors, saying they would take care of contacting them. That request ended the meeting."

Neither Donohue nor Kitts wanted to put the project into the hands of bureaucrats who didn't see the importance of promoting basketball's centennial.

"About a week later we received a phone call saying that we could go and try and secure a sponsor but from the tone of the voice at the other end of the phone, it was obvious that they didn't think we would be able to get the funding," Kitts said. "We arranged to go to Toronto and met with prospective sponsors and within two days we signed The Sports Network (TSN) as the corporate sponsor for the Naismith stamp," Kitts recalled.

Donohue never gave up his idea of establishing a professional league in Canada where national team players and hopefuls could play in the winter instead of trekking to Europe, Asia, and Latin America in order to prepare for the next Olympics or World Championships. He nearly got his goal fulfilled in 1994 when Ted Septien contacted him about forming a pro circuit in Eastern Canada. Septien was a former owner of the Cleveland Cavaliers and co-founder of the Global Basketball League, a professional league that lasted less than two years in the United States. Septien wanted Donohue to be the commissioner of the new league but in reality, the Cleveland businessman would be the boss and everyone involved knew that. Donohue was willing to promote the league but wasn't interested in any day-to-day activities. He liked Septien a lot, appreciated his business acumen but Donohue was too busy speaking and suggested Kitts for Stepien's front man in Canada.

"We had franchises ready to go in Moncton, Halifax, and Montreal." Kitts said. "Ted was very organized and knew what he was doing but he was also the reason why the league never got going."

Septien wanted to inundate the league with NBA wannabes and pay them a flat fee of $200 a week.

"I told them the government wouldn't let us do it that way, that we needed to pay minimum wage and withhold taxes," Kitts explained. "Ted said the Canadians were crazy but that killed the deal."

The league never became a reality but, the following year, professional basketball came to Canada and Donohue became a part of it. The NBA granted franchises to the Toronto Raptors and Vancouver Grizzlies and the Grizzlies GM Stu Jackson was quick to offer Donohue a position as Director of International Relations and Canadian Player Development. Over the years, Donohue turned down overtures from pro teams but the Grizzlies job was a perfect fit. He would work part-time giving speeches and represent the team at various functions. At age 64, he was back in the game but on his own terms.

"Contributing to the promotion and development of basketball at all levels is an essential part of the Grizzlies and Jack will be an important part of our work in this area," Jackson said.

The job was tailor-made for the former coach who basically served as a good-will ambassador touring the country and doing what he did best – talking to groups about basketball and succeeding in life.

CHAPTER 27

A Friend in Need

D onohue arrived at the trendy Vancouver restaurant at the appointed hour but didn't see his luncheon guest anywhere and decided to take a table in the no smoking area facing the waterfront. He was in town to give a speech and had arranged to meet Pat Hickey, the sports editor of the *Vancouver Sun*, for lunch. The pair enjoyed getting together and discussing the problems of the sporting world and inevitably their conversation led back to the New York basketball scene of the early 60s.

Hickey had attended Regis High School in Manhattan's East Side at the same time Jack was coaching Power Memorial on the West Side. Regis was a private scholarship school run by the Jesuits that prided itself on the academic achievements of its graduates while Donohue was establishing a standard of excellence with the Power Memorial basketball teams. Pat arrived 10 minutes late and was greeted by Donohue's usual upbeat demeanor.

"Hey chief, how is everything going?" He was taken back for a few moments by Hickey's unexpected reply. "Not that great, I've just been fired," he said glumly.

The announcement of bad tidings certainly surprised Donohue but he quickly rebounded with a classic line. "Well this could be a good thing," he said with an earnest expression on his face.

"I've been married for less than a year – my wife has just transferred to Vancouver from Ontario – we are moving into a new house in Whistler – a house that we can no longer afford – how can this possibly be a good thing?" Hickey asked.

They spent the next hour going over career changes, changes that Pat had never considered. Donohue constantly reminded Hickey that he had untapped resources within himself and that many men older than he, had successfully changed careers. By the end of the session, Donohue had given him a dozen different career options, none of which he followed up on. More importantly, he had Pat feeling good and confident about himself by the time they parted company. Within a day, Pat was back working, this time for a Toronto newspaper and later that year he was hired as sports editor for the *Montreal Gazette*.

"There isn't a better person to be with the day you get fired," Hickey would later remark.

Donohue loved to talk and hold court with friends or casual acquaintances but even more than that, he enjoyed helping people who were experiencing a difficult time.

It began when he volunteered his services for the St. Barnabas CYO teams and continued at Tolentine and Power where he was more than just a coach and a teacher. For many students, he became a father figure, a counselor and later, a friend who was available with an encouraging word or bit of advice.

"I was another one of Jack's boys who he impacted in a tremendous way," said Bobby Erickson, a star basketball and baseball player at Power. As a result of Donohue's guidance Erickson not only received a college degree but became an officer in the United States Air Force and later, a commercial pilot.

"Jack was a father figure who used to call my grandmother up and check on me to get my homework done and made sure I wasn't going out at night. Coach Donohue was a great coach but his biggest influences to me was not on the basketball court. He gave me direction, goals and opportunity to use the Power experience as a stepping stone in life. I never considered college an option, didn't have the money or the inclination to make academics important in my life but Coach D changed that. He planted seeds all the time and made sure I was making progress. I have had a wonderful life and I can say that he was my biggest influence. He was a great coach but most of all a great person."

Sometimes it was a simple pat on the back or words of encouragement and other times he would slip a few bucks to a friend experiencing tough times.

"A lot of people don't realize that whenever Jack took a trip across the country, he would always make a side trip to visit a friend who was down on his luck or experiencing trouble," Dan Pugliese said. "He helped so many people, and did it without anyone knowing about it."

* * * * *

When Ed Brown, the national team manager, first told Donohue in the spring of 1982 that he had cancer, the normally upbeat coach was devastated. Brown had always been a picture of vitality and his positive demeanor even surpassed that of the eternally optimist head coach. The two had grown close over the years and, whenever Brown was in the Ottawa area, he was a fixture at the Donohue household and a favorite with the kids. Each time he visited the house, he told Kathy that they were going to get married when she got older.

When he heard the news that there was no cure for Brown's malady, Donohue sought to ease the pain. "How can I help you?" Donohue asked point blank. "I have had one goal since I joined this team – to participate in the Olympics," Brown replied.

"Don't worry, we will be there together," Donohue told him.

The Olympics were more than two years away and the doctors didn't believe Brown had that much time left. Donohue lacked the power to restore his friend's health but he resolved to do everything possible to keep his dream alive. He knew that Brown was denied a chance to go to the Olympics once before when Canada boycotted the Moscow Olympics shortly after the team qualified for the 1980 Games. With each passing day, Brown's ability to function as team manager lessened but Donohue never thought of replacing him. Bruno Carvecchio was brought in to help with the managerial responsibilities during the '82 training camp and Brown traveled with the team to Knoxville and Cali. It was obvious that he wasn't physically up for the job but outwardly he maintained the same cheerful disposition while the staff and players pitched in to assist him when he made mistakes. His chances of remaining alive for two more years were slim, at best, but Donohue wasn't going to be the person to take Brown's dream away after it had been snatched away once before with the Moscow boycott.

Brown finished the summer and headed back to his beloved Newfoundland where his condition slowly deteriorated. He died that winter and Donohue, Mary Jane and Kathy traveled to St. John's for the funeral. Donohue delivered an emotional eulogy praising a man who did so much for others, a man very much like himself. Brown had passed away but he was not forgotten by his friends. Donohue placed a picture of Brown on the dresser in the coaches' dormitory room at the Los Angeles Olympics as a tribute and reminder of Brown's dedication to the National Team. "You couldn't come in or out of the room without seeing Ed's picture," Steve Konchalski said. "It was nice knowing that he was there in spirit." Donohue had kept his promise and brought that spirit to the Olympics.

* * * * *

Every time Kathy Donohue and her husband Denis Sicard would visit the Donohues' home in Kanata, he would hand Denis a stack of letters to mail. Whether he was home or on the road, Jack made it a point to touch base with friends and associates, dropping a simple line of encouragement or a making a phone call to see how they were doing. He felt it was important to keep lines of communication open with other coaches, friends old and new, as well as business contacts. Unlike many people, he preferred to talk with people who were struggling rather than ones who were sitting comfortably at the top.

"Every one talks to the guy who has just won or whose business is going well," Donohue explained to Denis. "But it is the guy who is struggling, who has just lost a big game or whose business is in a slump that needs to hear from his friends."

That's what he did on a daily basis, as he picked up the morale of those who had fallen on tough times, people who needed a helping hand to get back on their feet and not a kick in the butt.

When news of Donohue's illness became public, Jacques Martin, the coach of the Ottawa Senators, talked publicly about the time the retired coach contacted him during a particularly rough time. Martin had taken the Senators into the upper echelon of the National Hockey League but was constantly criticized in the local media for the team's failures in the playoffs. It was during one of these times when Donohue made an effort to contact the coach and offer his support.

"I first met Jack when I was coaching with the Chicago Black Hawks," Martin said. "He worked with the players and coaches and did an exceptional job. He was very good at motivating people. Later, when I joined the Senators he made it a point to stay in touch and always had a word of encouragement when things weren't going well."

Martin and Donohue would meet once or twice a month for breakfast and just talk about coaching. During one playoff run, the team retreated to Montebello prior to the playoffs and Martin asked Donohue to come and talk to the team. That same year, the Senators reached a new plateau in their short NHL history as they advanced to the Eastern Conference finals. The team was once again the talk of the town, this time in a positive light. Martin had suddenly transformed himself into a coaching genius with everyone in sight jumping on the Ottawa Senator bandwagon. As the team prepared for the Eastern Conference finals against the New Jersey Devils, Kathy Donohue asked her father if he was going to call Martin and congratulate him.

"No," her father replied. "He doesn't need it right now when everyone else is calling him and is in his corner. The time to call is when the person is down and no one is supporting him. That's when people need a phone call and a pat on the back."

Donohue also provided support to a former player who would later become one of the more successful coaches in the NCAA. When Ralph Willard graduated from Holy Cross in 1967, he was drafted into the Army and received orders to go to Vietnam.

"I had just finished basic training when I received an unexpected but very encouraging letter from Coach Donohue," Willard recalled. "He reminded me that I had been planning for the army during my days at Holy Cross and that the leadership qualities I learned while playing at Holy Cross were the qualities I would use in the army. Holy Cross was always about seeing the big picture and coach Donohue was great at that. The letter meant a lot to me."

Willard was spared a trip to Vietnam when the Paris Peace Talks signaled the end of the conflict but it was during his army days that Willard realized how much he missed basketball. After his discharge, he spent a year as an assistant coach at the Merchant Marine Academy before returning to his former high school, St. Dominic's in Oyster Bay,

New York in 1976. It was the start of a coaching career that would include stints at Kentucky, Western Kentucky, the New York Knicks and finally as the 20th head coach at Holy Cross College. When he returned to Worcester, Willard pointed to Donohue's genuine concern for people and his ability to instill character among his players as traits that he admired the most about his former coach.

*　*　*　*　*

Mary Jane and Jack always stressed to their children that people should be judged by their personality and actions, and not by their occupation or material possessions.

It was a point literally brought home one Sunday evening when Jack showed up for dinner with Darryl. Darryl was a porter at the Ottawa Airport, a man who did his job conscientiously with dignity and a pleasant outgoing personality. Jack took an instant liking to the man and whenever he flew into the Ottawa Airport, he sought Darryl to take care of his bags. Over the years, the pair developed a relationship and would talk about the National Team's performance, family and anything else that came to mind. Donohue described Darryl as a friend and although the two men appeared to have little in common, Jack made a point to find out more about the man, his family and finally brought the man home for Sunday dinner.

Of course bringing guests to Sunday family was commonplace at the Donohue home. Every Sunday before leaving church, Jack would invite the parish priests at St. Isadore's for dinner and it wasn't long before Father Gerry became a regular fixture at the dining table, but he would also extend the same courtesy to total strangers.

"We would be out eating in a restaurant and Dad would see someone eating alone and invite them to join us at the table," Kathy said. "He said no one should be eating out by themselves."

Donohue had a long-standing rule that he would not desert his friends when they were in trouble. He would never condone bad behavior – not from his team, family or friends – but he would offer support when someone he knew was in trouble. It began back at Tolentine when he would spend extra time with students who suffered from abuse at home or had trouble with alcohol or drugs. He would talk to the kids about the choices they needed to make and would often offer his father's home as a temporarily refugee from their daily problems. On at least two occasions, he enlisted the help of Detective McLaughlin, the father of Walter, Frank and Tom, to intercede on behalf of team members who got in trouble with the law.

"My father was a law-and-order guy," Walter McLaughlin said. "He knew Jack Donohue and knew that the players weren't getting off if they were placed in Jack's custody. Jack would, and did, discipline them."

On more than one occasion, Donohue served as a character witness when friends and associates found themselves in trouble with the law. When two of Jack's Canadian friends were sent to jail for white collar crime, Donohue remained friendly without condoning their actions. He kept in touch with each man during their respective incarcerations, accepting collect phone calls and offering encouragement and support. Donohue didn't agree with either man's illegal actions, but he wasn't going to turn his back on them when they needed his support the most.

*   *   *   *   *

Donohue was always penning a note to those experiencing trouble and the correspondence knew no boundaries, from sport figures to former student to politicians. He once wrote to Marv Levy, at the time the head coach of the Montreal Alouettes, and offered to help Johnny Rodgers who was having trouble catching passes. Levy replied that Donohue would be a big help if he could teach Rodgers to either "a) keep his eyes open when the ball is thrown, or b) keep his mouth shut after he drops it."

Donohue's public speaking and profile in Canadian media allowed him to develop relationships with many politicians, government officials and more importantly a succession of sport ministers. Still he was surprised one day to receive a call from the Prime Minister's office requesting his and Mary Jane's presence at Rideau Hall for dinner with Pierre Trudeau. Mary Jane stayed in Kanata to look after the kids while Jack took a government limousine and dined alone with the Prime Minister.

"He was very good and it was obvious that he was prepped by his staff," Donohue said afterwards. "He talked about the sports scene and the basketball team and he asked about Mary Jane. It was a nice evening."

Donohue always shied away from talking publicly about politics but he had a much warmer relationship with Trudeau's successor, Brian

Mulroney. Their paths would cross at charitable events and the two Irishmen took a liking to each other.

"We were at a charity softball and Jack was the umpire," Denis Sicard recalls. "Brian Mulroney would ground out but Jack would always call him safe."

Donohue received invitations for luncheons honoring Queen Elizabeth II and Soviet leader Mikhail Gorbachev.

"Jack didn't want go to the luncheon for Queen Elizabeth but I told him that I didn't think he had the option to decline," Mary Jane said. "They invite you, you have to go. He went and as usual had a great time."

Mary Jane and Jack were sitting at their table during the Gorbachev affair when Mulroney and the Gorbachevs stood up and began to exit the dining room to the sound of applause. Mulroney made a short detour to where Donohue was sitting, patted him on the back and said, "Not bad for a couple of dumb Irishmen."

When Mulroney's approval ratings began to plummet at the end of his second term as Prime Minister, Donohue sent him an encouraging note on the quality of leadership.

In a written reply, Mulroney thanked Donohue and added "I appreciate your comments on leadership and it certainly helps to hear it from others now and then. Occasionally, I get the chance to see your program on television. How would you like to exchange popularity ratings? With best wishes, Brian Mulroney"

CHAPTER 28

Heroes and Legends

During his travels across the Canadian landscape Donohue became aware that there was a need for heroes in his adopted country. Not the comic book variety or those seen defeating unbeatable odds in the movies or on TV and certainly not the highly paid professional athletes who often acted as if they were superior to the rest of society simply because of their athletic ability.

His heroes were ordinary people who overcame obstacles and disabilities to reach extraordinary goals. In his numerous meetings with his players, he would explain how Gandhi rose to power in a most unconventional way and defeated the British Empire through non-violent means. He would talk about Albert Einstein who overcame the stigma of being called an idiot by a grade school teacher to become one of the 20th century's greatest thinkers.

Donohue carried those same messages that he delivered to his players to schools and corporate boardrooms, preaching that everyone had the ability to make a difference.

In 1980, he became aware of a real live Canadian hero, an amputee named Terry Fox.

Fox was diagnosed with a rare form of bone cancer, steogenic sarcoma, while a student studying kinesiology. As a result, his right leg had to be amputated six inches above his knee. Fox spent little time feeling sorry himself and during his recovery, he developed an idea –a run across the country to raise awareness and funds for cancer research. Fox set his sights on crossing the country and began his "Marathon of Hope" run on April 12th 1980 in St-Johns, Newfoundland.

In the beginning, Fox drew little attention, but as time passed, his campaign gained momentum as donations began to steadily roll in. On September 1, 1980, in Thunder Bay, Ontario, after 143 days and 5,373 kilometers, cancer was discovered in his lungs and Fox was forced to stop his incredible run. It was during his Marathon of Hope, averaging 43 km a day through six provinces, that he inspired a nation, including Jack Donohue.

Terry Fox passed away on June 28, 1981, one month before his 23rd birthday.

His dream to collect $1 from every Canadian was soon realized and by the year 2006, the Terry Fox Marathon of Hope, which is held annually in 60 countries around the world with thousands of participants, had raised an estimated $400 million for cancer research. For his heroic efforts and perseverance, a mountain in British Columbia was named after him and he was made a Companion of the Order of Canada. His legacy has been preserved through numerous awards, movies, television specials and the annual Terry Fox Run.

Donohue used Fox as an example of a person who achieved greatness in spite of a tremendous handicap, a person who continued to inspire and help the fight against cancer long after losing his own personal battle with the disease. But Donohue did more than just preach about Fox's heroics, he took an active part in continuing Fox's legacy after his untimely death.

"For 18 years, Jack Donohue would come from Ottawa to Toronto to be the Master of Ceremonies for our main fundraiser – the Great Valentine Gala," Vim Kochher said. "He never took a cent for speaking or expenses. When we tried to give him money he would just give it back to us. He paid everything out of his own pocket. He insisted on paying his dues."

Donohue was later asked to serve on the selection committee for the Terry Fox Hall of Fame and once again he paid for all his expenses to Toronto for meetings.

"He impressed everyone on the selection committee with his dedication and once again he refused to take any expenses for his work or travel," Kochher said. "In charity, it is not how much you raise but how much you have after paying your expenses. When he was in town he would take my son to baseball and basketball games. Jack Donohue was a special person."

* * * * *

Jack never had the opportunity to actually meet Fox but that was not a case of another one of his personal heroes, Rick Hansen.

Hansen was another normal teenager growing up in his hometown of Port Albemi, British Columbia when a truck accident left him a paraplegic at the tender age of 15 years. He spent his 16th birthday in a hospital dealing with the fact that he would not be able to walk again. He had played high school basketball before the accident, turned on to the sport by the success of the national team and its head coach.

"What Jack Donohue did for this country was inspirational to me," Hansen said. "I saw the impact that he had on people like Billy Robinson and Jay Triano and was impressed with how passionate he was about Canadian sport."

Hansen had heard Donohue talk about overcoming obstacles and now he would use basketball to overcome the biggest obstacle of his life – paralysis. After a difficult transition period, Hansen began to see his situation not as a handicap but rather a challenge to overcome and refocused his athletic abilities to master wheelchair sports. He was an athlete and would use his athletic ability to restore his self-esteem and give purpose to his life. He began competing in wheelchair volleyball and basketball in 1976, the same year the National Basketball Team finished fourth at the Montreal Olympics.

"In those days, to compete in the Canadian Wheelchair Championships you had to compete in at least five events," Reg McClelland, director of Canadian Wheelchair Basketball said. "So Rick played wheelchair basketball, ran marathons and competed in other track and field events."

Hansen and McClelland were teammates on several Canadian basketball championship teams but eventually Hansen began to narrow his focus on marathons, winning nineteen international wheelchair marathons, including three world championships, and competing for Canada in the 1984 Olympics in Los Angeles. The following year, motivated by his success and a desire to make a difference in how people with disabilities were perceived, he embarked on the record-setting "Man in Motion World Tour". Along the way, he motivated others to pursue their own dreams while raising over $148 million for the fight against spinal cord injuries, monies that was used for research, awareness and rehabilitation.

Hansen soon found himself in demand as a motivational speaker as he shared his remarkable story and challenged others to make a difference. Donohue and Hansen teamed up as a broadcast team on cable telecasts of the Canadian Wheelchair Basketball Championships and the pair continued to be an inspiration to each other in the years to come.

In Hansen, Donohue saw not a man in a wheelchair but a true international hero and held him as an example to Canadians that everyone is capable of doing great things if they have the proper attitude and resolve.

* * * * *

Jack Donohue had become a media star in Canada – he was a regular on a TSN panel show called *Sports Talk* along with veteran sportscaster John Wells, player agent Bill Watters and Paul Beeston, the president of the Toronto Blue Jays. He provided color commentary for basketball games for both CBC and TSN and wrote a weekly column for the *Ottawa Sun* newspaper.

His sense of humor and ability to put sports in its proper perspective was refreshing and enabled him to build a loyal audience. However Donohue's talents were not truly utilized until 1991 when he teamed with producer Tom Aziz in a weekly television series called *Donohue's Legends*.

When Aziz first proposed the idea to Donohue, the coach saw the series as a vehicle to send a powerful message to the Canadian public. The two men hit it off right away and their professionalism was evident in the episodes that aired over a two-year period.

"The 40 shows we did together was the best professional experience of my career," Aziz said. "You can not fool the camera and Jack's honesty, integrity and genuine likeability is what made the series work."

Each segment was a half-hour show in which the retired coach went on location to interview some of the greatest athletes and teams in North America. But unlike similar shows that concentrated on athletic performances, Donohue focused on the athlete as a person, selected people who were not only great athletes but who also possessed strong character traits.

The show gave him an opportunity to go one-on-one with athletes whom he had befriended over the years or had admired from a distance. He also showed that he now understood that hockey was and will always be Canada's number-one sport as many of the segments were devoted to hockey celebrities or Stanley Cup winning teams. One episode chronicled the glory days of the Toronto Maple Leafs and there was a two-part piece on the Montreal Canadiens. He profiled Maurice Richard, Gordie Howe, Bobby Orr and Wayne Gretzky, hockey greats that he had met on the banquet circuit.

On the basketball side, he did episodes on Julius Erving, John Wooden and Kareem Abdul-Jabbar. There were shows highlighting Olympic athletes as well as TV personality Don Cherry, jockey Ron Turcotte, former NFL great Jim Brown and TV star Chuck Connors who was a two-sport professional athlete prior to his acting days.

The episode with Connors was one of Donohue's favorites because it allowed him to touch base with an athlete that he had admired as a youngster and also to fulfill a life long dream of playing a cowboy in front of a camera.

"Jack liked the Connors episode because it allowed him to be an actor for the opening scene and he really enjoyed that," Aziz said. "It was in the middle of the winter and we were spending several days in sunny California so Jack and the crew were in good moods and that was reflected in the final product."

There was an instant connection between the Brooklyn-born Connors and the Yonkers native and the pair soon became friends. Connors was a baseball/basketball star who played at Seton Hall University before joining the NBAs Boston Celtics and signing a contract with the Brooklyn Dodgers. He played briefly with the Celtics before concentrating on baseball. He bounced around in the minor leagues for several years before he got his break when he was sent to the Los Angeles farm club in the Pacific Coast League. Soon, his good looks caught the eyes of several movie producers who suggested that he give up baseball for an acting career. He appeared in small roles in several movies but it wasn't long before the Connors was a legitimate TV star – first in the *Rifleman* and later in *Branded*.

Donohue began the Connors segment dressed in a poncho and wearing a 10-gallon hat. He sported a grubby beard, had a cigar hanging from his mouth and carried a six-shooter, a villainous looking creature right out of a Sergio Leone western. As he walked down a deserted street town, he talked about the upcoming gun battle. Then as the music intensified, Donohue came to a stop and prepared to draw his gun as the camera switched to Connors' trademark opening scene from the *Rifleman* where he fires repeated rifle shots into the camera.

One night after the day's shooting was completed, Jack mentioned to Connors that Mary Jane was a fan of his TV shows and asked for an autographed picture. It was late at night but Connors insisted on calling her to verify the story.

"I received a call from a woman who asked me to hold for Chuck Connors and I was sure it was Jack playing a trick on me," Mary Jane said.

After listening for a few seconds Mary Jane realized that she actuality talking to the TV star.

"He told me that he wasn't going to sign the picture for me unless I promised to hang in on the bedroom wall, and I said 'Heck, I'm putting it under my pillow'."

Donohue's warmth was also evident in the Wayne Gretzky episode. He had first met Gretzky when the Great One was still a teenager and the pair took an instant liking to each other.

"I was 17 when we first met and we would talk anytime we got together for a banquet," Gretzky said. Gretzky knew as much about basketball as Donohue knew about hockey but the pair appreciated each other's talents and passion towards their respective sports.

"Everyone talks about James Naismith inventing basketball, but in my mind Jack Donohue was the architect of Canadian basketball and the reason why he has become so popular in Canada."

Donohue filmed a segment about Wayne that included a trip to Gretzky's hometown and a visit with his parents Walter and Phyllis.

"We were filming the beginning of the episode outside of the Gretzky house and it had to be 40 degrees below zero outside," Aziz recalled. "Everyone was freezing but of course Jack doesn't have a winter coat so I had to lend him my coat. The guy lived in Canada for 30 years and he never had a winter coat. Because of that I am out in the cold wearing nothing but a sweater, I nearly froze to death!"

Once inside the house Donohue and the Gretzkys hit it off as they discussed Wayne's career.

"My dad is a straight shooter and he and Jack became good friends," Gretzky said. "Jack had a great personality. When I first started running a charity sporting event he was the first person who called me up and offered his help."

Donohue was the MC for the first dinner and did such a great job that he was soon a fixture as Gretzky's fundraising event grew in stature.

* * * * *

The series also gave Donohue an opportunity to publicly address and make amends for the incident that had occurred three decades earlier.

Kareem Abdul-Jabbar was on the top of Jack's list of athletes to interview and it was during that show that the retired coach revisited a painful moment in his career and set the record straight about the half-time talk he gave nearly 30 years before. The show began chronicling Jabbar's career from high school star to collegiate player of the year, NBA champion and league Most Valuable Player. During the first part of the episode the two joked about Kareem's first love – baseball.

"You could have been an outstanding athlete in a lot of sports," Donohue stated as the interview began.

"I could have pitched, I definitely could have pitched if I had stayed with it and had worked on my control," Jabbar said in earnest.

That statement brought a smile to Donohue who wisecracked, "I was going to say there were some batters who didn't believe that you could have pitched."

As they both laughed, Kareem recalled his last official appearance on the mound.

"You weren't there but the last game we played in Little League we were getting slaughtered. I was playing the outfield and I used to relief pitch."

Jabbar was called in to mop up the game and the little leaguer set the tone for the rest of the game by throwing his first pitch over the batter's head and into the stands.

"They bring me in and the first batter comes up and the ball goes up in the stands rattling around the seats. I didn't give up any hits after that pitch."

"Of course not, everyone was afraid to come to the plate."

After a commercial break, Donohue addressed the issue that had caused a rift between the two men as he stood overlooking the Brooklyn Bridge.

"It was halftime of a game that we were losing, Lew Alcindor wasn't playing well. He and I had spent a lot of time talking about prejudice. I told him that 'there are people in the stands who are saying that this guy is playing like a nigger. He thinks I said 'you are playing like a nigger'. It was a problem between us that lasted a long time."

As the scene shifted back to a hotel room, Kareem talked frankly about the incident.

"Well, the way I remembered it you said that if someone was watching in the stands they would say I was being lazy and listless like a nigger'."

"And that is a bad word and that is a word their neither one of us enjoys," Donohue interjected.

"Yeah, it was such a shock to me and had a very traumatic and negative effect on me. I certainly never implied that you were a racist. I think the exact opposite; you have always been totally above board and ethical with your dealings with people. Really, I got a lot of value from that because at that age of my life I could see how racism was really something that hinders your ability to make sound judgments and I always took that with me. That was an insensitive remark, you were emotional. 99.8% of the things that you did with me were all for my own good and had a very positive effect on my life."

The interview then switched to Kareem's days at UCLA and the need for him to be a positive role model for young blacks. The episode ends in an outdoor park in Manhattan where his old coach challenges the NBA superstar for a final one-on-one game.

"You remember the rules?" Donohue asked.

"I remember the rules, I have to play basketball and you can wrestle," Jabbar responded.

The pair, wearing gloves and winter coats to starve off freezing temperatures on a November afternoon, spent several minutes jostling back and forth for position. As the cameras rolled, the pair traded friendly barbs and wild hook shots.

Finally the coach, huffing and puffing, calls an end to the contest saying "We're not proving anything here."

The show's credits begin to play as the coach and player walking off the court shaking hands, their friendship restored.

CHAPTER 29

The Summer of Michael Ri

Jack Donohue had been out of the coaching business for nine years when two Kanata businessmen, I, Wayne McKinnon and Gary Thom, approached him with an interesting proposition. The pair had started a sport agency a few years earlier and had a few junior and minor league hockey players in their fold under the auspices of Evergreen Sports. As luck would have it, a similarly named company located in Cleveland, Ohio was pursuing a North Korean named Myong Hun Ri whose anglicized moniker was Michael Ri. Little was known about the North Korean other than he was 7'9" and could shoot the basketball a bit. North Korean sport teams rarely ventured out of their own country but in the Jones Tournament in Taiwan the previous summer, Ri had an exceptional game against Wake Forest and their All-American center, Tim Duncan. When the Wake Forest coaches returned to the States they spoke highly of the North Korean center and Michael Coyne, president of the Cleveland-based Evergreen Sports, investigated the possibility of becoming Ri's agent.

There was just one slight problem. The United States did not recognize the North Korean government and it was illegal for Americans to deal with the communist country.

In fact, North Korea had isolated itself from the rest of the world and its only outside contact was with China, with whom it shared a common border and ideology. The Canadian Evergreen Sports Agency was contacted to see if would they be able to find someone to train Ri and at the same time help the North Korean acquire landed immigration status. The belief was that once he landed in Canada, entry into the United States would become a mere formality. Donohue was still well known in the States from his Power and Holy Cross days and had strong ties with the NBA. Add to the mix the fact that he had a major role in the development of Kareem Abdul-Jabbar and he was a natural to develop the world's tallest player. So, the Canadian Evergreen Sports approached Donohue with a unique offer – to train Ri during the summer months in preparation for the NBA tryout camps in September. With Donohue on board, they also felt that the chances for obtaining a landed immigrant card would be greatly enhanced.

Donohue was leery and intrigued by the project at the same time. He certainly didn't want to be tied down in a gym every day in the summer. He liked both Wayne and Gary, but this was their first foray into professional basketball and the savvy former coach had plenty of questions.

Did they know how much the project would cost? What if he didn't make it to the NBA? Did they know people who would help obtain landed immigrate status – after all that was the key to success. There were so many questions but the idea of supervising the program was appealing. Finally he agreed, to do it under the following conditions: 1) he would be able to hire the coaches, athletic therapist and any other support personnel that he felt were needed for the job; 2) he alone would be in charge of the training process, and 3) he would have a say in what team Michael would play for if he made it to the NBA.

* * * * *

The first call Donohue made about Ri was to Steve Konchalski. Konchalski was now the head coach of the National Team and they played North Korea in the same tournament that Duncan and Ri had matched up against each other. The news was not good. "I told Jack that he did nothing against us," Konchalski said. "He was just a big guy taking up space but I heard he played well against Wake Forest, so I passed the phone to Doc Ryan." Ryan, who did the scouting for the National Team, had seen Ri play several times, and presented a different picture. He said the Korean did play well against Duncan and with proper coaching; Ri could develop into a player. That was just what Donohue wanted to hear. He agreed to take on the challenge and began preparing his staff. Donohue saw the venture as an opportunity to work with former associates and family members as well as a chance to rekindle relationships with friends in the NBA. He enlisted Andy Pipe to handle any medical problems, Gunner would evaluate his fitness level, and Ryan would set up the daily programme. He had several coaches, including his son John Joe to run the daily workouts and he would oversee the entire operation.

The training sessions began in early May and consisted of the Mikan Drill, taps, offensive put-backs, a five-minute shooting drill and a series of post moves. The workouts were expanded as the summer progressed and Donohue gained a better idea of what exactly the NBA was looking for. The retired coach was constantly on the phone to his contacts, explaining what he was doing and looking for feedback. There were discussions with Layden, Abdul-Jabbar, Bill Walton, as well as Pete Newell, the guru of post players and a close friend of Bobby Knight. Donohue talked to several NBA scouts and arranged for them to take a look at the larger than life experiment. Everything appeared to be going well on the court. But off the court, cultural differences and Ri's Asian posse were causing problems. And after two months in Ottawa, Ri was getting no closer to the landed immigrant visa.

*   *   *   *   *

The original group that flew into Vancouver from Beijing in April included Michael, his North Korean basketball coach known simply as Coachee, John, a translator and obvious leader of the delegation and Carl. Carl was presented as Michael's fitness instructor but in reality he provided security for the group and wherever Michael went, Carl and John tagged along. No one was ever really sure whether Carl's job was to protect Michael from the evils of Western Civilization or to ensure that Michael would not succumb to the temptation of defecting, but he never let Michael out of his sight.

John the interpreter was an educated man who spoke English well, smiled a lot and was protective of Michael, particularly when the Canadian coaches were upset with their star pupil. Language was not a big problem on the court –it was always possible to demonstrate what one wanted Michael to do – but off the court it caused a lot of trouble. And on the rare days when Michael had an off practice session, it was clear that the Canadian coaches' messages of displeasure were not being forwarded to him.

Communication, or more aptly lack of communication, was just one of the problems. Because of Michael's size, he couldn't ride in a normal car so Jack arranged for a local car dealership to donate a van. All the back seats were taken out so Michael could stretch his huge frame across the van floor when he was transported back and forth from the gym. Sleeping was also a problem that was temporarily solved by buying additional mattresses and laying them across his bedroom. When he complained about being unable to sleep, it was discovered that he had placed the box springs on top of the mattresses. Finally, it took several weeks before size 23 shoes could be tracked down to replace the worn-out pair he brought from Korea.

The biggest problem, however, was Coachee who was bedridden a day after arriving in Canada and was causing his countrymen a lot of anguish as his condition got worse with each passing day. He saw several doctors but Western medicine was proving to be ineffective. Michael was having trouble concentrating on practice because Coachee was keeping him up late at night and Donohue decided that if Canadian doctors didn't know what was wrong or were unable to cure him, the best thing to do was to send him back home where he could be treated in familiar surroundings. But Coachee was not anxious to return to his native country, which at the time was experiencing a serious famine, and his inability to sit in a chair for more than 20 minutes made flying back to Korea a rather dubious proposition. Still, a ticket was booked and the entire North Korean entourage headed to the Ottawa airport one afternoon to see Coachee off. But when they tried to escort him on to the plane he refused to go, grabbing on to handrails on the door of the plane and yelling in Korean, scaring both the passengers and the crew. Attempts to quiet him and remove his grip on the handrails proved fruitless and just elicited more screams that brought both the airport security and RCMP to the scene. The RCMP officer recognized Jack and allowed him to defuse the situation. Fearing that the scene would lead the Koreans having their visas revoked, Jack brought Coachee back to Kanata. "I never realized how strong he was until I tried to get his hands off the plane door," Donohue said afterwards. "He doesn't want go back to Korea and the entire scene upset Michael. We are lucky we didn't get arrested."

Jack arranged for Coachee to leave on the next flight but Air Canada insisted that they would not put up with another screaming scene. The only solution was to medicate him so much he would sleep all the way to Vancouver. Arrangements were made to house him for a night in Vancouver and sedate him again before flying to Beijing. The plan seemed simple but nothing dealing with Michael Ri was simple. Jack, John the interpreter and Wayne McKinnon from Evergreen Sports, took Coachee to the airport the following day while Michael practiced. They were able to get him on the plane and seated when an Air Canada representative came to Jack and said there was a problem. Jack and John the interpreter were allowed through security and boarded the plane to find Coachee sprawled across the floor blocking the entrance to two washrooms.

"He can't stay there," a stewardess said.

"No, no, Coachee is comfortable there, he won't bother anyone," John the interpreter said.

After much discussion in various languages, Coachee was moved to a seat by himself. As the plane took off, Donohue emitted a sigh of relief. Now it was time to concentrate on basketball.

* * * * *

The Korean contingent resided in a townhouse in Kanata, minutes away from Jack's residence, to have better control of Michael when he wasn't on the court. One day he was sluggish in practice and reeking of beer and after much questioning, John explained to John Joe Donohue what had happened the night before.

Michael had gone to bed early while his two sidekicks drank. At one point, they knocked over a beer on Michael's practice jersey, waking up Michael in the process.

Annoyed, Michael spent the rest of the night trying unsuccessfully to get the smell out of the uniform. He arrived at the gym the next morning, refusing to wear anything but the beer-soaked jersey. After the practice, a conference was held with John and Carl.

They were both told that there was to be no more late night drinking for anyone and they had to get Michaels' practice jersey washed properly before the next session.

Meanwhile, Michael and the boys were becoming celebrities around Kanata. When they went to the local barbershop, they posed for pictures and on daily trips to the mall, Michael obliged autograph seekers.

Michael's skills were improving each day and Donohue was constantly adding things to challenge him. Lorne Goldberg, the strength coach of the National Hockey League's Ottawa Senators, accepted to work with Ri one hour a day, five days a week in addition to the daily practices. On the first day of weight training, Ri could hardly bench-press 55 lbs. His inability was due in part to a lack of technique but within a month he was bench pressing over 200 lbs and showing tremendous agility and overall strength. Donohue also hired a masseur for two treatments a week and a dietitian to help Michael bulk up his slender body. In June, some former university and college players were put together to try to simulate full court games at night and Donohue found several tall players who could play defense against Michael during practice sessions. One was a 6'9" African-born social worker named Makor Shayok who led the University of Dayton Flyers in rebounding during the 1990-91 season. He introduced Michael to the physical defensive style that he would have to get accustomed to if he played in the NBA. Makor was more than just a practice player; he developed a close relationship with Ri and was able to push him to work harder during the practice sessions.

Donohue enrolled a team in the University of Ottawa summer league but that experiment only lasted one game. There was a good crowd assembled in the gym to see Ri but the game was a disaster. Michael was continually beat up and down the court, lost his composure when fouls weren't called, and looked like a big clumsy overgrown man, not a prospective NBA player. Donohue failed to be dissuaded by Ri's poor play and used it as a motivational tool.

"We had a setback and that is all," he stressed. "We have to take this game and use it to our advantage. This will be a good learning experience for everyone."

* * * * *

In July, practices alternated between Holy Trinity High School in Kanata and Algonquin College, which meant that equipment, had to be moved when the venues changed. During one particular move, stopwatches that were used to time Michael's suicide runs at the end of the practice, were left at the other gym. Jack was livid when a manual clock had to be used and, the next day, he took the coaching staff aside and read them the riot act. After warning about becoming sloppy and complacent, he insisted that every drill was to be timed or recorded and then he hung the two stopwatches on the side of a portable board that was used to write motivational messages to Michael.

"Keep the stopwatches in the same spot and there won't be any problems," Jack said emphatically.

That day was an important one for Jack and the investors. A new potential financial backer was coming by to look at Michael and Jack wanted his protégé to practice well. As Michael sat on a small bench putting on his socks, Jack walked over to him with a bag.

"This is for Michael," Jack said to the group as he took a pair of extra large kneepads from the bag and handed them to Ri. "He must wear them every day so he doesn't injure his knees."

Donohue had become obsessed with the fear that all his work would go down the drain if Michael was injured before signing a contract. John the interpreter relayed the message as Michael eyed his present. When John was finished, Michael politely said "Thank you", bowed his head in respect and then proceeded to put on his sneakers while placing the kneepads off to the side.

"No, no," Jack protested as he raised his hands to the skies. "He needs to put on the knee pads before the sneakers."

"He will, tomorrow, he will put them on tomorrow," John explained. Donohue looked in disbelief, his face turning red as his body temperature rose to a boil. Finally, he erupted. "No, he is not wearing them tomorrow, because there will be no tomorrow. There will be no more practices; no NBA, Michael and the rest of you will be on a plane back to North Korea tomorrow morning, if not sooner."

With that, Jack took a ball he was holding and heaved it against the bulletin board, knocking it down and sending the aforementioned stopwatches reeling against the gym wall. John attempted to translate but there was no need. Michael understood the gist of Donohue's tirade and quickly took off his sneakers, put on the kneepads and relaced his sneakers. When he was ready to start practice Donohue had one last piece of advice.

"We just wasted 15 minutes screwing around with these kneepads, 15 minutes that we could have used preparing for the NBA. Don't let it happen again."

The prospective investor entered the gym a few minutes later and witnessed Ri's best practice in Canada. Michael practiced with energy to burn, hit all his shots and looked very much like a *bona fide* NBA player. "We didn't get off to a very good start but Michael certainly worked hard today," a beaming Donohue told a captive audience on the sidelines.

It was right before the final drill when Donohue received some bad news; the coaches were going to have to use the manual clock on the wall to time Ri's suicide runs.

"Why aren't we using the stopwatches?" Donohue asked his blood pressure rising once again.

"Well, Coach, it seems that the two stopwatches were smashed to bits when you hit the message board with the ball," he was told.

Donohue realized that their malfunction was a result of his temper tantrum. It was a small price to pay for the results he got on the court that morning.

"No big deal, use the clock on the wall," he said as his demeanor quickly changed. "If you get a chance later, pick up a few more stopwatches…and this time try to find some that don't break so easily."

* * * * *

Every time someone from the Evergreen group contacted Canadian Immigration they were told that the visa was in the works and it was just a matter of time before it would be issued. Meanwhile, Jack was getting a lot of publicity for Michael who had become a media celebrity for his height alone. The major Canadian dailies all carried stories as did local and national TV stations and cable sport channels. A sports writer from the *Washington Post* came up and spent three days with Michael and filed a story that made the front page of the *Post's* sports section. A picture of Michael also ran in *USA Today* and an application was made to the Guinness Books of Record to have Michael declared the world's tallest living human.

Initially, NBA teams showed interest but that cooled when the commissioner's office sent as memo stating that no clubs were to have direct contact with Ri. Dealing with a North Korean was a touchy subject with the U.S. government. In a newspaper interview, Marty Blake, the director of scouting for the NBA discounted Ri's ability to play in the league. However, several team scouts who came to Canada before the commissioner's ban or saw tapes of Michael told Donohue that he would be signed once he became eligible to enter the United States. But the bills kept coming in with no revenue to cover them. A sponsorship deal with a South Korean automobile company for a half million dollars was stopped by the South Korean government.

Donohue considered accepting an offer from a Turkish club team. Jack even met with the club president, a multi-millionaire who thought it would be great publicity to have the world's tallest man playing for his team. Donohue was impressed with the man, but in the end, he rejected the offer, saying it was counterproductive to Michael's dream of playing in the NBA. He also reasoned that the only way Evergreen Sports was going to recuperate all their expenses was by landing endorsements contracts for the NBA first Asian player.

In retrospect, the Turkish offer was probably Michael's last chance at a pro contract. As Ri appeared to be closer to a possible NBA tryout, Donohue began to worry about Michael's lack of English. The only thing certain was that all the information that Donohue wanted to get to Michael was not being forwarded. And, conversely, the information he was given often contradicted what was said the previous day. It appeared that John the translator would try to determine what answer would make Michael look best in Jack's eyes.

To make sure that the messages were translated properly to his star pupil, Jack hired a young South Korean teenage girl to act as Donohue's personal interpreter. That seemed to solve the communication problem but it soon became the source of a bigger concern when Jack asked the South Korean to conduct English lessons in the afternoon at Ri's Kanata townhouse. On her first visit to their townhouse, all hell broke loose. Minutes after the interpreter arrived, John called Wayne, and then, Donohue and the pair immediately rushed to the house and listened as John informed them of the peril facing Michael and the rest of the group. The North Koreans were all in grave danger. By bringing in a South Korean into their residence their security was breached and they could no longer stay in the house safely. On top of that, they had lost confidence in Donohue, for allowing such a situation to happen. In their minds, the girl was obviously an agent for South Korea. Donohue surveyed the situation and tried not to laugh.

"John you have lived in this house for over two months coming and going as you pleased," he tried to explain. "Michael is the only 7'9"

North Korean in Kanata and people see him every day, on the streets, in the gym, coming and going into this house. Every day he gets into a van that says 'Official Transportation of Michael Ri'. It is no secret that he is staying here."

But the look on John the interpreter was one of concern and Donohue realized that the North Koreans' minds their fears were real. North and South Korea had been at war for close to 50 years and their citizens had been raised to distrust each other. Donohue quickly assumed the role of diplomat as he tried to soothe the situation. He was sorry for not respecting their security. Nothing was done intentionally; he was just trying to help Michael. In the end not only did every one shake hands, but John agreed to let the girl come to the house on a daily basis for English lessons.

In July, Michael took, and passed, a medical physical and he appeared to be one step closer to obtaining his landed immigrant status. But the papers never came, hung up in bureaucratic red tape. Evergreen Sports were feeling the financial pinch of supporting three grown men and paying for Michael's training. They were encouraged by NBA scouts who stated off the record that Michael would be offered a contract as soon as he became eligible for entry in the U.S. But their Canadian visas were expiring soon and when the North Korean contingent suggested a trip home for a brief vacation, everyone agreed.

It appeared that despite statements to the contrary, the papers were not going to be issued and without those documents there wouldn't be a NBA contract. Donohue was told that training would begin again as soon as Michael returned from North Korea, but he knew that the deal was over.

"As soon as they boarded a plane for Beijing, the plan was doomed," Donohue said to his staff. "They are not coming back."

Everyone involved was disappointed except for Donohue who gave it his best shot but whose early fears were confirmed. "We didn't have a chance from the beginning," he explained. "But it was a good experience for everyone involved. The only people who lost out were the people who invested money and who footed the bill for everything."

A few months later, Jack sat down with John Joe and told him: "I never realized how good a coach you were until this past summer. Even though we didn't get Michael to the NBA, it has been an interesting experience that we got to share with people that we liked a lot."

CHAPTER 30

New Millennium, Same Old Jack

As Jack and Mary Jane Donohue prepared for the new millennium Maura was still living at home, while four other children were living within two miles of their house. Bryan had just accepted a job with a computer company in Indiana and moved there with his wife, Michele. They had four grandchildren with two more on the way and grandfather Donohue doted on each and every one of them although he didn't always get their names right. Jack continued his speaking engagements and was able to do travel extensively with Mary Jane. They visited Ireland with his sister Mary and cousin Anne, and took a dream vacation to Hawaii. And there was always the annual two weeks in Surf City on the Jersey Shore. Things could not have been much better for the man, who was still considered The Coach by all who knew him. When in Florida, he got together with old coaching buddies like Danny Buckley, Red Sarachuk and Billy Kirsch and wherever he went there was always time for phone calls to former players. On the West Coast he would touch base with Kareem and John Wooden.

"It was strange, one day Coach Donohue was in Los Angeles and called Coach Wooden when I was visiting," Kareem recalled. "Coach Wooden told Jack that he had someone in the house that wanted to talk to him. We spoke briefly and agreed to meet later. He came over to my house a few days later and spent some time with my father and myself. My father brought out a bottle of Bushmill's Irish Whisky and the two of them had a drink. Coach Donohue didn't drink much but he appreciated my father's gesture. We had a good talk and it gave me a chance to tell him I loved him and I appreciated all he did for me. That was the last time I saw him alive."

In the summer of 2001, Jack went out to the local park in Surf City with his children and grandchildren and started to show off with some trick shots on an outdoor basketball court. Suddenly, he felt a muscle ache and needed help back to their beach house complaining of severe pain with every step he took. The pain continued on the ride back to Canada and he immediately sought medical treatment. No one seemed to know what was wrong, but the ever-present pain persisted.

Confined to his bed in Kanata Donohue was feeling down about being laid up for so long but more upset over the fact that no one could tell him what exactly was wrong or how long the recovery period would be. He had been sick many times before, but the recovery time was never this long and doctors usually had an idea of how to treat the particular illness.

The man who had lifted the spirits of so many people was depressed and seemingly unable to pick himself up. Still he wasn't giving up, and with Andy Pipe's help, he found a doctor that correctly diagnosed the problem; he had indeed pulled some muscles in his back. The pain and lack of mobility would go away in time; he just had to be patient, never one of Donohue's strongest assets.

Meanwhile, Donohue had to cancel plans to return to New York City for the induction of the Power Memorial basketball team into the New York City Basketball Hall of Fame. When he first heard the news of the induction he contacted each of his former players and urged them to attend the ceremony.

"I remember getting a phone call from Coach and telling me that he was looking forward to seeing everyone at the dinner and that I should really try and get there," Charley Farrugia recalled.

Farrugia, who lives in Sugarland, Texas, where he is part owner of an Allied Van Lines franchise, was also looking forward to seeing his former teammates and coaches and was disappointed when Donohue's mysterious illness prevented him from traveling to New York.

"I belonged to the same country club as Kenny Smith, the great backcourt player for the Houston Rockets (who was an outstanding high school player at Archbishop Molloy High School) and he was being inducted into the Hall of Fame at the same time," Farrugia said, "We knew each other to say hi in the clubhouse and then one day I told him that I would see him at the induction ceremonies in New York. He asked me why I was going to New York for the ceremony and I told him that I was being inducted at the same time. He couldn't believe it."

Percudani accepted the award for Donohue who was also being inducted as a coach that evening. Art Kenney made a few brief comments and then introduced the team. As he stood at the podium, with Brian Winters on his right and Kareem to his left, Kenney told Kareem in a loud voice, "Hey, Kareem, Brian said that his Molloy team and Kenny Smith's Molloy team could have whipped our team's butts!" The former players had all moved on, several had became NBA all-stars while others were successful businessmen, but bragging rights established during their high school days were still of major importance. Kareem talked briefly and then it was time for pictures. As the Power team assembled for a team shot, Freddie Stegman took a prominent spot in the line-up.

"It took awhile to realize that Freddie the Spook was trying to get his picture with the team," Farrugia said. "We had to kick him out."

Each player received a plaque, which incorrectly stated that the team had won 19 straight games, not 71.

"Six months later I got a call that the corrected plaques were ready and at the same time Coach Percudani had become gravely ill from lymphoma and was bedridden at Memorial Hospital," Kenny said. "I brought his plaque to him at the hospital and after I handed him the corrected plaque, he sat up and gave an acceptance speech. The family chuckled at the fact that he was 'ever the coach, and was making an 'acceptance speech'. He said 'it was the players who deserved the recognition and were responsible for this honor because of all the hard work that they put in to earn it'. That was Perc (and Coach D and Coach Kuhnert), always giving credit to others! He passed away about two hours after I left the hospital."

Back in Kanata the healing process was slow but Donohue's spirits were lifted by the doctor's prognosis. He was still aching but his outlook changed and the speed of his recovery began to accelerate. One day, he received a package in the mail that brought a smile to his face and brought him back to his days at Friendship Farms, a blue polo shirt with a large T on the left breast, a present from Bobby Knight.

"It came in the mail one day with a little note saying that he always thought of me as one of the good guys," Donohue said with a satisfied smile.

* * * * *

Jack continued to support the National Team and became more involved when his long time assistant Steve Konchalski was selected to replace Ken Shields as the National Team head coach in 1995. He would show up at training camps and patrol the sidelines offering words of encouragement to coaches and players alike.

Anytime Basketball Canada or Konchalski asked him to attend a tournament, press conference or meeting, the Coach Emeritus was more than willing. Konchalski's squad came within one game of qualifying for the 1996 Olympics and Basketball Canada rewarded the new head coach with a five-year contract. Steve Nash led the Canadian team to a berth in the 1998 World Championships, where the team finished sixth, but a year later the team once again failed to qualify for the Olympics and the Basketball Canada Board of Directors fired Konchalski. One of the problems Konchalski encountered was an issue that Donohue and other national team coaches had faced for thirty years – being at the mercy of a volunteer board that changes every few years.

"The problem was that between September of 1997 and the summer of the World Championship in 1998, there was a complete turnover of the people in charge at Basketball Canada," Konchalski said. "All of those who agreed and bought into the five-year plan were gone. There was a new executive director, new president, new board of directors with a Toronto base, and a new marketing group that was very market-driven."

The new board didn't like what they saw in the Olympic qualifying round in Greece, a tournament that Canada played without Nash, and decided it was time to change coaches. Donohue was livid; not only with the decision, but also the way the board treated his long time friend. He encouraged Steve to challenge the decision and supported him publicly and privately. Konchalski fought the dismissal and had plenty of ammunition. Basketball Canada had not lived up to some of the provisions in Konchalski's contract and when he appealed the decision, an arbitrator reinstated him.

But once Konchalski was reinstated, the board members once again fired him and Konchalski gave up the battle. Basketball Canada then hired Jay Triano, who had been working for the Vancouver Grizzlies, as the new head coach of the National Team. While he still believed that Konchalski should be coaching the team, Donohue backed the appointment of his former captain. He had admired Triano as much as any player he coached.

When Triano took the team to Puerto Rico in the summer of 2003 to qualify for the 2004 Olympics, Donohue accompanied the team. While other former coaches would be inclined to offer advice and have trouble letting go, Donohue simply offered support without meddling.

"No press went, and we had no other fans there, he was the only one who came down to cheer for us," said Triano. "He was always there, just to show support."

Donohue's health was dealt another blow when he was diagnosed with diabetes, although in typical fashion he proclaimed that it was a positive experience in his life.

"I have Type 2 diabetes, which is very controllable and if I follow my doctor's advice I won't need dialysis or anything like that," Donohue said. "It is a positive thing because I now have a diet I have to follow and I check my blood twice a day. If the count is not right then I have to make adjustments. It is going to make me a healthier person."

He carried his blood counter wherever he went and took readings religiously, like a kid with a new toy. When someone asked how things were going they would get a ten-minute discussion about his blood count and his new diet. Of course, he modified that new diet to his own specifications.

"Jack asked me to go to a meeting with some nurses to see what he should be eating since I did the cooking," Mary Jane said. "After the meeting I came home and got rid of all the foods that had too much sugar and weren't good for him. So what does he do? The next day he comes home from the store with ice cream, cookies and cake explaining that we had run out of them, the exact things I threw out the day before."

Jack continued on the lecture circuit although he cut back to about 20 speeches a year and was spending more time traveling and receiving recognition for past contributions as he was inducted into the Canadian Olympic Hall of Fame, the New York State Basketball Hall of Fame, the

New York City Basketball Hall of Fame, the Ontario Basketball Hall of Fame and the Toastmaster Hall of Fame.

* * * * *

"Jack Donohue never really left New York City," Lou Carnesecca remarked after his death. "He was always a Bronx guy."

Indeed Donohue returned to New York on a regular basis, sometimes to speak or just to visit old friends. Often Richie Murphy would pick his former college coach at the airport and serve as his chauffeur. Murphy had become a successful nightclub owner and enjoyed taking time off to spend with Donohue and mutual friends. On one such occasion, when Murphy arrived at the airport, he had some bad news to deliver.

"Sorry to be the one to tell you Coach, I just heard on the radio that Al McGuire died," Murphy said in a somber tone.

Donohue took the news stoically and then talked about his final conversation he had with the basketball legend.

"I called him when I found out that he was sick," Donohue told Murphy. "We talked and were able to say our good-byes to each other."

Brian Boyle recalled the time that he and a bunch of friends visited Richie Mannion who was working at Ruynon's, a popular Manhattan restaurant.

"It was an unusual day at Ruynon's because there weren't a lot of people and we actually had a chance to talk to Richie," Boyle said. "We were getting ready to leave when Richie said Donohue was in town and on his way over. None of us had seen Jack for a while so we decided to stay. When Jack arrived, he made the rounds talking to each person and made everyone feel comfortable and important. It was really nice and it was the last time most of us saw him alive."

Donohue returned a year after Power Memorial's induction into the NYC Basketball Hall of Fame to receive his plaque. Mannion accompanied him to the dinner, a seven-course affair at one of the city's nicer hotels. Before the main course was served Mannion went to the kitchen and had them make an onion sandwich, which he delivered to Donohue, complete with a can of Pepsi, the same meal that Mannion would fetch for Donohue back at Tolentine forty years earlier.

"I'm not sure what they are serving for the main course Coach, but I figured you might want one of your old favourites," Mannion said.

Donohue smiled and quickly disposed of the sandwich and the drink with great satisfaction.

CHAPTER 31

I got a little cancer

The entire Donohue family was going to be in Kanata for Christmas 2002 (the number had grown to 21 counting in-laws and grand children) so Mary Jane decided it was time for an updated family portrait complete with printed T-shirts made especially for the occasion. There were, of course, problems.

Taylor, the resident teenager, said, "I'm never wearing that!", when presented the shirt that everyone was wearing for the picture. When his grandmother asked if he could wear it this one time as a favor to her, he consented with a tremendous lack of enthusiasm, "Okay, but never again, Grandma!" The end result was a generational color photo – Grandma and Grandpa in one color, the children and in-laws in another color, and the grandchildren in a third.

Donohue started the New Year with a trip to New York to meet with some NBA executives. He used the excursion to visit with his old friend, Frank Shiels, the driver the fateful night when Jack and Mary Jane first met. Shields still lived on Martha Avenue across from St. Barnabas Church in the Bronx. When he arrived at Frank's house, Jack suggested that they take a walk to Woodlawn Avenue to return a book to his cousin Peggy McCaffrey. As they strolled through the streets Donohue marveled at how little the old neighborhood had changed in the last 50 years.

It was still a predominantly Irish community and St. Barnabas Church and adjoining schools remained the focal point for the neighborhood inhabitants.

When Jack returned to Canada, Mary Jane noticed that he was tired and she reminded him that he was wasn't 21 anymore and needed to rest more after speaking engagements. He agreed but still had a hard time turning down requests. He had a busy 2003 planned with a trip to Winnipeg to speak to Bruce Pirnie's national Coaching Institute and was discussing a major project with John McConnachie, the former CIAU executive, who was now a public relations consultant. If he was slowing down, it was hard to tell, so Mary Jane insisted that he take some time off.

The couple planned a cruise with Mary and Ann in late January and the coach was looking forward to spending a week prior to the ship's departure catching up with old friends in Florida. Before leaving Canada, he had blood tests that showed his hemoglobin was too low, although his doctor attributed the low count to steroids he was taking because of the muscle pulls he had suffered the year before at Surf City. Another blood test was given before Mary Jane and Jack headed for Florida.

Their original idea was to get a hotel room in the Miami area where the ship was docked and then rent a car and visit Red Sarachek, Danny Buckley, Billy Kirsch and Danny Meagher. But as the couple prepared to leave Kanata, Jack became increasingly tired and they had to revise their plans. "We were able to see Danny Meagher and Les Kirschman, and then got into our motel," Mary Jane said. "Jack was exhausted, but we decided to go further north and see Red Sarachek and stay near him."

In the following week the Donohues and Saracheks met several times, but Jack was too tired to do anything else. "Both of us figured once he would got on the boat, he could go swimming and bake out whatever was ailing him, Mary Jane said. "Just before we left, we got the word from one of our children that his Doctor wanted to see him – his blood count had dropped further – but it could wait 'til we got home."

Once aboard the ship Jack ate well and rested a lot, but still suffered from fatigue. "He never went off the boat at the ports of call and would leave the dining room early to go back to the cabin to rest," Mary Jane said. "We did manage to see the shows and he enjoyed them as always." Something was wrong and Jack, remembering the problems he had two years ago, was determined to check it out as soon as he got home.

They arrived back in Kanata on the first Saturday in February. He had a blood test on Monday and was scheduled to see his doctor Tuesday afternoon after he attended a luncheon on Parliament Hill. He found a parking space close to the Parliament buildings but as he began to climb the steps leading to the government buildings he experienced chest pains. *Oh my God, I am having a heart attack!*

He quickly tried to assess the situation as best he could. He began to feel better when he returned to the car and decided to go home and rest. As fate would have it, he turned on the radio and heard how heart attack victims often think they should go home to bed when they really should be in the hospital.

That was all Jack needed to hear, he headed over to Ottawa Civic Hospital to see Andy Pipe. It was just a ten minute drive and he felt he had enough stamina to make it.

"Here I am with chest pains, thinking I am having a heart attack and instead of getting out of the car and calling ambulance or hailing a cab, I try to drive there," Donohue said later. "It was stupid."

As he drove across town his sense of direction failed him one more time and he missed the cut-off to the hospital. Rather that negotiate his way back to Civic Hospital, he continued to his doctor's office where he had a scheduled appointment for a blood test later that afternoon. When he arrived at the doctor's office, the nurse reminded him that his appointment was later but when he told her what he was experiencing chest pains she brought him in to see Dr. Morrissut. She decided that he was going straight to the hospital, but this time he would not be driving himself!

Someone from home would have to pick him up and take him to the hospital. "I was out shopping with Marybeth so Kathy and Carol picked him up and took him to the Civic Hospital where I met them later," Mary Jane said. "The kids went home to take care of their kids and John Joe stopped by on his way home from work. Jack was losing blood and they were trying to determine why and at the same time replenish the lost blood."

Marybeth, Kathy and Maura returned to the hospital that night after a basketball game and, after a second transfusion, they took their mother and father home. What Jack had experienced was not a heart attack but he was sick, a lot sicker than he could possibly imagine.

* * * * *

Donohue felt better the next day and made a return visit to Dr. Morrisut to learn the results of the various tests he had taken the day before. She explained that he had a hardened lymph node on the pancreas, she didn't know why he was losing blood and she was referring him to a lymphoma doctor at the General Hospital.

"We went there several times for a variety of tests – everything from blood tests to a liver biopsy to a bone marrow test." Mary Jane said.

The testing was tiring Jack out but his spirit and demeanor remained upbeat and positive. Mary Jane and Jack saw the lymphoma doctor several times and on February 25th the doctor discussed the results of the various tests. The good news was that he did not have lymphoma but there were spots on his liver and she was referring him on to another specialist. The doctor tried her best to explain in medical terms the severity of his illness but neither Mary Jane nor Jack truly understood how sick he was. They vaguely discussed various options with the doctor-including surgery and/or chemotherapy.

Jack finally asked, "What if I do nothing?" "You will not survive a year," was the blunt answer. "One last thing – if it was me, I would get my affairs in order," the doctor added as the couple prepared to leave.

"We left thinking that this next doctor would operate, use chemo, whatever," Mary Jane said. "Yes, it was serious, but we were prepared to do whatever to get Jack well again!"

As they headed home to Kanata Jack turned to Mary Jane and said, "I know I have asked you this many times before but now is the time. If there is anything you want to do together, we should do it soon." Mary Jane just shook her head and said the only thing she wanted now was to see her husband out of harm's way; that was the priority.

"Let's get you better and then we can go somewhere and celebrate," she told him.

They headed home to share the latest news with the kids. The five children living in the Ottawa area were all in attendance on Lismer Crescent that night as Mary Jane and Jack tried their best to explain the situation. They still believed that the cancer was beatable but expressed to the rest of the family that this would not be an easy fight.

When they were finished one of the children asked what effect the cancer would have on Jack in the short term.

"Well, he is going to tire easily and he will need a lot of sleep," Mary Jane said. "Nothing new about that!" one of the children, said and everyone laughed.

The family was facing their biggest crisis but they hadn't lost their sense of humor. Jack was literally in the most important fight of his life, a fight he wouldn't win. But in the next two months he demonstrated for a final time what an outstanding person he truly was.

* * * * *

Jack tried to keep a regular routine that included daily Mass and phone calls to friends.

"Jack loved to drive and really hated anyone else taking over the wheel," Mary Jane said. "But from the time we came home after his blood transfusions, I became the driver. Most every morning, we would go to St. Patrick's Church in Fallowfield for Mass and Communion and then off to McDonalds with a group of friends for coffee and talk. Then home and he would rest for a while, and if there were no doctor's appointments or tests, he would be on the phone talking to players, friends, etc."

As Jack weakened he took great comfort from his children and the support they were giving him. When Bryan heard that his father had cancer, he made a snap decision. He would quit his job, move the family back to Ottawa and take his chances of finding a job. He had been talking about trying to relocate back to the Ottawa area to be closer to the rest of the family for over a year but the hi-tech market in Kanata had taken a big hit and there weren't many employment possibilities.

"Wait a second, let's think this out,' Jack said. "I'm sure we can come up with a better solution than quitting your job. You have your family to think about."

Bryan had benefited from his father's advice before and agreed to explore other options. He went to his bosses the next day and explained the situation and suggested several options to the company. The soft-spoken boy who was often seen and not heard had a totally different persona at work where he established himself as an excellent manager with strong leadership abilities and the company did not want to lose him.

"I told them that I didn't know how long I would be away but they were very understanding, saying that family comes before work," Bryan said.

The company accepted Bryan's proposal move to Ottawa indefinitely and work out of the Jack's upstairs office. Within a week Bryan packed up his office equipment, and his family of four and moved back home to be with his dad and the rest of the Donohue clan as they faced the biggest crisis of their lives. They moved onto the basement of Kathy and Denis's house and Bryan spent the days on Lismer Crescent dividing his time between work and his father.

"I told him not to do anything rash but the thought that he would quit and come back home was nice. I am a lucky man," Donohue said as he condition began to deteriorate "My spirits are good; I am surrounded by my family, what more can I ask for."

* * * * *

One night, Mary Jane came to bed to find Jack totally disorientated. He was unable to work the TV channel changer and wasn't sure where he was. Mary Jane put on a program that he enjoyed watching but it didn't help. Mary Jane and Maura, who was still living at home, became concerned and after a call to a doctor friend, they decided to take him to the Civic Hospital.

"On the drive to the hospital Jack had some Pepsi with him, with a straw in it," Mary Jane said. "He would attempt to take a sip, even slurping it, but the straw was a foot from his mouth."

Maura tried to help the situation by telling him he had to hold it closer and he replied, "I know!" very curtly and then moved the can an inch or two closer and attempted to slurp again with the same results.

Once they got to the hospital Maura placed him in a wheelchair and took him to the Emergency Waiting Room. "We had to wait for quite a while, but he kept others entertained with his ramblings," Mary Jane said. "There was a hockey game on the TV and every time there was a roar he thought they were calling for him. Not the most patient person at the best of time, he wanted to know what would happen if we just went into the back and saw a doctor. When we explained that there was a cop sitting in the back and he would stop us, he replied he was just a rent-a-cop and couldn't do anything."

Eventually Maura convinced one of the nurses that there was something seriously wrong with her father and he was taken to a cubicle.

"Taking off his clothes and getting him up on the table was almost as bad as getting him dressed and down the stairs at home. He didn't have the strength for anything," Mary Jane said.

A young doctor finally came in and started asking questions to determine Jack's state.

"Have you been drinking?"

Jack replied matter-of-factly that no, but his wife was an alcoholic and sometimes he would drink so she wouldn't know how much she actually drank. Between laughter and tears, Mary Jane and Maura explained that he very rarely takes a drink.

Eventually, the blood tests came back and they discovered his sugar was way down and they hooked him up to a glucose solution and the change was miraculous. Within seconds, he was moving on his own, talking as intelligently as ever, but his condition would not stabilize and the hospital gave him several glucose transfusions before deciding to keep him overnight for observation. It would be several days before Donohue was allowed to return home but it didn't bother Jack a bit.

"He was comfortable entertaining the troops in his ward, so he was happy," Mary Jane said.

The Donohues went to see a second specialist, Dr Jonkers, on March 25th, a month after the first prognosis and the news was not good. "John Joe drove us to the hospital on his way to work, and then decided he would stay with us," Mary Jane said.

"By this time, Jack needed a wheelchair to move around the hospital – he was okay at home and in the doctor's offices. Dr. Jonkers had the dubious pleasure of meeting us for the first time and telling us that Jack had anywhere from one to five months to live. If he liked where he was, was comfortable with his present lifestyle, etc. chemo could give him another month or so."

Jonkers told the couple to go home, discuss their options, and he would schedule a chemo treatment in the next week, in case they wanted to go that route.

"We thanked him, and left, each with our own thoughts," Mary Jane recalled. "We dropped John off near his office and drove home. Jack and I talked. He hated where he was, in pain, unable to concentrate much, tired all the time. So, after thinking about it, he opted to forego any treatment.

* * * * *

The family was able to keep the news out of the media and those reporters who became aware of Jack's condition considered it a private, family matter. As the news spread throughout the basketball and sport community, friends called daily to see how he was doing. Jack took it upon himself to call his sister, cousin and close friends. One of the first persons he called was his old army buddy Ted Burns, who was a cancer survivor.

A few years earlier, Jack had helped Teddy in his own fight against the deadly disease and now Burns tried to reciprocate.

Donohue got a different response when he notified his mentor Red Sarachek. "Red hung up on me. But that is typical Red. He didn't give me permission to get cancer so I shouldn't have gotten it," he said with a laugh.

Steve Konchalski arrived in mid-March and spent several days at their home. Their plan of attending baseball games in Ottawa was no longer possible. Instead they spent several hours a day reminiscing about the good times they shared, the battles they fought and the friendship that began with a simple conversation in Montreal thirty years earlier. At one point, Jack turned to Steve and said, "I have no regrets; I did everything I wanted to do."

"But Coach you should have written a book," Steve replied.

"You know me Steve. I could never sit down long enough to write it."

As the days wore on, so did Jack. He received visits from Jay Triano and Eli Pasquale and then Mary Jane had to put a stop to anyone outside the family from visiting. Bill Wennington called as soon as he got the news that Jack was dying but was told it was too late to visit.

"In the beginning, we told people that if they were coming into Ottawa for another reason then stop by the house but don't come just to see Jack," Mary Jane explained. "If someone came on a bad day they wouldn't get to see him at all. The most important thing was for Jack to get his rest. It didn't make sense for people to come all the way to Ottawa and not be able to see him."

* * * * *

While many of the Donohue's high school coaching colleagues like Lou Carnesecca, Danny Buckley and Jim McDermott eventually moved to the college ranks, Jack Curran resisted numerous collegiate offers and stayed at Archbishop Molloy High School. He nearly renewed his on-court rivalry with Donohue in 1969 when Boston College courted him to replace Bob Cousy as its head coach, but Curran felt comfortable at the Queens high school. In over 45 years of coaching, Curran captured five city titles, coached three Olympians, seven NBA players and saw numerous of his former players establish themselves as successful coaches, lawyers, businessmen and clergy. In that span, he became the dean of NYC coaches and when he eventually retires, he will do so as the city's most successful high school coach. On the baseball field, he was equally successful and guided the Stanners to six city titles.

Such was Curran's impact on the city game that the *New York Times*, which rarely covers high school sports, devoted a two-page story on his career accomplishments in 2003. The article prompted a call from Donohue congratulating his long time friend.

In the course of the conversation, Curran asked Donohue how he was doing.

"Okay – I have a little cancer," was Donohue's understated reply.

Curran explained to him that there was no such thing as "a little cancer," and that he should come down and have it checked out at Lennox Hill Hospital in Manhattan.

"I have a good friend who is one of the top cancer specialists at the hospital and I told Jack that they would look after him there," Curran said.

"I got the best doctor in Canada looking after me," Donohue answered. "I will be alright."

After they finished the conversation Curran hung up the phone convinced that his long-time friend would get the needed treatment. Curran's confidence was shattered a few days later when he got a call from Richie Murphy. Murphy, who was Donohue's first captain at Holy Cross, had some bad news.

"Coach Donohue has terminal cancer," Murphy relayed to Curran.

"No," Curran protested, "I just talked to him a few days ago and he told me that he was getting it treated." A few days later, Curran called Donohue back and got the full story, Donohue had a few months, at best, to live. "I asked Jack why he didn't tell me and he said he didn't want anyone to worry about him."

*   *   *   *   *

Chris Critelli rehearsed the talk that she wanted to have with her former coach the night before she called the Donohue household. "I spent the night before practicing what I was going to say and to make sure that everything came out the right way," Critelli said. "The one thing I didn't want to do was to ask him how he was doing. So I called him early in the morning around nine because I figured he wouldn't be as tired then. And what's the first thing I say – 'Hi Coach, how are you doing?' I was so mad at myself."

She then proceeded to tell him how much he affected her life and helped make her a better coach and a better person.

"Coach, I just want to tell you how much you mean to me and how much I learned from you," she said.

"Well, Chris I want you to know how much I learned from you as well and thank you," Donohue replied. They talked a few minutes before Donohue said, "Listen Chris it has been great talking to you but I am getting tired and I am going to have to let you go." But Critelli, sensing that this was the last time they would talk, didn't want to hang up the phone. "I said 'No, no, don't go.'"

"I just wanted to talk to him a little longer; there were so many things I wanted to say to him. But I knew he had to hang up so I said 'Good-bye'. It was typical Jack. I was trying to give him a compliment and he turned right around and gave me the compliment. Even in his dying days he was always thinking of someone else."

Jack's health was failing but not his sense of humour or his feistiness. One afternoon, he was watching Judge Judy with Bryan and decided that his life would not be complete without a lawsuit against one of the family members.

"Bryan, do you know who I should sue in this family?" his father asked after watching a particular episode "It doesn't make sense to sue Carol or John Joe, because they don't have any money. I guess I could always sue your mother or maybe Maura." Bryan just shook his head.

On another occasion, he had a heart-to-heart with Mary Jane about his funeral arrangements. "You know how I feel about funerals?" he asked. "Yes, the same as me, you hate them," Mary Jane answered.

"Then we have one day for visitation," Jack proclaimed.

"No," was Mary Jane's blunt reply that surprised her husband to no end. "You have too many friends and family that live too far away and need some time to get here."

They compromised and decided on a two-day wake.

*   *   *   *   *

A week after the meeting with Dr. Jonkers, Jack was in constant pain and unable to do just about anything but sleep and eat and even his famed appetite for food was diminishing daily. As the end neared, the family spent as much time as possible with their ailing father. Word continued to spread throughout North America although Jack's many media friends continued to refrain from reporting the story out of deference for the feelings of the family. Several weeks after the first hospital visit, a reporter from a local newspaper called and asked about his condition.

"His editor had been fielding calls from people across the country and he wanted some kind of confirmation," Mary Jane recalled. "I told them we knew it was news and that we respected the fact that they had a job to report it. I asked them to do so with some thought for the family. His grandchildren knew that he was sick but they weren't told how serious it was. They didn't know he was dying. I asked him not to print that it was pancreatic cancer, asked for prayers and to tell people to give their families hugs."

That night Taylor Sicard was unable to attend the Ottawa Senators playoff game with his father and when he woke the next morning, he quickly checked the morning paper to see how his favorite hockey team had fared. On the front page of the Sports section, right next to the story of the hockey game, was the headline that Coach Donohue was dying!

"It was not exactly the way we wanted him, or the others, to find out," Mary Jane explained. "Taylor was the oldest of the grandchildren and went on a lot of trips with his grandfather," Mary Jane said. "I was not happy with the way the paper broke the news."

But the story was now officially out and the rest of the country's papers ran short stories explaining that the man known to a nation simply as "The Coach" had incurable cancer. No sensational headlines, just stories explaining that Donohue's time was growing short. The phone started ringing off the hook and each of the six kids visited daily to spend time with Jack and help field many of the calls.

Jack's sister, Mary, cousin Anne, and nephews Mark and Gene, all came to visit in the first week of April but as soon as they returned to the States, Jack's condition worsened.

"Mary and Anne were coming back for Easter, but I called them and told them I didn't know if he was going to make it," Mary Jane said. "So, Mary and her daughter, Mary Jo, drove back to Kanata the next day."

As Jack's condition deteriorated he asked for a priest to hear his last confession and deliver the last rites of the Catholic Church. "That was a major hassle," Mary Jane said. "He wanted a priest he knew, but he didn't want our parish priest because he knew him too well." Finally, it was agreed that Father Frank from a neighboring parish would perform the sacrament and they were administered at the Donohue home.

As she cared for her dying husband, Mary Jane was reminded of an eerie conversation that she and Jack had engaged in before he had fallen ill.

"Out of the blue he said to me 'I hope I go first because I don't know what I would do without you'," Mary Jane recalled. "It was very strange because he was in good health at the time. Now he was getting his wish." On one occasion, the entire family was in the room talking when Jack made a noise and started to wave his hands telling everyone to leave the room; he had enough of them for that day. "He was dying but he was still in charge," Mary Jane said.

Earlier in the year, the Toronto Raptors had named Donohue as the 2003 recipient of the Mac Award. This award is named after Coach John McManus and presented for outstanding contributions to Canadian basketball. "They wanted some member of the family to come to Toronto and accept the award," Mary Jane said. "The family decided that Bryan, who had missed out on so much living in the States, and grandson Taylor would do the honors. However, the day before the presentation, Jack took another downward turn, and Bryan didn't want to leave him. After some finagling, Taylor and his cousin Keith flew in and accepted the award at half time of the Raptors-Chicago Bulls game."

The next day, Wednesday, April 16th, everyone was in and out of the Donohue house throughout the day. Later that night the Donohue children were quickly summoned back to the house when Jack's breathing suddenly became worse. "Mary was holding one hand and I had the other," Mary Jane said. "We had all said the rosary earlier and I was telling him that I loved him that it was all right to go home. His Mom and Dad were waiting for him along with my parents and we would be all right." As she talked to husband for the final time, the six children and Andy Pipe came running into the room, tears rolling down their checks.

"Kathy and Maura were at his head, and he looked around, gave a little smile, turned towards me and mouthed 'I love you'," Mary Jane said as she recalled her husband's final moments. "He took a slow breath and then no more."

Andy Pipe pronounced Jack Donohue dead at 9:30 p.m.

CHAPTER 32

The End

The tears flowed down their checks as the family members said their goodbyes.

As Kathy eyed her mother crying she exclaimed "Mom, you really do cry!" a statement that immediately ended Mary Jane's tears. While the family waited for the funeral home to arrive, they gathered in the room besides their father and said a few prayers. After about twenty minutes, John Joe broke the somber mood by saying "I need a drink," prompting the males to head to the kitchen to prepare drinks for everyone.

As they reassembled in the bedroom, a form of Irish wake took place as each of the family members took turns telling stories.

"We talked, we laughed, we cried and hugged," Mary Jane would say later.

At one point, John Joe said it was ironic that the family roles have been reversed.

"Now we are the ones telling the stories and it is dad who is sleeping through them."

Jack died on the Wednesday prior to Easter, and as a result, his wish of a quick burial was frustrated by the Easter holidays. Mary Jane arranged for visitations on Easter Sunday and Monday with the funeral scheduled for Tuesday. The Donohue's parish church, St. Isidore's, was not large enough to handle the expected crowd so the service was relocated to Holy Redeemer Church, a newer, larger church located on the other side of Kanata.

Callers to the Donohue household inquiring about the funeral services or to offer condolences were treated to an unexpected but familiar sound as the phone was forwarded to an answering machine:

"This is Jack Donohue. I am not able to take your call so please leave a message. If this is the IRS, the check is in the mail; if it is the RCMP, not guilty; anyone else, please leave a message and I will get back to you as soon as possible."

It was a nice gift for friends to be able to hear his voice one more time and to laugh once again at one of his oldest lines.

Across North America, columnists were remembering the Coach in heartfelt stories. Friends and relatives came from every province and more than 16 states to attend the funeral while first-person stories about Donohue appeared in every major Canadian newspaper and all the New York papers. Wire service stories were carried in the major U.S. dailies. TSN, Canada's first national sport network, ran a special on Jack's life while journalists tried to put into words exactly what this transplanted American had meant to Canada.

At the Ottawa Senators playoff game, the man who knew so little about the intrinsic subtleties of Canada's most popular game was honored prior to opening face-off. Jacques Martin had not forgotten the man who was always there with a supporting word when things weren't going well. On Parliament Hill, the government passed a resolution recognizing Donohue's contributions to his adopted country.

The five Donohue residences in Kanata were soon packed with relatives and friends who came from near and far, not only pay their respects but also show support for Mary Jane and the kids. The following day, Kareem Abdul-Jabbar called up Richard Lapchick to talk about his former coach.

"Kareem had talked to Jack before he died and Jack told him that one of his wishes was that the two of us would try and stay in contact with each other a little more," Lapcheck recalled. "We talked for awhile and agreed that we would keep in touch, a promise that we have kept."

The two had first met at Friendship Farm and became close friends. Over the years, as they both made their mark in the sporting world, they had less contact with each other. Now, with the death of a close mutual friend they resolved to keep that friendship alive. Even after his death, Donohue was continuing to make an impact on those close to him.

* * * * *

Kareem and Wayne Gretzky were among the 1,000 people who sent flowers, or cards of sympathy while hundreds filled Holy Redeemer Church for the funeral Mass. From New York, former players and friends, including Richie Mannion, Richie Murphy and Steve Ryan, traveled to pay their respects although the atmosphere inside the church was anything but somber. A choir sang Irish songs as mourners stood in groups, telling stories prior to the service.

Ryan, Steve Konchalski, Teddy Burns and John and Vivian Restivo read passages from the Bible. There were four eulogies and each was more moving than the next.

The six Donohue children, who all sported one of their Dad's favorite ties, spoke first.

> We figure our father will be very impressed that we are working from a script that we wrote more than two minutes ago.
>
> First of all, we would like to: Thank you all for being here to help us say good bye; Thank all of you who called, sent cards and letters, the beautiful flowers and food, the thoughts, prayers and e-mails ... letting us know him in many ways. We were always aware of his other lives, outside of this family, but your messages have shown the extent of his impact on others, and we thank you for sharing them with us. As important as his "other life" was, as often as he was away, we always knew that family came first, and from your letters, it's obvious he let you know that too.
>
> Thank you for respecting our privacy over the last few weeks. As difficult as it was for us to be here, we realize it was also difficult for you to stay away.
>
> We'd like to thank the doctors, palliative care workers, and Victorian Order of Nurses for the incredible care provided for our father.
>
> Thank you to Aunt Gert, for running our household for the last few days. Aunt Mary and Aunt Anne – we thank you for all your support for Mom, and for being here for Dad. He knew you were here, and it meant as much to him as it did to us.

To Dan, Denis, Deanne and Michelle: there are no words. We love you. A special thank you to Andrew Pipe ... You always knew the right things to say to Dad, to Mom and to us. You were with us through it all, and you were our rock.

And our final thank you is to you, Mom. We should not have been surprised by your strength and courage, because Dad wasn't. We know he appreciated it, and so did we. You led by example, and we did our best to follow. It has been said that "The best thing a man can do for his children is to love their mother". Dad did this everyday of our lives together, and we did notice. We also would like to thank you and dad both for Long Beach Island and the Can-Am Olympics – for allowing us to get to know our cousins; we would not be as close to the Castelli's and Chomich's without those two weeks on the beach every summer. Those of you who have taken us up on our invitations to join us there know how important time together with family and friends is to all of us.

We had "Dad-isms"; some of you will know them as "Coach-isms" or "Jack-isms" but they are things he said and did that will stay with us forever. His infamous "Tips from the Top":

You can never have enough windshield washer fluid, club soda or toilet paper – but never pay more than 25 cents a roll.

Sub sandwiches, fried garbage, raw rhubarb for dessert ... and remember ... "It's all in the presentation".

Road trip songs, consisting solely of "Joe the Cowboy" and "Big Rock Candy Mountain"

Softball games growing up, even if anyone NOT on Dad's team was always "The Bad Guys".

In any game or sport: "Whoever is keeping score, wins."

His jokes and stories that we'd heard a hundred times, but would still make us laugh – Trying not to laugh or smile when we were mad at him.

And of course ... "I wonder what the poor people are doing today?"

Asking strangers who were eating alone in a restaurant to join us.

Quality time and quantity time – both are important.

Family meetings and "references".

Sundays are meant for family.

Hold hands when you say grace.

Kiss the people you love.

His most famous sayings to us include:

"Don't tell the others – you're my favourite"

"What great thing happened to you today?"

"Where do you see yourself in five years?"

"Find out what you love to do, and figure out how to make a living out of it – I never worked a day in my life."

"Dream Big Dreams"

"Shoot for the moon, because if you come up short, you'll still wind up in the stars"

"And always remember, God is good to dumb Irishmen"

Our father was an avid collector of poems and inspiring stories that he would pass on to others at any given opportunity. Often after a speaking engagement or presentation, he would receive calls or faxes requesting a copy of one of these literary treasures. We would like to close by sharing one of his favourites by Dan Baker:

You can love me, but only I can make me happy.

You can teach me, but only I can do the learning.

You can lead me, but only I can walk the path.

You can promote me, but I have to succeed.

You can coach me, but I have to win the game.

You can even pity me, but I have to bear the sorrow.

For the Gift of Love is not a food that feeds me.

It is the sunshine that nourishes that which I must finally harvest for myself.

So if you love me don't just sing me your song.

Teach me to sing – for when I am alone

I will need the melody.

Dan Baker

Jay Triano, speaking on behalf of the players, was next and stated that Jack's tenure with the Olympic team was about more than just wins and losses.

Coach was more than that. He taught us about life, about experiences, about a passion to play for your country. It's safe to say that as good as he made us on the floor; he shaped us to be even better off the floor.

Coach was so far ahead of everyone in the profession, and this was sensed at major tournaments. Whether in Olympic Villages or at international basketball events, no one knew the other coaches, but everyone knew Coach. We, as his players, were the envy of the other athletes.

Coach had an incredible way to get his point across – maybe it was his Kanata accent. You had to be able to take a joke, or accept the quick one-liner. You quickly learned how well he could motivate. We learned his language: 'Chop-Chop' meant hurry up and let's get going. 'Baby-Baby' meant he had found a new stash of food in his pocket

On every trip, one of the players would keep track of the number of meetings there would be. We would hear the same stories over and over, but it was Coach's way of teaching, inspiring – or practicing his one-liners. Those meetings also kept us out of trouble.

Along the way the team came to understand Donohue's unwritten rules

The first seat on the bus was always his

If there was growth on you face he would ask you to stand a little closer to the razor in the morning

No hats to be worn inside – ever

Running sprints in practice is a reward not punishment

If you came to watch one of our practices there was a good chance you would get thrown into a drill

With 86,400 seconds in each day there was time for everything and everyone.

We quickly learned that his family was of huge importance to him. Very seldom were his children not at our practices. Sometimes they had the opportunity to travel with us. Our annual baseball games in Kanata were highlights of our summer. We once got to play on the Blue Jays field at Exhibition Stadium.

I will never forget one player showing up at his first camp and looking over the competition on the floor. He said to me, 'My chances are pretty good. I am better that those two guys over there.' I let him know that the two guys were Bryan and John Joe Donohue who were just filling in for the day.

Coach had a great way of teaching. He let you know you were wrong, he corrected your mistake and you went away smiling and feeling good. One time a player was dribbling toward the half court line and he dribbled into a trap and threw the ball away. The other team scored. Coach stopped the play and said 'Tommy, Tommy next time you see a trap like that, take one dribble back and shoot the ball.' Tommy asked, 'Shoot the ball from center?'

'Yes,' said Coach, "if you shoot from center you have a better chance of scoring than if you dribble into that trap again.'

While in Ottawa, some of the players decided to break curfew one night and head to Hull. They were greeted at 3:00 a.m. by Coach, who wanted answers. The first player said he was young, immature, and stupid. Coach agreed and said he would deal with him in the morning. The second player said it was his idea, and he wanted to take all the blame. Coach said he would deal with him in the morning. The third player said it was not his idea; he was dragged along by the other players and accepted no fault. That player was sent home...he wanted people who would take responsibility and not bring others down.

Today's athletes want to distance themselves from a coach; that was not the case with Coach. You quickly learn that being around him or listening to his suggestions made for excitement...

He knew how to build teams, in the truest sense of what a team is, including everyone and making each role a role that mattered. Coach was effective because he lived what he taught.

No one was above the team

It was never about him.

He was as giving an individual as there ever was.

He set the standard on how to deal with people. Those of us who had the opportunity to play for him and know him can now relay his philosophy and beliefs to the next generation, and they in turn can do the same.

I can't think of a greater legacy.

Coach was proud of his teams, of his players, of how great a speaker he was, but he was most proud of his family – his Number One team.

Triano finished his stirring eulogy by thanking Mary Jane and the family for sharing their father and then it was Andy Pipe's turn to reminisce about the Coach.

Pipe, who became the Canadian team doctor by accident and one of Jack's closest friends by design, spoke of his humanity and strong sense of morality. In the ultimate tribute, he began by reciting some of Jack's better known one-liners, quips duplicated by many speakers including Pipe himself.

Patriotic, loyal to his roots and his heritage and at the same time a
passionate Canadian – immensely proud of his adopted country.
Devoutly religious, (A man who followed St. Francis' injunction to
'preach the gospel every day ... and sometimes use words') Jack's deep
Christian convictions found daily expression in deed and example.
Neither pious nor pretentious, his Christianity was muscular and robust
and lay at the core, the very centre of his being; his Catholic faith a
source of inspiration, the bedrock on which he built his life, and the site
of comfort, sustenance and reassurance during the time of his illness. A
phenomenal father, whose pride in the accomplishments and achievements of his family were revealed in nearly every one of his conversa-
tions. A coach whose example inspired and encouraged his colleagues
while serving to redefine the standard by which coaches will here after
be judged or compared. And finally, and most importantly, a man who
took what he did very seriously, but never, ever took himself seriously.

Pipe talked about Donohue's New York influence that stayed a part
of him long after he left the City.

I was witness to a wonderful tribute to the accomplishments of those
days and to this wonderfully warm, human and engaging coaching
style when while attending a basketball tournament with Jack and his
son John in Madison Square Gardens we were stopped by an excited
stadium employee. The man renewed acquaintances with Coach and
then turning to John said "son, whenever you are in New York City call
me ... you'll never have to pay for a ticket at the Gardens because your
father was one of the finest men who ever coached in this building". A
more genuine, spontaneous, and heartfelt tribute I could not imagine.

Jack's successful high school career led him to the college ranks and
Holy Cross College in Worcester Mass, where he was named coach of
the year in the Eastern region in 1969-1970. By now Jack had begun
conducting clinics in Europe and had become intrigued with the international aspects of the game ... Many years ago Almonte's James
Naismith left Canada and in Springfield, Massachusetts devised the
game of basketball; in 1972 in a reversal of circumstances a young
coach from Massachusetts journeyed to the Ottawa Valley and neither
the game of basketball in Canada nor the Canadian sport community
have been the same since.

Jack's skills had no equal. His ability to inspire, to enthrall, to engage, and to bring out absolutely the best in everyone came directly from the fact that he cared, passionately about his players and the other members of his teams. He cared, not just about their abilities as athletes or the results of their contests – fiercely competitive though he was – but rather he cared about shaping young lives, developing character and producing thoughtful, responsible and considerate human beings. "Thank you for teaching me that people don't really care what you know, until they know that you care" wrote one of those whose career in sport was galvanized by the example and the values of Jack Donohue.

He couldn't abide indifference or apathy and was frustrated by the fact that Canadians too often ignored or were blithely unaware of the accomplishments of their nation's own athletes.... He made believers of Canadians when in 1976 he inspired the Men's National Basketball Team to a fourth place finish in the Montreal Olympics ... and the magic had just begun. Over the course of the 16 years of his coaching career his teams qualified for every Olympic Game; in 1983 in an electrifying tournament, they defeated star-studded teams from the USA and Yugoslavia to a win the gold medal at the World University Games in Edmonton .But his magic, and his greatest talent, was to ensure that all those who entered into his world left it a better person. His influence was transformational ... his legacy lives on in the lives of those who grew, developed and matured under his influence. "Every day, in everything I do, I see the lessons, the phrases and the methods imparted to me by coach" said one athlete in a conversation last week. As parents, teachers, doctors, lawyers, coaches, and citizens, his players and colleagues now impart the same lessons and convey the same values that he communicated so powerfully and so pervasively. "I don't know what to say except thank you so much. I love you, and not a day passes that I don't think of the nine years I spent growing up with you. I will pass (all your lessons) on to my family" wrote one of his athletes. "He encouraged us to become responsible and accountable" said another. Not for Jack were athletes who would "snarl in victory and whine in defeat". "Values" and "perspective" characterized his approach and his career – and were reflected in the accomplishments and demeanor of his teams.

Then Pipe touched upon the very core of Donohue's life.

But while his accomplishments as a coach are legendary ... his achievements as a parent are his most outstanding legacy. To enter the Donohue household is to enter an oasis of warmth, boisterous good humour, ceaseless banter and an atmosphere of love and caring. To his wonderful wife Mary Jane – who met the man she was to marry just 41 years ago at "a CYO dance he didn't go to" go our thanks, our prayers and our sympathies. Your graciousness, strength and remarkable ability to maintain a sense of order in a lifetime of sharing Jack with us is very deeply appreciated. "I could not live without Mary Jane, she has been everything for me", said Jack in a conversation a few days ago in quiet, heartfelt acknowledgement of the love and support you so unstintingly provided.

Carol, John, Kathy, Marybeth, Bryan and Maura, you were a source of immense pride for your father who celebrated your accomplishments and your exploits every day. Your presence at practices and tournaments ... your travels and adventures with your Dad ... made us recognize and appreciate the very special bonds that unite a family. The people you have become and your own successes as parents and professionals are the ultimate tribute to the wonderful man we remember today. Thank you for sharing him with so many of us ... As I remember Coach, it will be as one whose influence was transformational; whose application of Christian values to daily life was inspiring and exemplary. I will forever recall a man whose greatest pleasures were to be found in the laughter and love of his children and his family. I will never forget his commitment to sport as a vehicle for the pursuit, not of victory alone, but of personal excellence through fair and ethical means. I will always remember the warm resonance of his laughter, the squeeze of his hand on your arm or at the back of your neck as he asked "how are things going?" and knowing that he really meant it. I will forever be grateful for the fact that he made me a better physician, parent and friend. Twenty five years ago I came under his spell. Oh, how I will miss him! But oh, how much better we are for having known him, for the lessons he taught, the experiences he shared, and the laughter he brought into our lives.

Coach was not perfect. He was human and had, as might be expected, his own quota of foibles and faults. He could be stubborn, had an inexplicable taste for a bizarre array of food choices including onion sandwiches, and a sense of direction that was non-existent! To drive with him was a religious experience ... your life flashed before your eyes every few minutes! And if he ever uttered a fashion statement ... it was unrepeatable and unpronounceable! All of us have memories of his favourite ensembles . was it the bedrooms slippers with the tuxedo? The stripes with the plaids? The collection of mismatched track tops and sweat pants?

In the past few weeks I have had the privilege of participating in the care of a wonderful man in the midst of a remarkable and loving family. Coach approached his illness with the same magical combination of determination, love and laughter that characterized every other facet of his life. We talked and we joked. About friends and about sport

Jack Donohue as a friend, coach, mentor and leader contributed immensely to the development of a stronger, more scrupulous and more gracious humanity. We must celebrate his life by rededicating ourselves to the values he espoused, by ensuring that they are shared with others, that they guide and influence our own lives and by rejoicing in the memory of his friendship and his love.

What a man! What a father! What a teacher! What a mentor! What a coach!

What a legacy!

The final eulogy came from Donohue's cousin Gene, the author of the Lives of the Fat and the Irish, who composed a song titled "Coach" which described Jack's life.

Jack's body was carried out of the Church to the tune of Sweet Georgia Brown and buried at the St. Isidore's Cemetery while friends and family gathered at the Church hall where once again stories of the Coach were retold long into the night.

CHAPTER 33

Legacy

Most of Jack's New York friends were unable to attend the funeral in Kanata, so Tom Konchalski organized a Memorial Mass in New York City in June.

The Mass was held at the Church of the Epiphany on the Lower East Side and over 100 former players and friends were in attendance. The priest, Father John Vesey, had played baseball for Jack at Power and told of the time that he got in trouble for using inappropriate language. "Coach Donohue was driving us back from a game in the Bronx and I used the word 'crap'," Vesey recounted. "Well, Coach stopped the car right there and made me get out. Not only did I have to find my own way home but I had to be in his office first thing the next morning to apologize."

Jack Curran read passages from the Bible while Art Kenney delivered the first eulogy.

Kenney, now a successful stockbroker remembered:

Coach Donohue was a teacher, a coach, a mentor, a role model, a father figure, in loco parentis, *a guidance counselor, and at times a confessor. The four years I spent at Power were a combination of* Camelot *and* The Wonder Years, *tranquility, interrupted by the turbulence of the Cuban*

Missile Crisis and President Kennedy's assassination. In those difficult times, it was reassuring to have the stability and support that Coach Donohue and his staff provided.

Coach Donohue let it be known that the Gold Star Gym was off-limits to any outside influences, and that rule allowed us to concentrate on being student-athletes and enjoy the experience. He told us that we were to be "tigers on the court, but gentlemen off the court."

Last year, Coach Donohue was inducted into the New York State Coaches Hall Of Fame in Glens Falls. My wife Jeanne and I were able to attend the event, and she was able to meet Coach Donohue and see how special he was. He touched the lives of so many people during his lifetime. We have been blessed for having had Coach Donohue as part of our lives; we are better people for the experience; he is part of who we are, and we will remember him forever."

Kenney was followed by Kareem Abdul-Jabbar who flew in from Los Angeles on a red-eye flight and was surprised when Konchalski asked him to speak. He spoke of the close relationship he had with Donohue and described long car trips from Manhattan up to Friendship Farm when they would discuss such diverse topics as the inhumanity of war and the hatred that fueled racial prejudice.

As he glanced around the church and saw familiar faces for the first time in years, Kareem talked of the pleasant memories he still had of his Power days, how good it was to see former classmates, teammates friends and how much Donohue had meant to him.

"Coach Donohue always told us to have a positive outlook," Abdul-Jabbar said.

Then, with a smile he added, "I guess I never really did listen that well."

When they returned to Kanata, the Donohue family was kept busy answering the hundreds of cards and e-mails that poured into the house following Jack's death. A letter from Rob Kent was typical of the numerous people who detailed how their lives were altered by a single meeting with Donohue. "Like many people, I had an encounter with the Coach many years ago which I still fondly remember to this day. Back in 1980, I was a 16-year-old teenager, working at Canada's Wonderland, an amusement park north of Toronto. I worked in a magic shop, where I would perform card and coin tricks for guests visiting the park. One summer day, Jack came into my store and watched the show. I have always been a big sports fan and recognized Jack as the coach of the Canadian Olympic team. After my show, I asked Jack if I could have his autograph. He replied that he would only provide me with his autograph if he could have mine. I readily agreed as this was a much better deal for me than it was for him!!! Jack was, and still is, the only person to ever ask me for my autograph. It's remarkable that such a small gesture could still have such meaning to me, even 23 years after the event. My entire encounter with Jack lasted no more than five minutes and yet, it is an experience I will remember for the rest of my life. I'm sure there are many people with similar stories of Jack's kindness to others. He was truly an amazing man and will be greatly missed."

The letter was similar to hundreds of others that the Donohue family received during Jack's illness and following his death. Letters from casual acquaintances who credited the Coach with helping them change their lives for the better, letters from former players who stated that Jack was a second father to them, or friends who benefited simply from time spent with Donohue.

*   *   *   *   *

At the time of his death, he belonged to eight Halls of Fame and was inducted into three more posthumously. Shortly after his passing, a gymnasium in Kanata was named after him as well as the University of Ottawa Invitational Basketball tournament and several basketball trophies in his adopted country. While a Donohue Way is likely to be included in one of Kanata's new housing subdivisions, the Ottawa School Board wasted no time in naming a new elementary school after the Coach.

The remembrance was not limited to Canada. The rejuvenated Power Memorial Alumni, which had begun to solicit funds for scholarships to high school students, remembered Donohue in a memorial Mass in conjunction with St. Patrick Day's festivities. The school was closed in1987 but the basketball team's induction into the New York City Hall of Fame helped revive school spirit and, in 2001, the Power alumni marched in the St. Patrick's Day Parade for the first time since the school's closing. Kenney was selected as the association's first president and quickly broached the idea of funding scholarships.

"The idea would be to solicit funds sufficient enough to provide for perennial scholarships for scholastically accomplished, but financially challenged young men so that they could attend a Christian Brothers High School in NYC (either Rice High School or All Hallows High School)," Kenney explained. "That way, we would ensure that the Power Memorial name would live on."

On the Canadian basketball scene, Donohue's legacy was unquestioned. In his 18-year tenure as the National Team head coach, his teams competed against the best in the world and the gold medal at the Edmonton Student Games was one of the great team achievements in the history of Canadian sport. He not only raised a country's consciousness about basketball but stressed the importance of the pursuit of excellence in any endeavor. He championed the cause of professional coaches at every level of sport.

Oddly enough, there were two distinctions that were denied the Coach during his lifetime. The first was induction as a member of the Order of Canada, the highest recognition handed down by the Canadian government to its citizens and it appeared Donohue's old nemesis, bureaucracy, kept him from receiving the distinguished honour.

The Order is presented to outstanding businessmen, politicians, doctors, lawyers, humanitarians and sports figures.

Dan and Carol Pugliese nominated Donohue on March 27th, 2003 mentioning in their application the fact that he wasn't expected to live much longer. That was an important piece of information since the Order is only presented to living people.

At their behest, a prominent former cabinet minister phoned the government with a similar message as did Andy Pipe, who was made a member of the Order several years earlier. On April 15th, the Puglieses received a thank you letter for their efforts, but Donohue died the next day and was no longer eligible for the honor. A few days later, Carol Pugliese received a phone call from the Governor General's office saying that Jack Donohue was dead and as a result the application could no longer be considered.

"No kidding," an irate Pugliese stated. "I worked for many years in government agencies and I couldn't help but think that if Jack had been 'someone of letters' and not a sports figure the application would have been pushed through with no problem."

But Donohue was so much more than a sports figure, a fact that Earl McCrae pointed out in his newspaper column. McCrae, a longtime Ottawa newspaperman and great admirer of Donohue, was incensed when he learned that Donohue's nomination was rescinded and launched a campaign in the *Ottawa Sun* to have Donohue named to the Order of Canada retroactively.

"If ever an exception should be made for a posthumous Order of Canada, it is Jack Donohue who took an anemic Canadian amateur basketball program and made it one of the best and proudest in the world, and if basketball had been hockey and he'd done the same thing, there'd be statues erected to him," McRae wrote.

What was just as startling as the government agency refusal to act quickly on the Donohue application was the fact that, over the years, none of the Canadian sport organizations nominated their most successful and visible coach. The government did make amends in 2005 when Donohue was named posthumously a Companion of the Order of Canada.

The other honor missing from Donohue's resume is an election into the Naismith Hall of Fame in Springfield, Massachusetts despite a remarkable coaching career at three different levels. He posted an impressive .610 winning percentage and a Coach of the Year award during his seven year tenure with the Crusaders, which added to his accomplishments at Tolentine, Power and with the Canada Olympic team, should make Donohue a shoo-in for entrance into the Springfield's Hall of Fame.

"There is no doubt that Jack Donohue belongs in the Springfield Hall of Fame," Frank Layden said. "Look at what he did in Canada. Without him the team would never have qualified for the Olympics, there would be no Steve Nash playing in the NBA. What he did as National Team Coach was simply unbelievable."

He was successful at every level he coached, from CYO to the Olympics, played a major role in the development of the game's greatest scorer, redefined a country's sport conscience and served as a basketball ambassador on six continents.

Without a doubt, his accomplishment with the National Team warrants induction. There are five international coaches in the Springfield Hall of Fame and each one gained entry because of their success on the international stage and their role in the development of basketball in their individual country. Yet, with limited resources and less talent, Donohue competed with, and on several occasion, defeated the Hall of Famers. He was a head coach of teams that qualified for four Olympics and four World Championships, an unprecedented feat in international competition. The four National Team coaches that followed were all Donohue disciples and while the talent level in Canada has increased over the years, the National Team programs have not reached the level of success or continuity it enjoyed under Donohue's watch.

"He should be in everyone's Hall of Fame," Jack Curran told *Newsday* following Donohue's death.

*   *   *   *   *

The honors will continue for Donohue but such tributes will not reflect Donohue's true legacy. It wasn't the games won or lost, awards and tributes received that defined the man. Rather it was his relationships with people and his ability to touch human beings from all walks of life for which he will best be remembered.

"He was wise, he was a philosopher, he was a teacher, he was a father, he was a disciplinarian," McRae recalls. "He had a way of making you believe in yourself and your capabilities, not only on the court of basketball, but on the greater and more important court of life, because those blessed to have known him and to have been associated with him, saw that he believed in himself and his ways, and they saw the successes of his beliefs in his everyday life, aside from just basketball.

McRae was not alone in his sentiments.

"Jack Donohue was one of the rare persons who was a giver," Morgan Wooten stated. "He delighted in giving his time and energy to help people. I remember seeing him at an all-star game and seeing him talk to players from other teams and offering his help. He was truly one of the great ones."

Jack Donohue approached life, with all its ups and downs, with an infectious sense of humor coupled with a genuine humane feeling towards others. He didn't change the world; he simply made it a much better place to live.

The young men that regarded him as a surrogate father, the players and students he inspired to greater heights, his 40-year marriage to Mary

Jane, the family that they raised together and the people he touched with a simple smile or encouraging word, his ability to say the right thing to the right person at the right time; such is the true legacy of the man they called Coach.

Epilogue

Throughout his life as a teacher, coach, parent and friend, Jack Donohue used stories and slogans to impart motivational messages, messages that were delivered to him as a youngster by his father in the streets of Yonkers, New York. One of his favorite slogans was to "Dream Big Dreams" because he firmly believed that without the ability to reach for the impossible, the desire to achieve beyond expectations, little of value can be accomplished in life.

At the 1976 Montreal Olympics, he made a cardboard medal and wore it around the Olympic Village to remind players that they were there to win a gold medal. At the 1984 Los Angles Games, he was constantly singing, off-key, lyrics to the *Impossible Dream*, from the Broadway play, the *Man of La Mancha*. The Canadian teams failed in their attempts to take home a medal in those two Games, but their ability to exceed expectations and their commitment to excellence were traits of Donohue-coached teams: he was never willing to just compete or accept mediocre effort.

It is only fitting that when he was laid to rest on April 22nd, 2003, his family had the following inscription engraved on his tombstone:

> JACK DONOHUE
> Born June 4, 1931
> Died April 16, 2003
> DREAM BIG DREAMS

Bibliography

Abdul-Jabbar, Kareem, *Giant Steps*, Bantam Books, New York, 1983.

D'Agostino, Dennis, *Garden Glory: An Oral History of the New York Knicks Triumph Books*, Chicago, 2005.

Dombrowski, Joseph and White, Matthew, *The History of the CHSAA Basketball Championships*, New York City, 1994.

Konchalski, Steve, Doherty, Bob and Walsh, Pat, *Silver to Gold*, Casket Printing and Publishing Company, 2001.

Lapchick, Richard, *Smashing Barriers*, Madison Press, New York, 1991.

Napolitano, Larry, editor, *Holy Cross Men's Basketball Yearbook*, The College of the Holy Cross, Worcester, 2002.

Newman, Steve, "Pathway to Gold", *Coaching Review*, September/October 1983, Coaching Association of Canada, Ottawa.

Rosen, Charley, *The Wizard of Odds, How Jack Molinas almost destroyed the game of basketball*, Seven Stories Press, New York, 2001.

Shouler, Ken *et. al.*, *Total Basketball*, Sports Media Publishing, Wilmington, 2003.

Power Memorial: The Legend of Kareem, directed by Michael D. Lardner, produced by Roman Gackowski, narrated by Fran Healy, 2002.

Donohue Legends: Kareem Abdul-Jabbar, directed by Tom Aziz, produced by Jack Donohue, narrated by Jack Donohue, 1992.

About the author

Mike Hickey grew up on Long Island, New York, watching the Power Memorial teams dominate New York City basketball in the early 1960s under Jack Donohue's direction. Upon graduation from St. Michael's College in Vermont, he embarked on a coaching career that brought him into direct contact with Donohue, who was then coaching the Canadian National team.

In his first year as a head coach at a Canadian university, Donohue proved to be a source of inspiration and over the next 30 years, he would serve as Hickey's mentor, employer, and close friend.

Hickey worked with Donohue and the National Team program for seven years and spent another six years coaching the Women's National Team culminating with the 1996 Atlanta Olympics.

Hickey began his journalistic career in the late 1970s and has written freelance sport stories for several major Canadian newspapers, focusing on basketball and hockey.